THE WALL STREET JOURNAL.

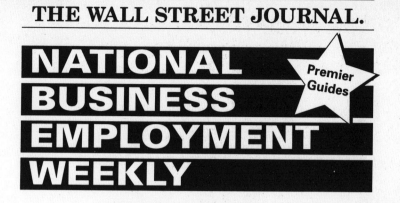

NATIONAL BUSINESS EMPLOYMENT WEEKLY

Premier Guides

COVER LETTERS

THE NATIONAL BUSINESS EMPLOYMENT WEEKLY
PREMIER GUIDES SERIES

Published:

Resumes, Third Edition,	ISBN# 0-471-32259-8 paper
Interviewing, Third Edition,	ISBN# 0-471-32257-1 paper
Cover Letters, Third Edition,	ISBN# 0-471-32261-X paper
Jobs Rated Almanac,	ISBN# 0-471-05495-X paper
Love Your Work,	ISBN# 0-471-11956-3 paper
Self-Employment,	ISBN# 0-471-10918-5 paper
Personal Best: 1001 Great Ideas for Achieving Success in Your Career,	ISBN# 0-471-14888-1 paper

COVER LETTERS

Third Edition

Taunee S. Besson

John Wiley & Sons, Inc.

New York • Chichester • Weinheim • Brisbane • Singapore • Toronto

To the memory of my parents,
Garvin and Lillian Snyder.

Library of Congress Cataloging-in-Publication Data:

Besson, Taunee S.
    National business employment weekly guide to cover letters /
  Taunee S. Besson. — 3rd ed.
      p.   cm. — (The national business employment weekly premier guides series)
  Rev. ed. of: Cover letters. 2nd ed. © 1996.
  Includes index.
  ISBN 0-471-32261-X (pbk.: alk. paper)
  1. Cover letters—Handbooks, manuals, etc. 2. Applications for positions—Handbooks, manuals, etc. I. Besson, Taunee S. Cover letters. II. National business employment weekly. III. Title. IV. Title: Guide to cover letters. V. Series.
HF5383.B434 1999   98-50853
808'.06665—dc21

Printed in the United States of America.

10 9 8 7 6 5 4 3 2 1

Foreword

In these days of instant communication, when a few strokes on a keyboard can connect you with people worlds apart, job seekers may wonder why they should bother writing cover letters to employers on fine grade paper. Why not just e-mail your queries about jobs—or for that matter, fax them? Surely hiring managers no longer care about the quality and appearance of the correspondence they receive from candidates.

Many corporate Web sites allow candidates to dispense with resumes and other traditional job-search correspondence and apply for jobs by completing online applications. However, for the majority of hiring managers, nothing can replace a well-crafted, persuasive and polished cover letter describing your interest in and qualifications for an available opening.

The high-tech recruitment practices sweeping the employment field work well for companies with an ongoing need to hire a particular type of candidate, for instance, sales representatives, broker trainees or telemarketing reps. But to find the best positions, particularly if you are a senior professional or executive, you need to search the old-fashioned way: through networking and personalized communications, such as tailored cover letters and resumes.

Taunee S. Besson stresses this maxim in her book on how to write cover letters. She explains how to create a powerful letter and other important job-search correspondence, such as the follow-up thank-you note. Writing well-organized, error-free letters can show a hiring manager that you:

☆ Care enough about his or her company to research its needs.

☆ Know how to synthesize and present important information logically.

☆ Are meticulous about details.

☆ Have high self-esteem and are persistent about achieving goals.

All of these are desirable qualities in candidates. Just by writing a letter, you have made a favorable impression on your potential boss.

Learning how to write good cover letters isn't difficult, as the 11 chapters in this book indicate. Taunee not only tells you how it's done, but also includes examples from real job seekers showing what works and why for specific audiences—from employers to recruiters.

To stay abreast of the constantly evolving Internet, this third edition also includes a new chapter about on-line job hunting. This section is authored by Peter D. Weddle, an Internet job-search authority who writes the *NBEW*'s weekly Web-site reviews and who has authored numerous books and newsletters on electronic job hunting and recruiting.

PERRI CAPELL
Managing Editor,
National Business Employment Weekly

Acknowledgments

Many people have been very helpful in putting together this book. While I cannot name them all, I would like to thank Tony Lee and Perri Capell of the *National Business Employment Weekly* for choosing me to write the book, editing it, and helping to solicit sample letters from readers.

Thanks to Peter Weddle, who did a tremendous job of updating this book's chapter on Internet job search. Pete is both an Internet guru and a great writer, two types of expertise rarely found in one individual.

Delores Smith, my office manager, deserves my heartfelt appreciation for spending days checking quotes, updating resource information, editing and typing revisions and generally keeping me on track. Her exceptional phone presence, eagle-eye attention to detail, perseverance and nurturing personality paved the way for this third edition getting to press on time and error free.

I also want to recognize Jane Smith of Options Career and Resource Center in Houston, Stephanie Ureate of Experience Unlimited in San Francisco, the Career Center at Southern Methodist University, Kevin Collins at the University of Pittsburgh and Karen Andrews at Kennesaw State University for their help in gathering cover letter examples from their clients and students.

David Westberry, C. Robert Morrison, Valerie Freeman, David Lord, Jim Caraway, Catherine Halvorson, Max Davis, Fred Asher, Larry Spivack and Dorothy Gallo all deserve kudos for offering their perspectives on the internal workings of executive search firms, college placement centers and corporate job-listing systems.

Chuck Wagner, Max Davis, Don Seaquist, Jim King, Christina Bublick, Bill Warren and Gary Cook receive a round of applause for their insights and advice on what the Internet can do for job seekers.

My own clients and newsletter readers deserve a tremendous thank you for allowing me to use their successful cover letters and showing uncommon understanding when I needed to concentrate on the book instead of on them. Richard Bolles has my gratitude for cultivating my healthy disrespect for run-of-the-mill resumes and inspiring my adaptation of his transferable skills exercise, which is no longer available. And thanks again to Tom Cheney for his wonderfully funny cartoons and Robert Half, the creator of Resumania.

Last, but not least, I must acknowledge the support of my family and friends who saw little of me while I was writing this book. While they've always been sympathetic to my need to spend lots of time with my clients and community, this past year has demanded a level of forbearance verging on saintliness.

About the Author

Taunee S. Besson is president of Career Dimensions, a Dallas consulting firm that helps individuals and companies with such issues as career change, networking, executive coaching, Internet job-search and recruiting techniques, small-business strategies, spouse relocation/ employment and outplacement. She also collaborates with corporations that want to enhance their recruitment, retention, promotion and marketing to women by establishing corporate advisory boards composed of prominent female nonprofit and business executives and entrepreneurs. Ms. Besson is an award-winning columnist for the *National Business Employment Weekly*, a frequent speaker and guest author, and a Certified Career Management Fellow. She has taught courses at numerous Dallas-area colleges and universities and is an active community volunteer.

Contents

Introduction   1

☆   Cover Letters Deserve Respect   2
☆   The Mission of This Book   3
☆   Nuts and Bolts   3
☆   A Note from the Author   4

1 **A Cover-Letter Quiz**   7

☆   Quiz   8

2 **Cover-Letter Basics**   21

☆   Formats   22
☆   Heading   23
☆   Inside Address   23
☆   Greeting   26
☆   First Paragraph   27
☆   Second Paragraph   28

☆ Third Paragraph   32
☆ Closing   33
☆ Enclosures and Copies   33
☆ Cover Letters Dos and Don'ts   33
☆ Other Important Tools   41

3 Determining Your Qualifications   43

☆ Accomplishments History   44
☆ Homecoming Chair   47
☆ Taking a Skills Inventory   48
☆ References   61
☆ The Catastrophic Expectation   62
☆ A Good Letter of Recommendation   64

4 Cover Letters for Direct-Mail Campaigns   67

☆ Choosing Your Recipients   67
☆ Researching Potential Employers   69
☆ Writing the Direct-Mail Cover Letter   73
☆ Other Cover Letters from Real People   75
☆ Two Different Cover Letters, One Candidate   81
☆ Human Resources Cover Letter   84
☆ More Direct-Mail Cover Letters   86

5 Cover Letters for Help-Wanted Ads and Job Hot Lines   93

☆ Interpreting an Ad   94
☆ Tailoring Your Cover Letter   96
☆ Interpreting a Tougher Ad   102
☆ Ads Requesting Call-In Responses   106
☆ Job Hot Lines   107
☆ Cover-Letter Examples from Real People   108
☆ Other Good Cover Letters Responding to Ads   118

6 Cover Letters for Search Firms, Temporary Agencies and College Career Centers   125

☆ Executive Search Firms That Work on Retainer   126
☆ Three Cover-Letter Attention Getters   128
☆ Cover-Letter Components for Retained Search Firms   128
☆ Example Cover Letters to Retained Search Firms   129
☆ Search Firms That Work on Contingency   133
☆ Components of Cover Letters to Contingency Search Firms   133
☆ Tips on Cover Letters for Contingency Recruiters   134
☆ Deciding Which Executive Search Firms to Contact   135
☆ Before-and-After Cover Letters for a Contingency Search Firm   136
☆ Cover Letters for Temporary Agencies   140
☆ Cover Letters for College Placement Centers   145
☆ Cover-Letter Examples from Graduating Students   147

7 Cover Letters for Networking Contacts   153

☆ Why Network?   154
☆ How to Use Contacts   154
☆ Cover-Letter Information from Networking Appointments   155
☆ Information Interview Evaluation Form   159
☆ Thank-You Note/Cover-Letter Example   160
☆ Cover Letter for a Direct Referral   162
☆ Networking Cover Letters from Real People   164
☆ Other Good Networking Cover Letters   170

8 Using the Internet in Your Job Search   179

☆ The True State of the Net   180
☆ Some Intriguing Statistics   180
☆ User Perspectives   181
☆ Using the Internet for Employment Purposes   182

☆ How to Hook Up   186
☆ The Difference between the Internet and the
   World Wide Web   187
☆ Netiquette   187
☆ The Best Resources on the Internet for Job
   Seekers   188
☆ Finding a Job on the Internet: A Short Illustration   194
☆ Future Trends   195
☆ The Last Word   196
☆ Bibliography   201

9 Cover Letters for Internal Corporate Use   203

☆ Reasons for Conducting an Internal Job Search   204
☆ How to Learn about Internal Job Openings   205
☆ Networking to Uncover Openings   205
☆ Example Cover Letters Derived from Networking   208
☆ Using Job Listings to Find Openings   211
☆ Published Job Listings   211
☆ Electronic Bulletin Board Job Postings   214
☆ A Final Note on Cover Letters   217

10 Market and Broadcast Letters   219

☆ Market Letters   219
☆ Broadcast Letters   224
☆ Advantages of Broadcast Letters versus Cover Letters
   and Resumes   224
☆ Disadvantages of Broadcast Letters   225
☆ Broadcast Letter Target Groups   225
☆ Selecting the Individuals to Receive Your
   Broadcast Letter   226
☆ Creating a Database   226
☆ The Mail-Merging Process   227
☆ Broadcast Letter Components   228
☆ Broadcast Letters from Real People   235

11 Thank-You Notes and Other Job-Search Correspondence   245

☆ Three Types of Networking Thank-You Notes   246
☆ Other Uses for Networking Thank-You Notes   256
☆ To Type or Write by Hand   256
☆ Thank-You Notes for Employment Interviews   256
☆ The Acceptance Letter   267
☆ The Landing Letter   270
☆ Other Follow-Up Letters   272

Appendix   Guide to Researching the Job Market   277

Index   281

"I'll level with you . . . the only thing I really like about your cover letter is your choice of typing paper."

Introduction

"There's only one thing I hate more than writing a resume, that's writing a cover letter."

"I have a good idea of what a resume should include, but I'm totally clueless about what to say in a cover letter."

"Everyone asks me for a resume. No one says anything about a cover letter. Why should I even bother with one?"

"Did I send a thank-you note after my interview? Uh . . . no. Am I supposed to do that? Isn't that kind of goody-goody?"

"How should I follow up after sending a resume or interviewing for a position? On the one hand, I don't want to be a nudge. But I don't want to be a Milquetoast either. What do employers want from me anyway?"

If resumes are the fair-haired children in the world of job-search correspondence, cover and follow-up letters are the neglected stepchildren. For every job seeker who lavishes hours of attention on creating a perfect resume, three others dash off a mediocre cover letter, while five or ten neglect to send follow-up correspondence altogether. If they only knew the real truth:

Cover letters and thank-you notes play a bigger role in attracting employers' attention and convincing them to hire candidates than do most resumes.

Cover Letters Deserve Respect

Hiring authorities expect you to put a lot of time and effort into a resume. That's why a good resume keeps you in the game, but having one is standard operating procedure for most job seekers these days. A truly memorable cover letter, on the other hand, stands out from the crowd. Employers know that candidates personally write each cover letter (unless they're unforgivably lazy). Consequently, interviewers view your letter as your best attempt to grab their attention and differentiate yourself from the hundreds of other candidates competing for the same position.

If an employer doesn't like your cover letter, she may automatically dismiss your resume. But if your opening words capture her interest, she'll comb your resume to corroborate her initial reaction. The old cliché about the first 60 seconds of the interview being the most important holds true for job-search correspondence as well. First impressions are lasting, even irrevocable.

A cover letter is a perfect vehicle for telling a potential employer why you're specifically interested in his company and job opening. While your resume may provide compelling reasons for a manager to interview you, it says nothing about your desire to find out more about him, the available position and the organization. Employers favor candidates who are genuinely enthusiastic about meeting them. Wouldn't you?

When someone uses your name in conversation, it probably makes you feel good. Employers are no different. Taking the time to address your cover letter to a specific person will generate the same response, especially if you had to dig to find his name. Your resume can't do this for you. Only your cover letter can create an initial spark of rapport between you and a potential manager.

Your cover letter also demonstrates that you're actively involved in your own job search. Resumes can't tell employers that you'll be calling them to schedule an appointment, but cover letters can and should.

Final impressions are important, too, especially when the competition for a position is keen. Hiring managers are just like the rest of us. They like genuine compliments. They appreciate candidates who appreciate them. Taking the time to thank them for a networking or employment interview isn't only polite, it's a strategic job-search technique. When there are two or three equally qualified candidates, but only one writes a thank-you note, whom do you suppose will receive the offer?

Follow-up correspondence can enhance your job-search efforts by giving you a chance to ask for the job, keeping your name in front of the employer, solidifying your relationship with networking contacts and confirming your understanding of the available position. As with many of life's pivotal moments, a little extra effort can mean the difference between your landing the job of your dreams . . . or not.

The Mission of This Book

The primary goal of this book is to provide the tools for gathering information and writing tailored cover letters guaranteed to grab a potential employer's attention. Producing a product worthy of your reader's interest requires knowing why you want to work for him and why he should hire you. Identifying what motivates both of you requires soul searching and research.

Like the *National Business Employment Weekly Resumes, Third Edition* (New York: John Wiley & Sons, 1999), this book offers a process-oriented approach for identifying the interests of job seekers and their potential employers. By the time you're finished reading, you should know how to gather salient information about yourself, job openings and organizations, and distill it into customized, concise letters destined to knock the socks off recruiters and employers. If you can do this by the end of Chapter 11, this book has fulfilled its mission.

Nuts and Bolts

Chapter 1   The first chapter provides a quiz on cover letters and follow-up techniques to test your acumen on writing job-search correspondence that gets results. Don't be too hard on yourself if you miss a few questions. The business world promotes many job-search myths that can confuse the savviest job seekers. After all, if you had all the answers, you wouldn't be reading this book.

Chapter 2   This chapter offers basic tips on writing an outstanding cover letter, starting with illustrations of the typical formats. It then shows you how to construct each section of your letter—from the heading to enclosures. Combining serious advice with comic relief, it ends with do's and don'ts and some hilarious excerpts from Robert Half's "Resumania" column in the *National Business Employment Weekly*.

Chapter 3   This chapter offers an accomplishments history and a comprehensive transferable skills exercise to help you determine which skills to include in cover letters. It also offers tips on coaching references to corroborate your skills and sell your achievements.

Chapters 4 through 7   Each of these chapters explains how to gather information about employers and openings, then write targeted cover letters that address four common job-search situations: mounting a direct-mail campaign, answering classified ads, working with search firms and other job brokers, and networking with contacts to uncover positions in the hidden job market. These four chapters explain how employers view these approaches and how to capture their attention with each strategy. A variety of cover-letter examples from real people are included.

Chapter 8   The Internet has made revolutionary changes in our day-to-day living. Its effect on your job search can be equally impressive. This chapter describes how employers are using the Internet to attract savvy candidates, and how job seekers can take advantage of this powerful new resource to learn about companies, industries, job postings and places to register their resumes. It offers some Internet do's and don'ts as well as key sites particularly geared to the needs of people searching for new opportunities.

Chapter 9   Formal and informal grapevines within companies are an important but sadly neglected source of job openings. Chapter 9 suggests that before looking outside your corporation for greener pastures, you should survey opportunities in your own backyard by networking and using job-posting systems to find openings that match your skills and interests. It also provides pointers on how to write a cover letter and/or application for a job you really want *without losing your seniority and benefits.*

Chapter 10   Many job seekers aren't aware that there are alternatives to traditional cover letters that accompany resumes. To provide other options, Chapter 10 defines and explains how to write market and broadcast letters. These approaches are somewhat unusual, but can achieve some dazzling results when properly used. Here again, letters from real people are included.

Chapter 11   To complete the text, Chapter 11 offers a host of follow-up letters for a variety of job-search purposes. Thank-you notes, acceptance and rejection letters, landing announcements, and so on are all intrinsic to a carefully planned job-search campaign. Be sure to read this chapter if you aren't familiar with how to use them to your advantage.

A Note from the Author

Approximately two weeks after I finished the *National Business Employment Weekly Resumes,* I received a call from Tony Lee, former editor of the *National Business Employment Weekly.* Fearing a major rewrite or some other unexpected catastrophe with the book, I picked up the phone . . . .

Tony was in a good mood. In fact, he sounded downright mischievous. "You won't believe what I'm going to ask you," he said, his voice betraying that he had a secret he couldn't wait to reveal. "John Wiley [the publisher] and the *National Business Employment Weekly* would like you to write another book, this time on cover letters. We're really happy with the one on resumes. And it makes sense that the person who did the resume book should author the one on cover letters, too."

Well, he was right about one thing for sure. The last thing on my mind was gearing up for the gestation of another book when I had just given birth to the first one. Besides, I couldn't imagine filling 280 pages with advice about cover letters, when I only had a pamphlet's worth to say. But Tony hooked my ego one more time. Against my better judgment, he charmed me into agreeing to another year of writing, writing, writing.

As with many major projects, once I started, the ideas came at a furious rate. Before I knew it, I had a book's worth of them. I decided to use some of the same approaches I had employed in the resume book, including letters from real people and a process orientation that explains both the how and why of writing a good cover letter. Having done some research on other cover-letter books, I found them to be long on examples and short on explanations. I wanted mine to be different. I think it's critical for readers to understand the reasoning behind:

☆ Putting together a targeted direct-mail campaign.

☆ Reading between the lines of an ad.

☆ Appealing to the enlightened self-interest of employers.

☆ Working effectively with employment brokers.

☆ Developing most leads from networking resources.

☆ Uncovering openings within a current employer.

☆ Taking an active approach when following up on leads to potential jobs.

☆ Using the Internet as part of a comprehesive job-search strategy.

☆ Writing follow-up letters to heighten interest or close the deal.

Just explaining the mechanics of writing good job-search correspondence wasn't enough. I wanted you to know why putting together targeted letters will exponentially increase your chances of landing a great job.

I hope I've succeeded. Let me know what you think.

TAUNEE S. BESSON, CMF
Career Dimensions
6330 LBJ Freeway, Suite 136
Dallas, Texas 75240
tsbcd@nstar.net

"Your cover letter is a joke . . . I'm impressed."

1

A Cover-Letter Quiz

How much do you know about writing cover letters? Are you a semipro who just needs a little fine tuning and a few constructive suggestions, or a neophyte who doesn't know where to begin? Or are you a job-search commando who assumes that knowledge of the subject will guarantee an easy win in cover-letter combat?

To find out if your perceptions are on target, spend a few minutes on the cover-letter quiz that follows. It includes 22 questions on subjects to be covered in later chapters. Don't be too hard on yourself if some of your answers are incorrect. If you were completely informed about this topic, you wouldn't be reading this book.

Quiz

Are the following statements true (T) or false (F)

_____ 1. One good cover letter will work for every employer.

_____ 2. The best source of information about potential employers and jobs is people.

_____ 3. A corporation's annual report is the most reliable written source of information on a company.

_____ 4. People are willing to network with you because it's to their benefit to do so.

_____ 5. The main role of an executive search firm is finding you a job.

_____ 6. Concentrating a lot of time on direct-mail campaigns is smart because you reach so many employers.

_____ 7. The percentage of people who find jobs through ads is quite small.

_____ 8. A cover letter should convey your personality, style and taste.

_____ 9. Employers don't expect perfection, so a typo in your cover letter isn't sufficient reason for them to reject your resume.

_____10. Every cover letter should include three main thoughts.

_____11. Because the Internet can help me reach thousands of companies around the globe, I should concentrate most of my job-search time online.

_____12. Employers think the Internet offers them a tremendous advantage in finding the most highly qualified job seekers.

_____13. Thank-you notes can play a critical role in your being chosen for a position.

_____14. Using the name of a former manager with whom you didn't get along as a reference will torpedo your chances of getting the job.

_____15. Employers expect a cover letter _and_ a resume whenever you write to them. If you stray from this combination, you'll automatically be rejected.

_____16. Follow-up letters generally annoy potential employers.

_____17. In a competitive job market, persistence may be more useful than expertise.

_____18. First-time job seekers can only attract potential employers through their education and raw talent.

_____19. Women returning to the workforce have a lot of marketable skills, even though they often don't realize it.

_____20. Employers are primarily looking for specific job knowledge. They don't think transferable skills count for much.

_____21. Employers want to know your entire work history.

_____22. If you pick a cover letter in this book that you really like and use it as your own, you're bound to get positive results.

Answers

False   **1. One good cover letter will work for every employer.**

Your cover letter and resume should be targeted sales tools, not generic bits of prose that attempt to be all things to all people. Consider how a good salesperson approaches a customer about her product or service. She first determines the client's specific needs, then prepares a verbal or written proposal highlighting how she'll fulfill them. She knows that promoting extraneous products would be a waste of everyone's valuable time.

Job hunters whose cover letters fail to address a potential employer's needs and expectations generally have poor track records. If you want your cover letter and resume to lead to an interview, do the necessary research and tailoring it takes to grab the recruiter's attention and make him want to see you.

If you don't know how to do this, be sure to read Chapters 2 through 7.

True   **2. The best source of information about potential employers and jobs is people.**

Doing library research to learn about industries and companies is a worthwhile but arm's-length activity. When you want to find out the real scoop on an organization, people will always be your best resource. Humans are social beings who are constantly forming professional alliances, information conduits and personal relationships during their daily activities. They're generally eager to share facts, insights and opinions with anyone who shows a genuine interest. By taking advantage of human nature while researching the job market, you'll gain access to inside information on companies, industries, job openings, personalities and contacts.

For more information on networking, read Chapter 7.

False   **3. A corporation's annual report is the most reliable written source of information on a company.**

While it's true that annual reports must adhere to accounting and Security and Exchange Commission (SEC) rules, corporations have a habit of "spinning" their stories to convey their situations in the most favorable light. Who can blame them?

To gain a more balanced perspective, gather information about corporations from trade publications, business journals and directories, the 10-K reports filed with the SEC, prospectuses and other specialized resources. If you haven't used the library for serious research since preparing your last college term paper, don't despair. Go directly to a librarian and ask for assistance. Librarians live for juicy projects and love to help the unannointed seek the truth.

You can access everything on the Internet you would find in the library, plus a whole lot more. There is a plethora of resources awaiting your fingertips, if you understand how to look for it. Both America Online and the World Wide Web provide direct links to corporate Web pages and thousands of articles about everything you could want to know about companies.

If you decide to do your own research, be sure to read Chapter 4 before you head for the library and Chapter 8 before you start surfing the Net.

True   **4. People are willing to network with you because it's to their benefit to do so.**

Most job seekers have difficulty understanding why total strangers are willing to take time out from their busy schedules to meet with them. They don't recognize that networking is a two-way street offering advantages to both parties.

Put yourself in a potential employer's shoes for a moment, keeping in mind that 80 to 90 percent of all openings are filled through networking contacts. Would you rather interview someone who has been recommended and used personal initiative to see you or someone known to you only through a resume? If you're like most managers, you'll feel more comfortable talking to the more familiar person.

What would you do if a friend of a friend called and asked for 30 minutes of your time to discuss how you chose your career and company, and what the future holds for your industry? You would probably see him because you want to accommodate your friend, aid someone who can genuinely benefit from your input and enjoy being perceived as an "expert."

Professionals like to help friends, serve as mentors, expound on subjects they know well and hire people they expect to contribute to their organization. Networking allows them to perform all these activities simultaneously.

For more information on using networking as an information-gathering tool, see Chapter 7.

False **5. The main role of an executive search firm is finding you a job.**

This dangerous myth lulls many candidates into thinking that signing up with a few search firms will produce a job for them. What these job seekers don't understand is that headhunters don't represent individuals. Instead, they look for candidates to fill positions for client companies.

If you decide to make search firms a part of your job-search strategy, either work with those you already know or cultivate a selected few who specialize in your career or industry. Before making contact, try to arrange an introduction through a credible third party. Don't waste time and money sending cover letters and resumes to a long list of recruiters unless you enjoy feeling frustrated and neglected.

If you aren't sure how to approach executive search firms about matching you with a potential job opening, see Chapter 6.

False **6. Concentrating a lot of time on direct-mail campaigns is smart, because you reach so many employers.**

Typically, direct-mail campaigns generate a 1 to 5 percent response rate. Consequently, you would have to mail at least 100 targeted cover letters and resumes to land between one and five interview invitations.

To achieve the best results with unsolicited cover letters, tailor them to companies that genuinely need your expertise. Use library and Internet research to locate organizations with the structures, missions and jobs that match what you want and have to offer. Mentioning what you like about these companies and how your experience could benefit their bottom lines may lead to interviews that allow you to further expand your credentials.

Following up on your initial contact may also substantially increase your chances of getting together with a potential employer. Always mention in your letter that you'll be calling to schedule an appointment, then follow through on your promise. Employers like to be pursued by worthwhile candidates.

For more information about mounting a successful direct-mail campaign, see Chapter 4.

True   **7. The percentage of people who find jobs through ads is quite small.**

Statistics vary concerning the percentage of people who find positions through want ads. Some surveys indicate that as many as 18 to 20 percent do. However, 1 to 4 percent is probably a more accurate range. If you decide to respond to want ads as part of your job-search strategy, keep these numbers in mind.

Also, recognize that one of the reasons the statistics are so dismal is that job seekers often send the same resume—even the same cover letter—in response to every ad. When employers receive 100 to 200 replies to their ads, they can afford to be finicky about whom they choose to interview. They'll only give a cover letter a 30- to 60-second scan, so it had better grab their attention. Otherwise, they won't even read the accompanying resume.

To put punch in your cover letter, be sure it addresses the most important requirements listed in the ad and gives a unique reason for your interest in the company. Beginning your letter with "This letter is in response to your ad in the *Morning News* dated November 3" and then adding, "I know my qualifications are a good match for the position," hardly starts an employer's hiring juices flowing. In the battle to be chosen for the interview stack, you must tailor or die.

If this concept is new to you, don't answer any ads until you've read Chapter 5.

True   **8. A cover letter should convey your personality, style and taste.**

Cover letters written by professional cover-letter writers can be deadly, especially if you provide little or no input concerning their content. All of us have pet phrases and formats that we use. If you give a resume consultant a free hand in composing your letter, you may not recognize yourself in the finished version.

To assure that your letter represents you personally, write it yourself or, if you're consumed by writer's block, collaborate with a savvy professional. Your ideas and phraseology should play a pivotal role in helping your letter stand out from the crowd and giving the recruiter a tantalizing glimpse of your potential contribution to his organization.

For more ideas about how to construct effective cover letters, see Chapters 2 and 4 through 7.

False   **9. Employers don't expect perfection, so a typo in your cover letter isn't sufficient reason for them to reject your resume.**

Even the most understanding employers will be critical of typos in your cover letter and resume because they assume these documents represent your best effort. If they see mistakes, it's only natural that they'll question your attention to detail and concern for quality.

Before you give or send a cover letter to anyone, ask a friend to review it. Because you wrote it yourself, you may automatically read what you intended to say, rather than what's actually on paper. Friends, on the other hand, have no preconceived notions about the letter's intent. Therefore, they're more likely to catch a missing "and" or misspelled word.

If you pay a service to mail letters and resumes, always check each document before it's sent. Just as taxpayers' returns may be audited if their accountants make mistakes, the buck stops with you. While your cover-letter preparer may feel terrible about making an unfortunate glitch, it's your career that's on the line.

Chapter 2 deals specifically with the nuts and bolts of cover-letter content and format.

True   **10. Every cover letter should include three main thoughts.**

Were you bamboozled by the word "every" in this question? Did you assume that "every," "always" and "never" are dead giveaways to a false statement? This question is a good example of how the exception proves the rule.

All good cover letters should include:

☆ Why you're specifically interested in the potential employer.

☆ Why the employer should be particularly interested in you.

☆ When and how you'll be contacting your addressee to follow up on your letter and schedule an appointment.

This approach sets you apart from your competition, states exactly why an employer needs to talk to you and makes clear your intention to proactively pursue this opportunity.

Unfortunately, this isn't a perfect world where you always know the names of companies and individuals you're contacting, as well as the qualifications required for the job. If you're replying to a blind ad that gives only a box number or provides a hazy or nonexistent job description, you can't compose an ideal cover letter.

Given the poor response rate to queries sent to people you've never met, ask yourself whether a semigeneric letter prepared from partial information is likely to yield positive results. If the opening is worth pursuing, by all means, go for it. However, don't waste your time on marginal possibilities.

For more tips on writing cover letters in both ideal and less-than-optimal situations, see Chapters 2 and 4 through 7.

False **11. Because the Internet can help me reach thousands of companies around the globe, I should concentrate most of my job-search time on-line.**

Job seekers and employers who regularly use the Internet agree that, while it's a powerful new tool for matching candidates to jobs, it's no substitute for person-to-person networking. Just as a 10,000-piece direct-mail campaign may not generate the interviews you expect, plastering the Internet with your resume won't guarantee job-search nirvana. The Internet is just one more way to make yourself visible to people who might need your expertise. If you treat it as a great tool, rather than a cure-all, it will amaze you with its convenience, global scope, time-and-option flexibility and potential results.

Read Chapter 8 to learn more about what the Internet can and can't do to assist you in your job search.

True **12. Employers think the Internet offers them a tremendous advantage in finding the most highly qualified job seekers.**

Employers view candidates accessed through Cyberspace as more intelligent, forward-thinking and educated than those who don't use the Web. Using the Internet reflects a willingness to try new approaches and endure frustration. Employers like perseverant innovators, too.

True **13. Thank-you notes can play a critical role in your being chosen for a position.**

How do you feel when someone writes to thank you for a gift, valuable item of information or the opportunity to talk with you? If you're like most people, you appreciate being acknowledged and elevate the writer to a category reserved for people who deserve your continuing attention.

Candidates who send thank-you notes after interviews reiterating why their qualifications are great matches for available positions compliment their interviewers and make them feel admired. Their letters also remind the recruiters about the high points of the interview.

When employees interview several candidates with equally impressive qualifications, they search for reasons to give one applicant an edge over another. A thank-you note is a powerful tool that can persuade a vacillating manager to choose you for a job.

Read Chapter 11 for some great examples of thank-you notes.

False   **14. Using as a reference the name of a former manager with whom you didn't get along will torpedo your chances of getting the job.**

Many job seekers who leave previous positions because of a downsizing, personality conflict with management, politics or because their performance didn't meet expectations worry that their former managers are itching to tell potential employers the real and imagined bad news about their work. This rarely happens for two reasons:

1. No matter what your former boss thought of you, he'll probably try to put the best face on your relationship and performance and not say nasty things about you. Most people choose to avoid giving negative feedback because venting anger and hostility is unprofessional and emotionally draining.

2. While it's true that a few unbalanced or diabolical types live to sabotage their colleagues, they have little reason to cause trouble once their target leaves the company. A small minority will give negative reports to potential employers, but such instances are rare.

Most companies limit discussions about former employees to basic facts concerning their job titles, dates of employment and, if they want to be especially accommodating, a simple "yes" or "no" as to whether they would hire the person again. Consequently, if you're concerned that your manager is waiting to assassinate your character, you're probably creating unnecessary anxiety for yourself.

Rather than obsessing about it, ask a friend to call your former manager or human resources department for a reference on you. Then you'll know whether you actually have a problem or not.

If you would like more information on selecting, coaching and checking out references, be sure to read Chapter 3.

False   **15. Employers expect a cover letter and a resume whenever you write to them. If you stray from this combination, you'll automatically be rejected.**

While sending a cover letter and a resume is the traditional way to contact a potential employer by mail, it's not the only way, especially if you're initiating the communication. Unless a company specifically asks for a resume, you can send a broadcast letter that's shorter and therefore quicker to read.

A broadcast letter is a hybrid between a cover letter and a resume. It's longer than a cover letter, shorter than a letter and resume combined and makes the same points as a cover letter:

☆ Why I'm interested in your company.

☆ Why your organization should be interested in me.

☆ Let's get together to discuss how we can be mutually beneficial to one another.

The broadcast letter includes more detail on the first two topics than a cover letter and reads somewhat like an executive summary. Some job hunters prefer the format because it's a relatively unique way to capture an employer's attention.

To learn more about how to compose a broadcast letter and review some successful examples, turn to Chapter 10.

*False*___ **16. Follow-up letters generally annoy potential employers.**

Potential employers like to be admired and pursued as much as anyone. When you send a follow-up letter to a resume, networking appointment or interview or as a reminder of your continuing interest, it gives your contacts a lift and reinforces your interest in building long-term relationships with them.

There are a variety of ways to slant follow-up correspondence. Various approaches—thank-you notes, FYI (for your information) newspaper or magazine articles, interesting sites on the Internet, "this-is-what-I've-done-since-we-last-talked" letters and inquiries to confirm receipt of your resume—can remind potential employers that you want to become better acquainted.

Review Chapter 11 for more information on when and how to write follow-up letters.

*True*___ **17. In a competitive job market, persistence may be more useful than expertise.**

Are you beginning to see a pattern here? People like to feel important. Your persistence in conveying an interest in them fosters their interest in you.

While American businesses openly emphasize their need for individuals who have specific skills, education and work experience, hiring managers have a hidden agenda that's actually more important. Professionals who make hiring decisions want to work with colleagues who are enthusiastic about their companies, jobs and relationships. They instinctively know that employees who may not have ideal backgrounds but are excited about their jobs can make greater contributions than applicants with perfect backgrounds and nonchalant attitudes.

Your persistence in pursuing a position reinforces your interest and indicates that you're an individual who doesn't give up easily. In a world of mediocre performers who view careers only as ways to fill time and make money, those who show persistence and enthusiasm are unique, refreshing and highly marketable.

If you don't have a clear understanding of how and when persistence pays in a job search, read Chapter 11.

*False*___ 18. **First-time job seekers can only attract potential employers through their education and raw talent.**

There are many places to gain marketable skills and experience besides classrooms. Paid or unpaid internships, extracurricular activities, hobbies, volunteer work, travel and family activities are some of the many venues for cultivating expertise. Unfortunately, many graduates who participate in these activities don't understand how their experience translates into applicable accomplishments. Cover letters, resumes and interviews are excellent vehicles for highlighting nontraditional experience if you know how to use them effectively.

If you think you have nothing to offer potential employers except a degree in anthropology, see Chapters 3 and 6.

*True*___ 19. **Women returning to the workforce have a lot of marketable skills, even though they often don't realize it.**

How true this statement is, yet very few career-changing homemakers give themselves credit for experience gained in their former profession. Perhaps they don't think their skills are marketable because they weren't paid for them. Or perhaps our culture has given them a clear, but erroneous, message that the more money you make, the more you're worth.

Like first-time job hunters, homemakers can use their nonpaid achievements to show employers they're capable of getting the job done, but, they must first believe their career is a noble and marketable profession. This is a perfect scenario for the Pygmalion Effect. If you feel your volunteer work has prepared you for a paid position as a fund raiser, meeting planner or project manager, potential employers will probably agree with you. If you think you have little to offer, interviewers will sense your feelings of inadequacy and evaluate you accordingly.

If you don't know how to convert your unpaid experience into marketable skills, read Chapter 3.

False   **20. Employers are primarily looking for specific job knowledge. They don't think transferable skills count for much.**

Networking contacts, executive recruiters and potential employers will all tell you that, besides technical skills, professionals should have good communication and organizational abilities.

But working cooperatively on a team and setting priorities are skills that come naturally to some and not others. These are intrinsic aptitudes that improve with use. Like other transferable skills—initiative, creativity, empathy, physical coordination and attention to detail, to name a few—we're either born with them or we're not.

Fortunately, all of us have valuable functional skills to market along with our technical knowledge. And as we progress from hands-on tasks to management, these skills become increasingly important, until they eventually overshadow our technical expertise as critical indicators of our ability to perform a job. Have you noticed how many boards of directors have chosen CEOs with fresh ideas from other industries to run their corporations? When selecting these individuals, board members are more interested in a candidate's personality and ability to get the job done than his background in potato chips or high-tech widgets.

Don't delude yourself into thinking that technical knowledge will be the deciding factor in whether you're chosen for an opening. Be sure to sell your transferable skills as vigorously as your specialized ones in your cover letters and resumes, because a combination of both is usually expected in a winning candidate.

If you aren't sure what your transferable skills are or how to sell them, Chapter 3 will be particularly useful.

False   **21. Employers want to know your entire work history.**

Interviewers are only interested in what you can do for them. While this attitude may sound self-serving, it gives you the freedom to:

☆ Delete unrelated or obsolete experience from your work history without feeling guilty or dishonest.

☆ Structure your cover letter and resume so that they focus specifically on the employer's needs.

☆ Showcase unpaid experience that applies to the position you're pursuing.

Sticking to related background and omitting irrelevant experience is especially useful for seasoned professionals who have 15 or more years with one company or industry. In general, employers are most interested in what you've been doing for the past 10 years. They'll consider experience gained before this time as outdated or assume it is beneath your current capabilities. Consequently, if you're concerned about your age or longevity with an organization, concentrating on recent activities in your cover letter and resume will be helpful to both you and your potential employer.

For more tips on how seasoned professionals can make the most of their many years of experience, see Chapter 10.

False 22. **If you pick a cover letter in this book that you really like and use it as your own, you're bound to get positive results.**

Never copy someone else's cover letter. Granted, there are times when using shortcuts or creatively adapting another document is the most intelligent option. But this isn't one of them. Using a form letter with your resume is lazy and insulting to employers. If you aren't convinced of this by the time you finish Chapter 11, read this book again or write "tailor or die" on your legal pad as many times as it takes to make you a believer. If you learn nothing else from this book, sear in your brain this ironclad rule: *Tailor your letters or die.*

"Miss Nettles, send in the young man who had enough gall to fax in his cover letter."

2

Cover-Letter Basics

Given a choice between swimming with sharks and writing a cover letter, many job seekers would rather head for the beach. Why? Perhaps they're poor writers. Maybe they don't have a clue about what their next job should be. Maybe they're trying to make one letter be all things to all people. Or like the dreaded college research paper, their cover letter represents such a prodigious effort, they feel defeated before they start. Perhaps they're simply unfamiliar with the basic guidelines for preparing good cover letters.

The philosophy behind writing cover letters that get results is elegantly simple. In fact, it's so elementary that most people overlook it in their quest for the "perfect letter." Then when they learn the process, they say, "Of course . . . why didn't I think of that before?"

The secret they seek is this: *You must tailor each cover letter you send, if you want it to have maximum impact.* Granted, this approach takes more time and effort than writing a single letter to use with all employers, but the results are worth it.

If you consider that hundreds of people reply to one classified ad, it's easy to figure out how recruiters reduce the candidates to a reasonable number. Of necessity, the process goes something like this:

First, the recruiter will specify job criteria that his company absolutely requires, plus some other prerequisites that are advantageous, but not critical. Then he'll flip through the stack of cover letters to see which ones mention these important items. Those that don't will automatically go to the round file. He'll also form quick impressions of the writers by how their letters look: Do they have typos? Are they neat? Do they use good grammar and understandable language? The ones that don't meet these tests will join the other rejects. Having eliminated the bulk of the candidates, the recruiter then scans the remaining resumes for how the writers' experience meshes with the requirements of the job.

Ergo, job seekers whose cover letters don't specifically address the recruiter's needs become job-search statistics, no matter how wonderful their resumes or experience may be.

To give yourself the best chance of surviving the cover-letter purging process, your letter must entice an interviewer to get to know you better. Tell her why you've chosen her company over the many others that might employ you. Impress her with your desire to discuss the exciting possibilities waiting for you at her firm. Make her feel special. People respond to positive feedback, even (maybe even especially) when they're plowing through a boring stack of cover letters.

Suppose you're the person sorting candidates into no, maybe and yes piles. Mechanically plodding through the deluge, you suddenly discover a cover letter that says nice things about your company. You feel a sudden tingle of appreciation. This candidate has class. He's done his homework. His business philosophy coincides with yours. He's a good communicator. He deserves an interview!

And, if he's really savvy, his letter states that he'll follow up with a call to confirm receipt of his resume and schedule an appointment. Employers like to be pursued. They admire candidates who have initiative and enthusiastically go after what they want. This is perfectly understandable because they're just like the rest of us. They want to be loved (or the professional equivalent thereof).

So much for cover-letter philosophy. Let's take a look at the nuts and bolts.

Formats

There are two main formats for a typical business letter: indented and block. Job seekers can use either of these models when writing cover letters, since recruiters don't have a special preference for one over the other.

An example of the indented format, which places the date and closing near the right margin and has indented paragraphs, is shown on page 24. If your address isn't preprinted on the stationery, position it directly above the date.

If you don't want to deal with tabs and indentions, you'll prefer the block format shown on page 25, since all its elements begin at the left margin. The two exceptions in this example are your preprinted address and the bulleted items, which should always be indented regardless of the letter's format.

Please refer to Willis Griffeth's letters (pages 24 and 25) as we review the following elements of a good cover letter.

Heading

As with any other letter, a cover letter's heading should include your address and the date. Many people include their phone and fax numbers and e-mail addresses as well. While this sounds straightforward, choosing what phone number and e-mail address to use and determining where to receive faxes can get complicated.

For instance, a potential employer who hears a bad rendition of Elvis on your home answering machine won't be favorably impressed. Nor will a current employer appreciate your taking calls from prospective companies on his time. One can only imagine the repercussions of getting faxes from employers on a machine that's closely monitored by a departmental secretary also known as the Gossip Queen.

Decide where you want to receive calls, correspondence and e-mail. Even if you have to rent post office and voicemail boxes or contract with an Internet server, the extra trouble and expense will be worth it if it ensures your communications with potential employers will be professional and confidential.

Some job seekers choose to have their name, address, e-mail address, phone and fax numbers printed on their stationery with their name and address printed on matching envelopes. This is a nice touch, as long as the letter's heading agrees with the one on the resume. Usually, preprinted headings are placed at the top of the page, either centered or stretched across the page. See the cover letter examples for illustrations of typical headings.

Inside Address

The inside address includes the name of the letter's addressee, title, company and business address. If you're sending your cover letter to a contact, search firm or direct-mail recipient, these facts are easy to locate and confirm.

Example/Indented

WILLIS E. GRIFFETH
2781 Preston Oaks #201
Dallas, TX 75257
214-233-0607

December 21, 1999

Mr. Tom Campbell
Stallings National
P.O. Box 2543
Dalworth, WI 54306-2545

Dear Mr. Campbell:

When I read your ad in the *Dallas Morning News,* it caught my attention for two reasons:

- I enjoy working for an organization that wants state-of-the-art management and operations systems.
- You are opening your new facility in Dallas, where I have lived for the past 18 years.

Consequently, I decided to send you my resume for the position of operations supervisor.

As warehouse manager for Carillon Systems, I have:

- Supervised 20 people of diverse cultural backgrounds.
- Managed the receiving and shipping of over 200 million pounds per year domestically and internationally.
- Spearheaded and implemented numerous projects to improve productivity and save money.
- Used both WIP and JIT processes to track inventory.
- Kept current with state-of-the-art techniques through continuing education courses.

I look forward to discussing your opportunity in operations management to determine if my background will be beneficial to your company. I will call next week to confirm your receipt of my resume and determine a mutually convenient time for us to get together.

Sincerely yours,

Willis E. Griffeth

Enclosure

Example/Block

WILLIS E. GRIFFETH

2781 Preston Oaks #201   **Dallas, TX 75257**   **214-233-0607**

December 21, 1999
Mr. Tom Campbell
Stallings National
P.O. Box 2543
Dalworth, WI 54306-2545

Dear Mr. Campbell:

When I read your ad in the *Dallas Morning News,* it caught my attention for two reasons:

- I enjoy working for an organization that wants state-of-the-art management and operations systems.
- You are opening your new facility in Dallas, where I have lived for the past 18 years.

Consequently, I decided to send you my resume for the position of operations supervisor.

As warehouse manager for Carillon Systems, I have:

- Supervised 20 people of diverse cultural backgrounds.
- Managed the receiving and shipping of over 200 million pounds per year domestically and internationally.
- Spearheaded and implemented numerous projects to improve productivity and save money.
- Used both WIP and JIT processes to track inventory.
- Kept current with state-of-the-art techniques through continuing education courses.

I look forward to discussing your opportunity in operations management to determine if my background will be beneficial to your company. I will call next week to confirm your receipt of my resume and determine a mutually convenient time for us to get together.

Sincerely yours,

Willis E. Griffeth

Enclosure

If you're replying to a want ad, the name of the company, hiring manager or recruiter isn't always included. However, you may learn these details by doing a little investigating. If the company is listed in the ad, call the main number or send an e-mail to the person in charge of human resources or recruiting, or whomever's collecting resumes for this particular job opening. Then use his name and title in your letter. A potential employer will be impressed that you've taken the time to discover his name, because your extra work shows uncommon initiative and perseverance.

Have you ever responded to an ad that doesn't even include the company's name? Pretty frustrating, isn't it? These so-called blind ads, which ask you to respond to a box number, are used when an organization doesn't want an incumbent to know he's being replaced or when it is seeking to avoid a deluge of unwanted phone calls. But if you're persistent, you may be able to circumvent this tactic, and set yourself apart as a really resourceful candidate.

While postal authorities don't have to disclose names of employers renting postal boxes, they may do so anyway if you ask nicely. Call the post office for the zip code listed in the ad and ask for the name of the company using that number.

If the box listed in the ad belongs to the newspaper, you aren't likely to learn who rented it. However, if you're concerned that your own employer may have placed the ad, you can write to the newspaper's classified advertising manager and ask that your resume not be forwarded to a certain company.

Always make sure that the addressee's name, title, company and address are current and spelled correctly. It's easy to embarrass yourself and ruin an interview opportunity by sending a letter to someone who has changed departments, been promoted or left the company. Many references—including company directories—are only updated annually or biannually, so they aren't totally reliable sources. So, before you send a letter to the wrong person, do what they do on *Home Improvement*—"Measure twice, cut once."

If a friend provides a name, confirm the spelling with him or verify it with the company's receptionist. No matter how carefully you construct your letter, a misspelled or incorrect name can doom you to the reject pile. Potential employers take misspellings personally.

Greeting

If you know the addressee's name, use it in the greeting. If you don't, settle on an upbeat phrase such as "Good Morning," which can give the subtle impression that you're bright, chipper and up every day at a reasonable hour.

Other greetings commonly seen on cover letters include: To Whom It May Concern, Dear Recruiter, Dear Person, Responsible for the Job and Dear Sir or Madam. None of these gets you off to a very professional start. In fact, they tend to breed hostility. If you don't know a specific name, don't "Dear" anybody.

First Paragraph

Your first paragraph explains why you're contacting the reader. It's your opportunity to initiate rapport and convince her you're a candidate worth interviewing. Your wording will vary depending on how you heard about the position. The following examples refer to typical job-search situations.

Referral from a Personal Contact

Dear Mr. Denton:

At the Investor Relations Forum yesterday, I was talking with Bill Bailey, who was a colleague of mine at Tablor and Springer. He told me about his position with your firm and how much he has enjoyed working on your team this past year. He also mentioned that your company is currently developing a new product line and might need someone with my expertise in telecommunications. When he strongly suggested that I send you my resume, I decided to follow his recommendation.

Follow-Up on a Networking Appointment

Dear Susan:

Thank you so much for getting together with me to discuss the philosophy and programs of the National Lung Association. Ever since my grandfather died of emphysema, I have been interested in how I might contribute to the exceptional work of your organization. Now that you have told me about your "plate full" of programs, I find myself particularly drawn to your efforts to raise community awareness about the effects of secondhand smoke. I've given our conversation a lot of thought, and have developed a proposal I would like to share with you.

Direct-Mail Campaign

Dear Mr. Stewart:

Having recently left the military, where I was extensively involved with the logistics of moving personnel and equipment quickly to remote locations, I was particularly intrigued by your company's decision to explore for oil in Siberia as featured in an article in last Monday's *Wall Street Journal*. According to the *Journal,* this is Tandom Drilling's first foray beyond U.S.

borders. Now that you are heading north, where your corporation has limited experience transporting large amounts of people and heavy equipment in frigid, inhospitable international environments, it might be worthwhile for us to get acquainted.

Newspaper Ad

Dear Ms. Junkins:

DLC is a company I've been watching for the past several years, both because I own stock and because it's a bona fide true-to-life example of the phoenix rising from the ashes. In the past few months, I've noted several articles about DLC's new contracts with major customers in the Northeast and Mexico, so I wasn't too surprised when I saw your ad for a Technical Support Rep in the paper last Sunday. Given my ongoing interest and stake in the company, I've decided I would like to become a more active member of the DLC team.

Notice how each of these first paragraphs is carefully tailored to capture the interest of the reader and entice him to offer an interview. When you're competing with hundreds of other candidates, it's essential to give a potential employer a compelling reason to see you. If you suggest his company means more to you than just a job opportunity, he'll appreciate your uncommon perception and offer you a chance to expand upon your observations in person. If you begin your letter with the usual bland, "Enclosed is my resume" statement, you give him no reason to recognize you as the unique and insightful person you are.

Second Paragraph

Most job seekers do better in the second paragraph than the first, because they assume that somewhere in the cover letter, they should summarize their relevant experience. However, while they may list what they perceive to be their most important accomplishments, they often don't consider what a potential employer would find most intriguing about them. It's no wonder they achieve such a poor response for their efforts.

Tailoring a cover letter is even more crucial than customizing a resume. If your letter doesn't literally grab readers by the throat and scream, "Look at me! I'm the answer to your prayers!" then the world's most wonderful resume may be relegated to the round file without ever being read.

Use the following methods to identify the most important reasons why an employer would want to hire you.

Following Up on a Lead from a Contact

If a contact gives you a lead about a position, ask him what the company is looking for, then feature your skills and experiences that match these criteria in your second paragraph. For example:

> I was very interested to hear from Jim that you are looking for someone with extensive experience working with the elderly and their families. For the past 10 years I have been an occupational therapist with the Binghamton Hospice where I serve as case manager for approximately 250 patients a year.
>
> In conjunction with a team of medical professionals, I arranged for a variety of social services, such as Visiting Nurses, The Senior Citizens Center, and The Family Guidance Center, to provide in-home care, regular visits by volunteer seniors and counseling for the dying patient and his family. I strongly believe in helping humans die with dignity, surrounded by people and possessions that are familiar to them. From Jim's description of you and your organization, it sounds like we share the same philosophy.

Networking Appointment Follow-Up

If you're mailing a thank-you letter and resume after a networking appointment, refer to your meeting notes and summarize the skills, experiences and personality traits that parallel your interviewer's description of a successful employee. For example:

> I really enjoyed our conversation concerning your interest in transforming your in-house training department into a profit-making entity. Having spent the past six years with Techno Learning Systems, I have developed a great deal of expertise in designing programs to meet the needs of customers in a variety of industries. I'm particularly adept at customizing the high-tech sales and customer service training programs that you plan to make your primary product.

Direct-Mail Campaign

If you're tailoring letters for a direct-mail campaign, look at the information you've gathered from your library research. Then compose a few sentences about yourself that illustrate why a firm should talk to you. For example:

> I was particularly impressed by an article I read about Thompson Interests in *The Wall Street Journal* discussing your quest for depressed properties that have the potential to be wonderful inner-city dwellings. Turning dilapidated warehouses, obsolete office buildings—even abandoned fire houses—into affordable downtown housing is my passion.

ROBERT HALF'S RESUMANIA

WHAT MAKES RESUME READERS LAUGH?

A fill-in-the-blanks format like the following one will generate a lot of attention as it's passed around Personnel with a note saying, "Can you believe the nerve of this guy?" It may even make "Resumania" but it won't get you an interview.

1234 Seven Street
Walleye, Oklahoma 22222

April 1, 1999

Mr. _____

     _____

     _____

Dear Mr. _____ ,

As discussed in our conversation of _____ , I am seeking a new position. I am extremely interested in working for _____ .

The job seeker goes on to talk about some of his qualifications. Then he includes the following section:

Any of the following industries are acceptable to me. I have checked the one that applies to you:

Import and Export ( )

Pharmaceuticals ( )

Distribution ( )

Petroleum ( )

Food Processing ( )

Chemicals ( )

ROBERT HALF'S RESUMANIA (Continued)

The list was long. To his credit, he did check "Petroleum."

He also made another long list of places to which he would consider relocating. They were all big cities. To accommodate this particular employer, he wrote in "Oklahoma," no doubt to highlight his flexibility.

Finally, he added this section: "Willing ( ) Not Willing ( ) to travel. Percentage of time willing to travel for business (_____%)." He checked the box indicating he would travel for this company, and wrote in "20%."

The personnel director who sent me this example of what *not to do* was tempted to include the following in his reply:

- Have ( ) Have not ( ) received your resume.
- Am interested ( ) Am not interested in hiring you ( ).
- Will ( ) Will not ( ) keep your resume on file.
- Would like ( ) Would not like ( ) to hear from you again.

Please—no form letters with resumes. Ever.

As an architecture student at UCLA, I worked with a local firm to convert several unoccupied warehouses into retail and living space. My senior thesis detailed the process for renovating an old factory into lofts for artists and other urbanites who want large multipurpose living areas. (I've included an executive summary for your perusal.)

Newspaper Ad

If you're answering an ad, underline its requirements, then condense corresponding experiences from your background into a few carefully constructed sentences you can augment in your resume. For example, in response to an ad for a warehouse supervisor who has managed a large-scale operation employing diverse people and has a hands-on style and knowledge of state-of-the-art techniques:

> As Warehouse Manager for Carrollton Systems, I have:
>
> - Supervised 20 people of diverse cultural backgrounds.
> - Managed the receiving and shipping of over 200 million pounds per year, domestically and internationally.
> - Spearheaded and implemented numerous projects to improve productivity and save money.
> - Kept current with state-of-the-art techniques through continuing education courses.

To determine what to put in your second paragraph, you must decide which of your skills, personality traits and values are most important and marketable to each potential employer. Chapter 3 describes the self-assessment tools you'll need to determine what you have to offer an employer, and Chapters 4 through 7 explain how to decide what an employer wants in each of four key job-search situations.

Third Paragraph

Wherever your cover letter is going, its third paragraph should mention that you plan to take the initiative in making the next contact with the employer whenever possible. Many job seekers abdicate this responsibility because they don't want to be perceived as overzealous or desperate. Unfortunately, their inaction forces them to sit by the phone hoping for the best. This negatively impacts their job search because:

> ☆ It leaves them in limbo about their status in the interviewing process.
> ☆ Sitting tight does nothing to strengthen their position versus other candidates.
> ☆ Waiting for a reply can become an excuse to avoid exploring other possibilities.

To make paragraph three an important part of your job-search strategy, seize the initiative in developing a relationship with your prospective employer. Tell her you'll be calling in a week or two to confirm that your resume arrived, answer her immediate questions and discuss whether scheduling an interview would be mutually worthwhile. She'll be expecting to hear from you and, because of your proactive effort, will probably extend an interview offer. Even if she says you aren't an appropriate candidate, hearing a firm "no" is preferable to a lingering "maybe."

Closing

A simple "Sincerely yours," is a good way to close your letter. You should also type and sign your name at the bottom.

Enclosures and Copies

If the designated addressee of your letter isn't your potential manager, you may want to find out your potential boss's name and send her a copy, too. Indicate you've done this by using *copy: Sarah Addison* at the bottom of the letter.

If you want to include enclosures such as writing samples, required salary history, references or a proposal, write *Enclosures* at the bottom under *copy*.

Cover Letters Do's and Don'ts

Now that we've discussed the major cover-letter components, let's look at some important writing techniques that can make or break your chances of landing an interview.

Talk about Accomplishments, Not Responsibilities

In our bottom-line culture, people are more interested in hearing about results than process. Consequently, when you have only 10 to 30 seconds to grab a potential employer's attention, you want to spotlight accomplishments rather than responsibilities. Consider the following two statements written by a communications consultant:

Repositioned a regional commercial real-estate firm for national growth. Conducted market research, developed a five-year marketing plan and communications strategy, eliminated unnecessary expenditures and refocused public relations, direct mail and business development.

Repositioned a regional commercial real-estate firm for national growth. Results include a dramatic expansion in media coverage and market share, a 20 percent increase in annual sales and national penetration into two new markets.

Which of these statements gives you a better feel for how successful this candidate was in achieving her desired outcome? You probably picked the second one because of its specific results.

Remember this when you select key phrases to highlight your relevant experience to a potential employer. Brag a little. Modesty may be a worthwhile virtue, but it won't get you interviews.

Quantify Your Accomplishments

There's nothing like a good, juicy number to attract a recruiter's attention. More concrete than words, numbers are ideal for describing a project's scope and success. For instance, which of the following statements piques your interest more?

Implemented an aggressive public relations strategy for the State of New Mexico Bureau of Tourism.

Implemented an aggressive public relations strategy for the State of New Mexico Bureau of Tourism resulting in a 10 percent increase in tourists annually.

There's no contest between the two. The quantified statement wins hands down. Besides percentages, the following can be used to quantify your achievements:

☆ *Increase in inventory turns:* "From three to six per year."

☆ *Dollar amount saved:* "Chaired a quality improvement task force that decreased supply costs from $1.2 million to $900,000 per year."

☆ *Number of clients, states, departments and so on served:* "In my four years as an account executive with Quasar Systems, served 20 key accounts in an eight-state region."

☆ *Increase in dollar volume:* "Increased training department sales to outside client companies from $25,000 to $400,000 in three years."

☆ *Defects reduced:* "Led the team that developed a method for making widgets in one-half the time with a 40 percent decrease in rejected product."

By using some creativity, you can quantify just about any task. Be forewarned, though: If your figures are insignificant, don't use them. Quantification only works when the numbers are impressive.

Drop Names

While bandying about names of rich and famous friends might offend Miss Manners, mentioning well-known clients, employers, peers, states, regions and so on in cover letters (unless your business specifically frowns on it) is a great way to explain the scope and value of your expertise. For example:

Conceived and coordinated the taping of a national advertising campaign.

Conceived and coordinated the taping of a national advertising campaign for Motors Insurance Corp., a division of General Motors. Recruited Tom Landry as spokesperson.

What a difference a name makes, especially when it belongs to someone everyone loves and respects—like Tom Landry!

Sprinkle Your Letter with the Right Buzz Words

I will never forget the day I received my first *Training and Development Journal.* Splashed across its cover in four-inch type were the letters "OD." As I was new to the training field, I wasn't sure what these letters meant. My first thought was overdose. While I realized drug abuse was a problem in corporate America, I didn't think it was so severe that it merited the cover story in a training magazine. Spurred by curiosity, I turned to the first page of the article. After reading a few paragraphs, I realized it was about organizational development (OD).

At my next chapter meeting of the American Society of Training and Development, I used "OD" liberally, almost as though I had learned the password to an exclusive secret club.

This story illustrates the good and bad news about jargon. If you're seeking a new position in your current field or industry, you probably know many necessary buzz words. But if you're making a career change, you may need to revamp your jargon to be in sync with a new employer. Even people who remain in their fields, but switch to different companies, may have to update their professional vocabulary, especially if the new employer has invented proprietary terminology.

One of my colleagues agreed to serve as the human resources director of a start-up medical products firm. Each day, she attended meetings at which the top brass talked about the need to SMURF various projects. It was obvious that SMURFing was critical to the company's success, so it wasn't about the activities of a bunch of little blue cartoon characters. What did it mean? She was too embarrassed to ask. Finally, after listening carefully for a while, she realized that SMURFing was an acronym for applying a rolling financial forecast and cash-flow analysis to ongoing projects. Her management team was accustomed to using this term and expected her to know it as well.

Jargon obviously can be a powerful tool in cover letters if it matches specific buzz words used by a potential employer. If it doesn't, it can be a disaster. So you don't make mistakes, conduct advance research to learn the right pass words for each company's inner sanctum.

Use Humor with Caution

Have you ever heard someone begin a speech with a joke that bombed or had no obvious bearing on the topic? What did you think of the speaker? Did he seem inappropriate? Pathetic? Forced? Awkward? Whichever adjective applies, the speaker probably didn't inspire your confidence or your desire to hear more.

Humor is like the little girl with the little curl right in the middle of her forehead: When she's good, she's very, very good. And when she's bad, she's horrid.

When a potential employer gives you 30 seconds to make your case about why he should offer you an interview, you can't afford any missteps. Unless you're absolutely sure that a funny story or phrase will help you build rapport with your reader, leave comedy to the experts.

Here are some examples of cover-letter humor gone awry from the *National Business Employment Weekly's* "Resumania" column, by career expert Robert Half:

> I am the Prince of mythology, the King's Champion, Defender of the Faith, and Guardian of the Castle.

Gee, I'm sorry, but our company is looking for an accountant.

> Three factors prompt me to apply for a job with you:
>
> 1. My wife left me.
> 2. My mother doesn't want to see me anymore.
> 3. I decided that accounting might be fun after all.

Could this guy be related to Rodney Dangerfield?

For these job seekers, the joke's on them!

Be Brief and Concise

Your cover letter should be a summary of why you're interested in a company and why that company should be interested in you, not a dissertation on your life history. One page is plenty of space for even the most seasoned job seeker to tell a potential employer why he should rush to the phone to schedule an interview.

While you should never play hard to get when you're looking for employment, a tinge of mystery is both intriguing and enticing to a recruiter. If you give him a glimpse of your talents in your cover letter, reveal more in your resume, then postpone the rest until the interview, he'll keep coming back for more.

Some writers think that using big words or purple prose will impress their reader. If you get the urge to replace common vocabulary with unfamiliar phrases, remember this simple rule: If you have to look up a word because you don't use it in everyday conversation, keep it out of your correspondence. In the following examples from "Resumania," the writers suffered the consequences of violating this rule. If you were an executive recruiter, how would you react to these excerpts from their cover letters?

> The soil of my job search vineyard is rich and fertile, tilled in glistening rows from dawn-til-dusk, hard work, sweat and heightened expectations. For the vines to bloom and produce fruitful blossoms, my vineyard must have cool, fresh water to give life to its branches and fullness to its leaves. But I see no real rain clouds in sight.
>
> I really need you to help carry buckets of water for me, water in the form of contacting acquaintances and making inquiries, calls, contacts, and even sending out additional letters with my resume in search of the right job situation for me. Buckets of cool refreshing water to give support and help to one whose thirst is great for fulfillment and success.

Is this guy applying for a job or membership in the Bad Poet's Society?

> CONCLUSION: This association initiates the foundation of the forming of idealistic principles governing such an organization resulting in the firm stability of the company and the employees that make this stability possible, of which I am part. This, I feel, is part of the underlining principle of the evolution of mankind.

HUH?

Write Your Own Cover Letters

You'll notice that this book includes letters from all over the country. A diversity of styles and stories is more interesting and informative than made-up examples. Corporate recruiters appreciate variety and individuality, too. They enjoy receiving cover letters tailored to their needs and written in a job seeker's own unique syntax, rather than canned, fill-in-the-blank formats.

When you compose your cover letters, keep in mind that they must capture your professional essence in a few short sentences. Unless you're using a truly empathic resume service, no one can convey your message more effectively than you.

No Errors, Please

Very few things in life are black and white, right or wrong, good or bad. In most instances, we tend to give people the benefit of the doubt because, after all, nobody's perfect. Unfortunately, company representatives who review cover letters are rarely so magnanimous. They're looking for reasons to eliminate candidates. To them, typos, misspellings, bad grammar and improperly used words are clear indications that the writer is a sloppy imperfectionist who doesn't deserve their attention.

Unless you're one of those lucky individuals for whom typos and grammatical snafus leap off the page, ask one or more of your nit-picking friends to read your letters and resumes before you mail them. Not only will your perfectionist buddies delight in finding your bloopers, they'll revel in the opportunity to help you land a job you'll really love. Otherwise, you may end up making deadly mistakes, like these "Resumania" writers:

> Started my own computer software business with three other collies.

Must have been a pretty hairy experience!

> I am sending you a copy of my new resume. Please disregard the previous one because I found some mixtakes in it.

Not to worry. Everyone makes an occasional mixtake now and then.

> My current job requires that I be extremely indiscreet due to the large amount of confidential and very personal information handled.

Loose lips sink ships.

> I look forward to hearing from you shorty.

Let's hope the recruiter doesn't have a Napoleon complex.

Omit Negative Information

Why is it that some job seekers are compelled to tell a potential employer about the personality conflicts, rotten working conditions, slave-labor compensation, stupid systems, or sexual harassment they endured at the hands of their former management? Why do they feel duty bound to discuss the reasons why they left each of their former jobs or may not be qualified for the one they're pursuing? Catharsis may be good for the soul, but it's deadly in a job search.

If you're openly angry with a past employer and condemn him with a litany of complaints, you risk the chance of your potential manager siding with her peer. If she doesn't know either of you, it's only human nature for her to identify with the one who walks in her moccasins.

While you want to be truthful about your capabilities, there's no need to offer a list of possible ways you may fall short of recruiter expectations. You're responsible for deciding if you can handle the job and telling the interviewer why you would be a good match. She's responsible for evaluating your experience and skills versus her requirements and determining if you're the best person for the position. In our imperfect world, no candidate is perfect for an opening and no job is the epitome of a candidate's dreams.

Filling a position is a collaborative compromise between two equally responsible parties. Your hiring manager has the intelligence and judgment to make her own decisions. Don't "rescue" her with confessions of your shortcomings.

Curb Your Anger

A job search can produce a tumult of emotions. Some days you'll be king of the mountain, on others, you can crawl under a snake wearing a top hat. It's likely that you'll prepare cover letters during some of your lowest moments. Be careful not to foist your negative feelings on innocent readers. This is unfair to the addressee and severely detrimental to you. How would you feel about a job seeker who put the following paragraph in his cover letter, as did this "Resumania" writer?

> After careful consideration, I regret to inform you that I am unable to accept any refusal to offer me employment with your organization. I have been particularly fortunate this year in receiving an unusually large number of rejections. It has become impossible for me to accept any more, and your rejection would not meet with my needs at this time. Therefore, employ me as soon as possible. Best of luck in employing future candidates.

Don't Make Demands

Recruiters don't take kindly to demands, especially when they first hear from you. While you have every right to ascertain if a job is going to use your best skills and allow you to flourish, it's best to discuss these issues face-to-face. People who state in their cover letters that they must have an office with a view, four weeks of vacation, a designated parking space or a 20 percent increase in compensation come across as self-absorbed malcontents who would be constant irritants to any employer unwise enough to hire them. Here are a few "Resumania" examples that speak for themselves:

The enclosed resume tells it all insofar as my work experience is concerned. But let me make one point very clear, I refuse to work with has-beens and the mediocre. If you aren't the best, there is no sense in responding.

Should you hire me, it will not be necessary to offer me an employment contract. But I do insist upon a letter stating that if I am discharged due to no fault of mine, I will receive six months' termination pay if discharged during my first year of employment with you, and an additional six months' termination pay for each succeeding year.

Requirements: A minimum salary of $40,000 with appropriate executive perks, incentives, etc. I need absolute minimal supervision, flexible hours and methods, a variety of duties, a comfortable office, no unneeded stress, honest and cooperative coworkers, and all the necessary tools to get the job done (e.g., a state-of-the-art computer with the latest Windows).

Make Your Cover Letter Easy to Read

Have you ever written a report or a proposal, then edited it repeatedly to make it succinct and compelling? What were the techniques you used to improve it? If you're like most professionals, you carefully considered both the appearance and the content of your product. You evaluated the balance of copy versus white space, the readability of the typeface, the caliber of the words and the cadence of the text.

Each of your cover letters is a concise document critical to the success of your job search. Consequently, you must lavish the same attention on it that you would give a career-advancing report. Look at it with an aesthetic eye. Develop a pleasing format with sufficient white space for easy reading. Use a typeface and size that whispers professionalism. Select words that precisely convey your meaning without being pedantic. And refine your text to give it a natural rhythm that flows effortlessly in tune with your message.

A few tips on how to achieve the right combination of visual ingredients that readers will find appealing follow:

☆ Select high rag content stationery and matching envelopes in a neutral color. You can usually tell fine-quality paper by its watermark—a faint logo stamped on each sheet. If you don't want to fold your cover letter and resume, send them in a 9-by-12-inch envelope. However, a large envelope probably won't match your stationery. You'll have to decide which approach is more aesthetically pleasing to you: a totally coordinated package or a cover letter and resume without folds.

☆ Many job seekers choose to preprint their name, address, e-mail address and phone number on their stationery and envelopes. While this isn't necessary, it can save time and provide a finished quality that lends an added touch of distinction.

☆ You'll naturally prefer some typefaces over others. Because your letter should represent you personally, choose software that offers your favorite font. A good word-processing package should provide a reasonable selection of type styles and sizes, as well as allow you to italicize and boldface key words or phrases.

☆ Given the choice between preparing letters on a typewriter or computer, the latter is the obvious winner because it allows you to mix and match paragraphs and make quick corrections, as well as store, categorize and reproduce information easily. If you don't have a computer, rent or borrow one from a friend, college lab, outplacement center or copy business (where they rent them by the hour).

    If you're computer illiterate or can't put your hands on a PC, check the prices and turnaround times for cover-letter preparation at resume services and executive suites in your area. If you will require an answering and mailing service as well, try to negotiate a package for all.

☆ Along with a good software package and computer, you'll need access to an ink-jet or laser printer. Dot matrix ones have that "sixth-grade English theme" look that brands users as amateurish and unprofessional. If you don't own a high-quality printer or can't afford to buy one, take your disk to a local print shop and ask for a hard copy on your stationery. You'll be charged a small processing fee, but the results are well worth it.

Other Important Tools

In addition to your stationery, software, computer and printer, you should have the following at your work space:

☆ A dictionary or thesaurus for checking spelling and word meanings.

☆ Stamps, both first and third class.

☆ A wall or desk calendar for scheduling appointments and blocking out time for job-search activities.

☆ A Rolodex (manual or computerized) for quick reference to contacts and company names, addresses, and phone and fax numbers.

☆ A reliable system for keeping track of job-search activities and the follow-up needed for each.

Now that we've outlined the process of writing a cover letter, let's look in Chapter 3 at what must be done in advance to prepare an outstanding piece of correspondence.

"Didn't you read the ad? They're looking for a specific type."

3

Determining Your Qualifications

Just as you gather resources to prepare for any worthwhile project, from making a presentation to a key client to building a patio deck, you'll need to do some advance preparation to create an outstanding cover letter. As mentioned in Chapter 2, the best letters explain why you're interested in a prospective employer and why that company should be interested in you. It takes thought to maximize your case in these areas, but with practice, the process will become easier.

This chapter provides a step-by-step method for identifying your most important skills and experiences. Armed with this information, you'll be able to confidently answer ads and write to job-search contacts, executive search firms and companies you've targeted for a direct-mail campaign because you'll know which of your assets will be most valuable to each of your readers.

Accomplishments History

The best vehicle to use when determining your most marketable and enjoyable skills is an accomplishments history, which includes significant achievements from your paid career, volunteer work, hobbies, classes, organizations and other life experiences. When you are deciding what to include in your accomplishments history, keep in mind that "significant" is a loaded word, subject to a variety of interpretations.

Since we're talking about *your* history, you get to use *your* definition. If teaching your child how to hit a baseball is important to you, include it. If one of your most satisfying projects was planning a surprise party for a friend, use that, too. Don't restrict yourself only to those experiences that have a direct connection with work.

The following examples of accomplishments could logically appear in someone's history. They represent both paid and nonpaid experiences, written in abbreviated or outline formats.

Sale to Criterion Corporation

Two years ago, I sold an order of 500 PCs and servers to Criterion, a company with offices throughout the United States and Mexico. I had pursued this account for a number of years and had placed orders here and there, but nothing major. Even though Criterion hadn't been a big moneymaker for me, I continued to make calls because of its great potential.

One day I received a call telling me that Jim Hancock, the company's CIO, wanted to see me before the end of the week. Since I wasn't working on anything with them at the time, I wondered what was going on and hoped this would be my big break. Sure enough, Jim said his company had a mishmash of computers that couldn't talk to one another, and that upper management had finally agreed to replace the bits and pieces with compatible hardware and software. He asked me for a proposal for the 500 PCs and servers and the installation to connect them.

Naturally, I had to do a lot of research before I could whip together a proposal this large. I had to spend time with Jim to find out how many offices Criterion had, where they were located, how the computers would be allocated, how their planned installation schedule looked, what the company wanted these computers to do, what types of software they would be running, and a zillion other things. After three months of hard work with my manager and my company's technical people, I put together and delivered a proposal.

A week later, Jim called to say he was impressed and eager for me to present my ideas at a meeting with the top brass. Now that I knew I had a real chance of getting this contract, I started to get a little nervous. This was the biggest deal I had ever pursued.

Spurred by the extra energy caused by my adrenalin, I decided to try something really innovative to capture the Executive Committee's attention. I asked our company's interior designer to use extra furniture and fixtures stored in one of our warehouses to create a prototype of a typical small field office. Then I worked with the technical people to plan and install a computer system for the model.

When the big day came, we hosted Criterion's executives at our regional office. In the morning, I gave the usual dog-and-pony presentation of our proposal. Then, after a great lunch, we opened the doors to the room where we had set up the field office and invited them to try our LAN on for size. The role-play exercise worked perfectly. I got the order, coordinated the installation, and collected a big commission check as well as lots of kudos from my management and client.

ROBERT HALF'S RESUMANIA

When writing cover letters, too many job seekers rely on metaphors to describe their objectives and accomplishments, but they don't work and shouldn't be used. Employers are looking for facts, not rhetoric.

Some metaphors simply don't make sense, especially when you consider the jobs the candidates seek. For instance: "I am looking for a company that is looking for a man who plants corn instead of weeds and reaps corn instead of weeds because his experience in management has taught him the difference."

Corn and weeds? Grass and weeds might have made more sense. The metaphor is more apt for someone seeking a job as a farmhand, not an accountant looking for work with a public accounting firm.

Here's another: "Although I am not a horse, I have an excellent track record."

Makes you wonder what his time is for the mile.

Building the Wall

Not long after we moved into our first house, we noticed that there was no privacy wall behind the houses on our side of the street. Yet there was one constructed behind the homes across the road. This situation caught our attention when one of the young children in the neighborhood suddenly took off through the space between the houses and headed for the six-lane road behind the alley. (Fortunately, we caught him before he ran into the street.)

This incident got us thinking about the danger of not having a wall between our yards and the busy street beyond. Several of us decided to pursue building a wall at the developer's expense. But first we had to find out who the developer was. With the help of a realtor friend, we located the developer and wrote to him asking why our wall was missing. He said the original homeowners didn't want one because they were afraid they would hit it when backing their cars out of the alley.

What the developer didn't mention was that the properties were misplotted, leaving no room for a wall on the tiny strip of private property behind the driveways. We would have to get permission from the city to construct it on the publicly owned easement between the alley and street.

The city was willing to give us permission only if we had a petition stating that every homeowner involved wanted a wall. So we conducted a meeting of 30 homeowners, explained the situation, including the increase in home values a wall would bring, and collected the needed signatures.

Then we went back to the developer to present the city's documented permission and the homeowner's petition. After several months of putting-off phone calls, he agreed to pay for the wall if we made the arrangements.

We called a number of construction companies, solicited bids, looked at other walls, selected the best option and gave the contract to the developer to sign. The wall was finished one year from the day we started the project, on city property, at the developer's expense.

Marketing Strategy for Ralston Real Estate

Repositioned regional commercial real-estate company and six divisions for national growth at a time when market share was declining and the economy was depressed.

Conducted market research, developed budget and refocused dollars in public relations, direct mail and business development.

Created targeted national sales strategy, developed A/V sales presentation materials.

Trade and consumer media coverage increased dramatically, market share increased, and company expanded into national markets, with all divisions experiencing 20% annual growth.

Homecoming Chair

I. Nominated and elected by chapter.

II. Find a fraternity partner.

    A. Talk with friends in other fraternities.

    B. Call or be called by fraternities interested in working with us.

    C. Make final decision on partner.

III. Work with Northwestern's general Homecoming Committee. Attend informational meetings.

    A. Learn the parade route.

    B. Make "insurance" deposit for the float.

    C. Find our position along the parade route.

    D. Publicize other Homecoming events to the chapter.

IV. Build the float.

    A. Choose and motivate volunteer Homecoming committee.

        1. Sound excited.

        2. Use bribes, call in chips.

        3. Foment guilt.

    B. Brainstorm ideas.

        1. Work with fraternity's committee to come up with float idea to fit Homecoming theme and size parameters.

        2. Make sure float can be built: Get engineering majors to help with structural design.

    C. Get supplies.

        1. Coordinate with fraternity's chair to divide purchases.

        2. Persuade someone to drive me to buy supplies.

    D. Construct the float.

        1. Set up daily schedule.

        2. Build the frame of the globe and field goals.

        3. "Pomp" chicken wire signs.

        4. Put chicken wire around the globe's frame to make it round.

   5. Pomp or tissue paper the continents with green paper and hope it doesn't rain.

   6. Paint the field goal frames, finish signs and other details.

E. Put the float together on the truck.

   1. Confirm reservation of truck.

   2. Recruit *lots* of friends to help.

   3. Lower the globe from the second floor of the house to the ground.

   4. Anchor globe, goals, and signs on truck.

   5. String Christmas and neon lights all over the float.

   6. Find someone to make the stereo work.

   7. Position globe-turners (two people) inside the globe.

   8. Drive to the parade location making last minute changes along the way.

F. Ride on the float, wave to the crowd and have fun!

Taking a Skills Inventory

Once you gather a variety of experiences, break them down into marketable and enjoyable skills. The following skills exercise will make this process easier for you. Notice how many skills each of the preceding achievements used, regardless of whether they were paid or unpaid.

   If you are a first-time job seeker or a homemaker returning to the paid workforce, most of your significant accomplishments will probably come from volunteer work, hobbies or organizations. Don't discount their validity simply because you weren't paid a salary. They're as marketable as paid work, if you give yourself credit for them.

FUNCTIONAL AND TRANSFERABLE SKILLS INVENTORY

DIRECTIONS:

☆ On this skills exercise, put the title of your first experience at the top of Column 1. Then, keeping in mind its step-by-step process, look at each box of transferable skills. If you used one or more of the skills in a box, put a check in Column 1. If you enjoyed using the skill(s), make a second check (*in the same box*).

☆ Your completed exercise will give an excellent picture of your transferable skills, where they cluster, and which ones are most satisfying.

Skill Boxes	Sale to Criterion	Building the Wall	Strategy for Ralston	Homecoming Chair			
	1	2	3	4	5	6	7
I. THE SOCIAL THEME (People and Idea Skills)							
A. Written Communication Skills							
Love of reading voraciously or rapidly. Love of printed things.							
Comparing. Editing effectively.	✓		✓✓				
Publishing imaginatively.			✓✓				
Explicit, concise writing. Keeping superior minutes of meetings.	✓		✓✓				
Uncommonly warm letter composition.							
Flair for writing reports. Skilled in speechwriting.							
Writing promotions and proposals for funding purposes.	✓✓						
B. Verbal Communication Skills							
Effective verbal communication. Expressing self very well. Making a point and cogently expressing a position.	✓✓	✓✓	✓✓	✓✓			
Encouraging communication and participation.	✓✓	✓✓	✓✓	✓✓			
Thinking quickly on one's feet.	✓✓	✓✓	✓✓	✓✓			
Translating. Verbal skills in foreign languages. Teaching languages. Adept at translating jargon into relevant and meaningful terms to diverse audiences or readers.							
Summarizing. Reporting on conversations or meetings accurately.		✓		✓✓			

	Sale to Criterion	Building the Wall	Strategy for Ralston	Homecoming Chair			
	1	2	3	4	5	6	7
Informing, enlightening, explaining, instructing, defining.	✓✓	✓✓	✓✓	✓✓			
Developing rapport and trust.	✓✓	✓✓	✓✓	✓✓			
Adept at two-way dialogue. Ability to hear and answer questions perceptively. Accepting differing opinions. Helping others express their views.	✓✓	✓✓	✓✓	✓✓			
Listening intently and accurately. Good at listening and conveying awareness.	✓✓	✓✓	✓✓	✓✓			
Dealing with many different kinds of people. Talks easily with all kinds of people.		✓✓	✓✓				
C. Instructing, Guiding, Mentoring Skills							
Fostering stimulating learning environment. Creating an atmosphere of acceptance. Patient teaching. Instills love of the subject. Conveys tremendous enthusiasm.			✓✓				
Adept at inventing illustrations for principles or ideas. Adept at using visual communications.	✓✓		✓✓				
Coaching, advising, aiding people in making decisions.	✓✓		✓✓	✓✓			
Consulting.	✓✓		✓✓				
Mentoring and facilitating personal growth and development. Helping people make their own discoveries in knowledge, ideas or insights. Empowering.							
Clarifying goals and values of others. Puts things in perspective.	✓✓	✓✓		✓✓			
Fostering creativity in others. Showing others how to use resources.				✓✓			
Group facilitating. Discussion group leadership. Group dynamics.		✓✓		✓✓			
Training. Designing educational events. Organizing and administering in-house training programs.							
D. Serving/Helping/Human Relations Skills							
Relating well in dealing with the public/public relations.		✓✓	✓✓				
Helping and serving. Referring (people). Customer relations and services.			✓✓				

	Sale to Criterion	Building the Wall	Strategy for Ralston	Homecoming Chair			
	1	2	3	4	5	6	7
Sensitivity to others. Interested in/manifesting keen ability to relate to people. Adept at treating people fairly. Consistently communicates warmth to people. Conveying understanding, patience and fairness.	✓✓	✓✓		✓✓			
Perceptive in identifying and assessing the potential of others. Recognizes and appreciates the skills of others.				✓✓			
Remembering people and their preferences.	✓✓		✓✓				
Keen ability to put self in someone else's shoes. Empathy. Instinctively understands others' feelings.		✓✓					
Tact, diplomacy and discretion.	✓✓	✓✓	✓✓	✓✓			
Caring for. Watching over. Nurturing.							
Administering a household.							
Shaping and influencing the atmosphere of a particular place. Providing comfortable, natural and pleasant surroundings.	✓✓			✓✓			
Warmly sensitive and responsive to people's feelings and needs in social or other situation. Anticipating people's needs.	✓✓						
Working well on a team. Has fun while working and makes it fun for others. Collaborating with colleagues skillfully. Treating others as equals without regard to education, authority or position. Motivates fellow workers. Expresses appreciation faithfully. Ready willingness to share credit with others.	✓✓	✓✓	✓✓	✓✓			
Refusing to put people into slots or categories. Ability to relate to people with different value systems.		✓✓					
Taking human failings and limitations into account. Dealing patiently and sympathetically with difficult people. Handles prima donnas tactfully and effectively. Works well in hostile environment.	✓	✓		✓			
Nursing. Skillful therapeutic abilities.							
Gifted at helping people with their personal problems. Raises people's self-esteem. Understands human motivations, relationships and needs. Aware of people's need for supportive community. Aids people with their total life adjustment. Counseling.							

	Sale to Criterion	Building the Wall	Strategy for Ralston	Homecoming Chair			
	1	2	3	4	5	6	7
Unusual ability to represent others. Expert in liaison roles.				✓✓			
II. THE ENTERPRISING THEME (People, Idea and System Skills)							
A. Influencing/Persuading Skills							
Helping people identify their own intelligent self-interest.	✓✓	✓✓	✓✓	✓✓			
Persuading. Influencing the attitudes or ideas of others.	✓✓	✓✓	✓✓	✓✓			
Promoting. Face-to-face selling of tangibles/intangibles. Selling ideas or products without tearing down competing ideas or products. Selling an idea, program or course of action to decision makers.	✓✓	✓✓	✓✓	✓✓			
Making and using contacts effectively. Resource broker.	✓✓	✓✓	✓✓	✓✓			
Developing targets/building markets for ideas or products.	✓✓		✓✓				
Raising money. Arranging financing.							
Getting diverse groups to work together. Wins friends easily from among diverse or even opposing groups or factions.		✓	✓✓	✓✓			
Adept at conflict management.				✓			
Arbitrating/mediating between contending parties or groups. Negotiating to come jointly to decisions. Bargaining. Crisis intervention. Reconciling.		✓✓		✓			
Renegotiating. Obtaining agreement on policies, after the fact.		✓✓		✓			
Recruiting talent or leadership. Attracting skilled, competent, creative people.			✓✓	✓✓			
Motivating others. Mobilizing. Stimulating people to effective action.	✓✓	✓✓	✓✓	✓✓			
Leading others. Inspiring and leading organized groups. Impresses others with enthusiasm and charisma. Repeatedly elected to senior posts. Skilled at chairing meetings.		✓✓	✓✓	✓✓			
Deft in directing creative talent. Skilled leadership in perceptive human relations techniques.			✓✓	✓✓			
Bringing people together in cooperative efforts. Able to call in other experts/helpers as needed. Team-building. Recognizing and utilizing the skills of others.	✓✓	✓✓	✓✓	✓✓			

	Sale to Criterion	Building the Wall	Strategy for Ralston	Homecoming Chair			
	1	2	3	4	5	6	7
Directing others. Making decisions about others. Supervising others in their work. Contracting. Delegating.	✓✓		✓✓	✓✓			
Recognizes intergroup communications gaps. Judges people's effectiveness.	✓✓	✓✓	✓✓	✓✓			
B. Performing Skills							
Getting up before a group. Very responsive to audiences' moods or ideas. Contributes to others' pleasure consciously. Performing.	✓✓	✓✓	✓✓	✓✓			
Demonstrating. Modeling. Making presentations.	✓✓	✓✓	✓✓				
Showmanship. A strong theatrical sense. Poise in public appearance.	✓✓		✓✓	✓✓			
Addressing groups. Speaking ability/articulateness. Public address/public speaking/oral presentations. Lecturing. Stimulating people's enthusiasm.	✓✓	✓✓	✓✓	✓✓			
Making people laugh. Understanding the value of the ridiculous in illuminating reality.	✓✓		✓✓	✓✓			
Acting.							
Conducting and directing public affairs and ceremonies.							
C. Initiating/Risk-Taking Skills							
Initiating. Able to move into new situations on one's own.	✓✓	✓✓	✓✓				
Taking the first move in developing relationships.	✓✓	✓✓	✓✓	✓✓			
Driving initiative. Searching for more responsibility.	✓✓	✓✓	✓✓	✓✓			
Excellent at organizing one's time. Ability to do work self-directed, without supervision.	✓✓	✓✓	✓✓	✓✓			
Unwillingness to automatically accept the status quo. Keen perceptions of things as they could be, rather than passively accepting them as they are. Promoting and bringing about major changes. A change agent.	✓✓	✓✓	✓✓				
Seeing and seizing opportunities. Sees a problem and acts immediately to solve it.	✓✓	✓✓	✓✓	✓✓			
Dealing well with the unexpected or critical. Decisive in emergencies.	✓			✓			

	Sale to Criterion	Building the Wall	Strategy for Ralston	Homecoming Chair			
	1	2	3	4	5	6	7
Adept at confronting others with touchy or difficult personal matters.		✓	✓				
Entrepreneurial.							
Showing courage. Willing to take manageable risks.	✓✓	✓✓	✓✓				
Able to make hard decisions.	✓		✓✓	✓			
D. Planning and Management Skills							
Planning, development. Planning on basis of lessons from past experience. A systematic approach to goal-setting.	✓✓	✓✓	✓✓	✓✓			
Prioritizing tasks. Establishing effective priorities among competing requirements. Setting criteria or standards.	✓✓	✓✓	✓✓	✓✓			
Policy formulation or interpretation. Creating and implementing new policies.							
Designing projects. Program development.	✓✓	✓✓	✓✓	✓✓			
Skilled at planning and carrying out well-run meetings, seminars or workshops.	✓✓	✓✓	✓✓	✓✓			
Organizing. Organizational development and analysis. Planning and building. Bringing order out of chaos.	✓	✓✓	✓✓	✓✓			
Scheduling, Assigning, Setting up and maintaining on-time work schedules. Coordinating operations/details. Arranging.	✓	✓✓	✓✓	✓			
Producing. Achieving. Attaining a goal.	✓✓	✓✓	✓✓	✓✓			
Recommending courses of action.	✓✓	✓✓	✓✓	✓✓			
Making good use of feedback.	✓✓	✓✓	✓✓	✓✓			
III. THE ARTISTIC THEME (Idea Skills)							
A. Intuitional and Innovating Skills							
Having imagination and the courage to use it.	✓✓		✓✓	✓✓			
Operating well in a free, unstructured, environment. Bringing new life to traditional approaches.	✓✓		✓✓				

	Sale to Criterion	Building the Wall	Strategy for Ralston	Homecoming Chair			
	1	2	3	4	5	6	7
Ideophoria; continually conceiving, developing and generating ideas. Inventing. Conceptualizing.			✓✓	✓✓			
Improvising on the spur of the moment.							
Innovating. Perceptive, creative problem solver. Willing to experiment with new approaches.	✓✓	✓✓	✓✓	✓✓			
Love of exercising the creative mind-muscle.	✓✓		✓✓	✓✓			
Synthesizing perceptions. Seeing relationships between apparently unrelated factors. Integrating diverse elements into a clear, coherent whole. Ability to relate abstract ideas.	✓✓		✓✓				
Deriving things from others' ideas. Improvising, updating, adapting.	✓✓			✓✓			
Relating theory to a practical situation. Theoretical model development.	✓						
Generating ideas with commercial possibilities. Seeing the commercial possibilities of abstract ideas or concepts. Creating products or services.	✓✓						
Showing foresight. Recognizing obsolescence before it occurs. Instinctively gathering resources even before the need for them is evident. Forecasting.	✓✓			✓			
Perceiving intuitively.	✓✓		✓✓				
B. Artistic Skills							
Showing strong sensitivity to, and need for, beauty in the environment. Instinctively excellent taste.			✓✓				
Expressive. Exceptionally good at facial expressions used to convey thoughts without (or in addition to) words. Using voice tone and rhythm as unusually effective tool of communication. Accurately reproducing sounds (e.g., foreign languages spoken without accent).							
Good sense of humor and playfulness conveyed in person or in writing.	✓✓		✓✓	✓✓			
Aware of the value of symbolism and deft in its use. Skilled at symbol formation (words, pictures and concepts). Visualizing concepts. Creating poetic images.		✓✓	✓✓				

	Sale to Criterion	Building the Wall	Strategy for Ralston	Homecoming Chair			
	1	2	3	4	5	6	7
Designing and/or using audiovisual aids, photographs, visual, spatial and graphic designs. Illustrations, maps, logos.	✓✓		✓✓				
Perception of forms, patterns and structures. Visualizing shapes, graphs, in the third dimension.			✓✓	✓✓			
Spatial memory. Memory for design. Notice quickly (and/or remember later) most of the contents of a room. Memory for faces.							
Exceptional color discrimination.							
Designing, fashioning, shaping, redesigning things. Styling, decorating.							
Writing novels, stories, imaginative scripts, ad campaigns. Playwriting. Assisting and directing the planning, organizing, and staging of a theatrical production.							
Musical knowledge and taste. Tonal memory. Uncommon sense of rhythm. Exceedingly accurate melody recognition. Composing, making music. Dancing, singing, expert at using the body to express feelings.							
IV. THE INVESTIGATIVE THEME (Data and System Skills)							
A. Observational Learning Skills							
Highly observant of people, data and things. Keen awareness of surroundings.	✓✓		✓✓				
Intensely curious about people, data, things.	✓✓						
Adept at scanning reports, computer printouts or other sophisticated observational systems.	✓						
Hearing accurately. Keen sense of smell. Excellent sense of taste.							
Detecting, discovering. A person of perpetual curiosity. Delights in new knowledge. Continually seeking to expose oneself to new experiences. Highly committed to continual personal growth and learning. Wants to know why.	✓✓						
Learning from the example of others. Learns quickly.				✓✓			
Alert in observing human behavior. Studying other people's behavior.	✓✓	✓✓		✓✓			

	Sale to Criterion	Building the Wall	Strategy for Ralston	Homecoming Chair			
	1	2	3	4	5	6	7
Appraising, assessing, screening. Realistically evaluating people's needs. Accurately assessing public mood. Quickly sizing up situations and their political realities.	✓✓	✓✓		✓			
Intelligence tempered by common sense.	✓✓	✓✓	✓✓	✓✓			
Balancing factors. Judging. Showing good judgment.	✓✓	✓✓	✓✓	✓✓			
B. Investigating/Analyzing/Systematizing/Evaluating Skills							
Anticipating problems before they occur.	✓	✓✓	✓✓	✓✓			
Recognizing need for more information before a decision can be made intelligently. Skilled at clarifying problems or situation.	✓✓	✓✓	✓✓	✓✓			
Inspecting, examining, surveying, researching exhaustively, gathering information.	✓✓	✓✓	✓✓	✓✓			
Interviewing people. Researching personally through investigation and interviews. Inquiring.	✓✓	✓✓	✓✓				
Researching resources, ways and means.	✓✓	✓✓	✓✓	✓✓			
Dissecting, breaking down principles into parts. Analyzing needs, values, resources, communication situations, requirements, performance specifications, etc.	✓✓	✓✓	✓✓	✓✓			
Diagnosing. Separating "wheat from chaff." Reviewing large amounts of material and extracts essence.	✓✓						
Perceiving and defining cause-and-effect relationships. Ability to trace problems, ideas, etc. to their source.		✓✓	✓✓				
Grouping, perceiving common denominators. Organizing material/information in a systematic way. Categorizing.	✓✓		✓✓				
Testing an idea or hypothesis.							
Determining or figuring out, problem solving, troubleshooting.	✓✓	✓✓	✓✓	✓✓			
Reviewing. Screening data. Critiquing, evaluating by measurable or subjective criteria (e.g., programs, loans, papers, quizzes, work, staff, records, program bids evidence, options, qualifications, etc.).	✓✓		✓✓				

	Sale to Criterion	Building the Wall	Strategy for Ralston	Homecoming Chair			
	1	2	3	4	5	6	7
Making decisions based on information gathered.	✓✓	✓✓	✓✓	✓✓			
Reevaluating.	✓	✓✓		✓			
V. THE CONVENTIONAL THEME (Data and Method Skills)							
A. Detail and Follow-Through Skills	✓✓	✓✓	✓✓				
Following through, executing, maintaining.	✓✓	✓✓	✓✓	✓✓			
Good at getting things done.	✓✓	✓✓		✓✓			
Implementing decisions. Providing support services. Applying what others have developed.	✓✓						
Precise attainment of set limits, tolerances or standards. Brings projects in on time and within budget. Skilled at making arrangements for events, processes. Responsible.	✓✓	✓✓	✓✓	✓✓			
Expediting, dispatching. Adept at finding ways to speed up a job.	✓✓	✓✓	✓✓	✓✓			
Able to handle a great variety of tasks and responsibilities simultaneously and efficiently.	✓✓	✓✓	✓✓	✓✓			
Good at getting materials. Collecting things. Purchasing. Compiling.				✓✓			
Approving, validating information.	✓	✓✓	✓✓				
Keeping information confidential.							
Persevering.	✓✓	✓✓	✓✓	✓✓			
Following detailed instructions. Keen and accurate memory for detail. Showing careful attention to, and keeping track of, details.	✓			✓			
High tolerance of repetition and/or monotony.							
Checking, proofreading.	✓		✓				
Systematic manipulation of data. Good at processing information. Collates/tabulates data accurately, compares current with previous data. Keeping records. Recording (kinds of data).			✓				
Facilitating and simplifying other people's finding things.							

	Sale to Criterion	Building the Wall	Strategy for Ralston	Homecoming Chair			
	1	2	3	4	5	6	7
Organizing written and numerical data according to a prescribed plan. Classification skills. Filing, retrieving data.	✓						
Clerical ability. Operating business machines and data processing machines to attain organizational and economic goals. Reproducing materials.							
B. Working with Numbers							
Numerical ability. Expert at learning and remembering numbers.							
Counting. Taking inventory.		✓		✓			
Calculating, computing, arithmetic skills. Rapid manipulation of numbers. Rapid computations performed in head or on paper.							
Managing money. Financial planning and management. Keeping financial records. Accountability.			✓✓	✓			
Appraising, economic research and analysis, cost analysis, estimates, projections. Comparisons, financial/fiscal analysis and planning/programming.	✓✓		✓✓	✓			
Budget planning, preparation, justification, administration, analysis and review.	✓✓		✓✓	✓			
Extremely economical. Skilled at allocating scarce financial resources.				✓✓			
Preparing financial reports.			✓✓	✓			
Using numbers as a reasoning tool. Very sophisticated mathematical abilities. Effective at solving statistical problems.							
VI. THE REALISTIC THEME (Thing and Method Skills)							
Working with Your Hands and Body							
Molding, shaping, making.				✓✓			
Preparing, clearing, building, constructing, assembling, setting up, installing, laying.				✓✓			
Lifting/pushing/pulling/balancing, carrying, unloading/moving, delivering.				✓			
Handling/feeling. Keen sense of touch. Finger dexterity. Manipulating things.				✓✓			

	Sale to Criterion	Building the Wall	Strategy for Ralston	Homecoming Chair			
	1	2	3	4	5	6	7
Precision working. Showing dexterity or speed.				✓✓			
Feeding, tending.							
Controlling/operating, blasting, grinding, forging, cutting, filling, applying, pressing, binding.							
Using small or large tools, machinery. Operating vehicles or equipment.							
Fitting, adjusting, tuning, maintaining, repairing. Masters machinery against its will. Troubleshooting machine problems.				✓			
Producing things.			✓✓	✓✓			
Motor/physical coordination and agility. Eye-hand-foot coordination. Walking, climbing, running.				✓✓			
Skilled at sports.							
Physical recreation. Outdoor survival skills. Creating, planning, organizing outdoor activities.				✓✓			
Traveling.							
Cultivating, planting and nurturing growing things. Skilled at planting/nurturing plants.							
Farming, ranching, working with animals.							

References

Now that you're fully prepared to highlight your key skills and experiences in cover letters and resumes, you'll need to gather names of other people who can back up your claims. It's likely you'll want to put managers and colleagues at the top of your reference list, because they're in the best position to evaluate your paid work.

Unfortunately, company policy may prohibit them from discussing your performance, because employees who receive poor references may sue. Even if you made a tremendous contribution and received consistently excellent reviews, access to your colleagues may be restricted. Why would you want to sue anyone over a positive reference? You wouldn't, but many companies feel safer blocking employees and managers from discussing any former employee's performance, good or bad. While there's no doubt this policy frustrates many to protect few, you aren't in a position to change it.

However, other sources besides your former employer can vouch for your excellent work. If you're in sales, clients make terrific references. Purchasing managers or buyers can rely on suppliers to corroborate their experiences. If you've had regular professional contact with anyone outside your company, don't hesitate to ask him to serve as a reference for you. If someone thinks you did a good job, he'll usually be honored and happy to sing your praises.

If your position is strictly an inside job, ask for a reference from a former colleague, manager of another department or an executive in a field or corporate office that's removed from your day-to-day operations. Fellow task-force members also are in an excellent position to discuss your initiative, follow-through, team skills, creativity and so on. Because they don't work with you directly, they may be less restricted in communicating with a potential employer than your manager. Supervisors or peers who worked closely with you and have since left the company also can be great references, and they're under no obligation to toe the "no comment" company line.

ROBERT HALF'S RESUMANIA

Here's an interesting character reference: "Joseph is the type of person that every father hopes his daughter will marry."

So how come his daughter didn't marry Joseph?

If you're employed and looking for another position on the QT, you probably won't want to give your current manager's name as a reference. Most potential employers understand this and accept names of others who can vouch for your performance and integrity. Some of the venues that produce favorable references include volunteer work, hobby groups, university classes, neighborhood groups, political campaigns, extracurricular activities, sports teams, church congregations, alumni and professional organizations, and private clubs. References from leaders in these groups can be useful, especially if you've made an important contribution. Officers, board and committee chairs and members are more memorable and praiseworthy than someone who only attends general membership meetings. When it comes to references, the old adage that "You get out what you put in" is only too true.

While you won't be listing references in your cover letter or resume, it's wise to have them primed and ready for when you become a top candidate for a position. Before starting your job search, decide whom you want to vouch for you. Then call to see if the people you have chosen are willing to discuss your qualifications with potential employers. This approach is courteous and smart because it alerts references to the important role you want them to play in your job search, and it provides you with the opportunity to verify their names, titles, addresses, phone numbers, and e-mail addresses.

Another important bit of protocol involves contacting references to forewarn and prepare them for possible inquiries from ABC Company regarding your performance. Just as savvy job seekers tailor cover letters, they customize references' comments for two reasons:

☆ References appreciate being briefed on the opening so they know what experience, skills and personality traits are required.

☆ References will then highlight the job seeker's strongest skills to each employer.

In other words, it helps both you and your references to brief them on what to expect when they get "the call." They want to present you in the best possible light. Help them do it.

The Catastrophic Expectation

Most people can think of at least one person with whom they have a major personality conflict. Unfortunately, that individual is often their boss, college department head, biggest client or volunteer coordinator—in other words, the person they most need to ask for a reference.

THE ART OF LYING: RECOMMENDATIONS FOR LOUSY JOB CANDIDATES

In a recent article, *The Wall Street Journal* included excerpts from the book, *The Lexicon of Intentionally Ambiguous Recommendations* (LIAR) by Lehigh University economist Robert Thornton. When writing a recommendation for a candidate with interpersonal problems, he suggests saying: "I am pleased to say this person is a former colleague of mine." For the lazy worker: "In my opinion, you will be very fortunate to get this person to work for you."

The book, published by Meadowbrook Press in Deep Haven, Minnesota, also suggests writing the following recommendations for a criminal: "He's a man of many convictions" and "I'm sorry we let her get away." For the untrustworthy candidate: "Her true ability is deceiving." And for the inept worker: "I most enthusiastically recommend this person with no qualifications whatsoever."

Many job hunters suspect these references are eager to sabotage their job search because their relationship has been so miserable. This dilemma causes many candidates to worry incessantly about their characters being assassinated.

If this scenario sounds familiar, don't be embarrassed. You'd be surprised at the number of otherwise rational people who whip themselves into an emotional frenzy obsessing about potential catastrophes when a little reality testing would put their fears to rest.

If you're concerned that someone will blackball you, ask a friend or executive recruiter to call that person for a reference. In almost every instance, he'll either lavish you with praise or pass the call along to personnel. It's rare for even a really nasty colleague to give negative feedback on someone who's left an organization. Now that you aren't bugging him anymore, he can afford at least to be charitable, if not downright complimentary. Few people are comfortable destroying a person's reputation, especially if there isn't some reward for them in doing it.

Should your friend hang up the phone and confirm your worst fears, you have three possible courses of action:

☆ You can confront the perpetrator with his accusations and threaten him with a lawsuit for libel. This isn't your best choice, because it's time consuming, emotionally draining and expensive.

☆ You can ask another person at the company with whom you have a good rapport to serve as your reference instead.

☆   If the organization is large enough, you can resolve the situation by telling potential employers to call human resources for a reference. While legal policies may restrict HR staffers from giving you a recommendation, they won't destroy your reputation either.

People who leave companies under adverse circumstances often work out agreements with management stating exactly what the company will tell a potential employer about their work and why they left. If you've been fired or terminated because of a reorganization or downsizing, ask your boss for this agreement as part of your severance package. Unless you've done something truly egregious, he'll be relieved to corroborate a mutually agreeable account of why you left and how you benefitted the company (providing legal policies allow him to give more than your name, rank and serial number).

Many job seekers think *letters of recommendation* are the best vehicles for impressing potential employers. Generally, this isn't true. Why? Because generic letters of recommendation aren't tailored to the needs of a particular company. It's similar to the resume or cover letter that tries to be all things to all people, and ends up not being much of anything to anybody. And because it's addressed, "To Whom It May Concern," it lacks the credibility of a personal phone call. Unless you're going to a foreign country or you're asked to provide a letter of recommendation, rely on verbal references. They're more personal and focus on why an employer would be fortunate to hire you.

A Good Letter of Recommendation

Occasionally you may need a letter of recommendation. You and your reference may be leaving the company at the same time because of a downsizing. You may be moving to another part of the country or the world. You may be terminating under rather unhappy circumstances and you want a letter in hand because you frankly don't trust what a phone call might divulge. Or because someone has specifically asked you for one.

For your letter to be really effective, you'll need to advise your reference on what to emphasize. Think ahead to the positions you'll most likely pursue and the skills, background and personality traits they require. Then ask your reference to speak to those particular issues when describing your qualifications.

The following letter of reference is for a woman who wants to move from an administrative assistant position to a translating, interpreting and teaching job in international business. She asked her supervisor to put together a letter highlighting her applicable experience in those areas.

Letter of Reference

Good Morning:

Carmen Culpepper has been with START (name changed) since August 1992, when she joined us as a member of the Paratransit team, which administers the program for the physically and mentally challenged population. In her role with this department, Ms. Culpepper specialized in serving as a liaison with the public, prominent business executives, government and community leaders and foreign dignitaries in providing information about the HandiRides program and the agency as a whole.

Because of her facility with Spanish, French, Italian and Portuguese, we regularly called on her to interpret at conferences and public meetings. She also has given program presentations to the community and translated letters, manuals, pamphlets, news releases and notices for both internal and external use in Spanish.

Her dedication and zeal for excellence have made Ms. Culpepper an invaluable part of the Paratransit team, and her initiative and creativity in communicating the agency's mission to others has been praiseworthy. While she is most cooperative as part of a group effort, she can definitely think on her feet and meet deadlines under pressure as an individual contributor.

I strongly recommend her for a position of trust, especially one that uses her facility with languages and her affinity for a diversity of people.

Sincerely yours,

Jim Tamblin (name changed)

"So, tell me . . . what motivated you to seek a position with us?"

4

Cover Letters for Direct-Mail Campaigns

Choosing Your Recipients

As mentioned in Chapter 1, direct-mail campaigns aren't the most effective way to secure interviews, especially if you flood the job market with identical cover letters and resumes. However, direct contact with companies can be worthwhile if you select the employers carefully and then tailor your correspondence to capture their attention.

Some careers are highly specialized (e.g., petroleum engineering), so determining employers who need this type of expertise is a no-brainer. On the other hand, many fields and functions, such as human resources, sales, accounting, and public relations, are important to a variety of industries. If your career is one of them and you've decided to use direct mail, you must narrow your targets to a manageable number. A good rule of thumb is to calculate how many employers you can personally call to confirm receipt of your resume, then mail only to that number. The following sections describe techniques to begin the winnowing process.

Consider Your Current Industry

If you're in telecommunications and you get a real kick out of a high-tech environment, it makes sense to stay within your industry, not only because you enjoy it but because you have experience in that arena. Begin your job search by listing your current or most recent employer's top competitors. This group of organizations should comprise your most viable direct-mail targets.

Make a List of Your Favorite Products and Services

I once had a client who loved airplanes so much that he wanted to be involved with them professionally. While he didn't know much about aircraft, his enthusiasm more than made up for his lack of information. After considering various ways to apply his skills to the air transportation industry, he focused on companies that leased and serviced private jets for international clients. Because he had previously been an anthropologist, he had many international government and business contacts who might want to maintain their jets in the United States. During his first year with the firm, he doubled its international business.

If you've become an unofficial cheerleader for a particular product or service, you might want to work for the organization that makes it. Enthusiasm can be a valued substitute for specific experience, especially if you know how to court a team you truly admire.

Look for High-Growth Opportunities

You don't have to be an economist to know that high-growth companies and industries create more jobs than declining ones. Or that major, healthy industries in any city or region will employ more people than those with a limited presence.

To learn which local or national enterprises are important and growing, head for the library and locate these resources:

☆ **The U.S. Industrial and Trade Outlook** Published by the Department of Commerce, this reference volume provides an excellent thumbnail sketch of industries including sales performance during the previous seven years, primary issues affecting their ability to compete, annual and long-term forecasts and other sources of information.

☆ **Infotrac or the Readers' Guide to Periodical Literature**   Infotrac is a computerized database of magazine articles published during the previous three years. Users can search for articles by subject, author or title and learn the name of the periodical, issue, title and page number. You also can request synopses of various articles. The *Readers' Guide to Periodical Literature* is a similar resource for articles in hard-copy form.

☆ **Encyclopedia of Business Information**   This reference lists each industry's encyclopedias, handbooks, indexes, almanacs, yearbooks, trade associations, periodicals, directories, computer databases, research centers and statistical sources.

☆ **The Gale Directory of Publications**   This directory lists national, local and trade magazines alphabetically and by state.

☆ **Business Magazines**   Publications such as *Forbes, Business Week, Fortune, Inc., Money* and *Financial World* contain a wealth of information on business trends and individual industries and companies.

☆ **Local and National Newspapers**   Particularly useful newspapers to read for industry trend information are *The Wall Street Journal, Barron's, USA Today,* local weekly business newspapers and daily papers in larger cities.

☆ **Trade Journals**   Every industry and profession has at least one publication devoted to it. Ask librarians or research the preceding resources for the names of those covering your targeted industries. (For more references on industries, see Appendix.)

Researching Potential Employers

Investigate Companies You Admire

Have you ever aspired to work for a particular company but thought your goal was unattainable? This may be a good time to learn if the organization is what you've envisioned and if you have talent and experience it considers useful. After all, I never expected to be writing a column for the *National Business Employment Weekly,* let alone two books.

Identify Organizations That Are Most Likely to Need You

Once you've made a "most-wanted" list of a few industries and companies that you like and/or have identified 10 to 20 products or services that you admire, do

---

ROBERT HALF'S RESUMANIA

Explaining her reason for leaving a company, an Oregon woman writes: "I took this job, and picked up and moved to a new city based upon the expectation of rapid advancement. Instead, I was met with a constant string of broken promises and lies, as well as cockroaches, which was simply too much for me to bear. So I returned home and now seek a job with a company that lives up to its promises and provides clean and sanitary working conditions."

Just another example of a company not being sensitive to the needs of its employees. The least it could have included in its benefits package was a monthly supply of roach traps.

---

some research to discover which firms need your particular combination of experience and skills and can provide you with an opportunity to make a satisfying contribution. Start your investigation by learning about each company's culture along with such facts as size, philosophy, product line and locations. References you can use to gather this information include:

☆ **Corporate Annual Reports** Publicly held corporations produce these handsome booklets to impress and attract current and potential investors, suppliers, employees and other interested readers. The reports include information about financial performance and products and services, and publicize the organization's business, community and charitable activities. The reports are authored by the firm itself, so they're generally highly positive. However, they're worth reading as long as you keep their intrinsic spin in mind.

☆ **Dun & Bradstreet Million Dollar Directory** A listing of approximately 160,000 U.S. businesses alphabetically, geographically and by product classification.

☆ **Moody's Complete Corporate Index** If you want a lengthy description about a particular company, this publication is for you. Moody's provides extensive details about companies and their histories—ranging from financial information to when the companies were founded.

☆ **Online Services** America Online, Compuserve, Yahoo!, Excite, Altavista and a variety of other online resources will link you to an overwhelming amount of information on companies, industries and careers. You can access them through your computer's modem at home, work or your local library. (For specific information about online services, see Chapter 8.)

☆ **The Thomas Register of American Manufacturers; Thomas Register Catalog File** By looking up a particular product or service, you can find almost every company that provides it in this 26-volume publication. Published annually, Thomas's includes data on branch offices, capital ratings, company offices, addresses and phone numbers and company catalogs.

☆ **Yearbook of International Organizations** Lists 27,000 international organizations that are active in at least three countries; they are indexed by name, address and description.

As you're doing research, take notes on each company that might need your services. The following example shows a completed form that summarizes the data you'll need when writing a cover letter and resume. With this information, you can write an intelligent letter to a hiring manager explaining why you're interested in her organization and why you're a good candidate.

Company/Agency Research

Name of Company	Environmental Technologies Inc.
Address	2222 Rimer Road, Irwin, PA 15146
Phone Number	412-686-3000
Contact Name	Gene Cunningham
Title	President

1. **How old is this organization? How did it get started?**
   Environmental Technologies was started in 1984 by Gene Cunningham and John Berry, both environmental engineers. They foresaw the increasing need for environmental consulting, particularly among companies in the heavy industries that were gradually closing plants in the Pittsburgh area.

2. **How has it grown; slowly, quickly, internally, by acquisition?**
   The company has grown quickly for several reasons. It had an excellent niche in its market. Management knows how to sell its expertise. The need for environmental consulting continues to grow, especially now that the Soviet Bloc has dissolved and the United States and Mexico have signed NAFTA.

3. What are its sales volume, annual budget and number of employees?
While the company is privately owned, I did find some interesting statistics in a local business directory. Its annual sales are about $100 million, and it employs about 100 people.

4. What is its profit, return on investment and market share?
Profit and return on investment figures weren't available, but market share in this region is about 45 percent, especially in water, smokestack filtration and toxic chemical management. In the past three years, the company has established a presence in Mexico and Poland, but market-share figures aren't available for those countries.

5. Where are its plants, offices, stores, corporate headquarters?
The corporate headquarters is in a suburb of Pittsburgh. It has branch offices in Mexico, Poland, Detroit and Los Angeles.

6. What are its products and/or services, especially major areas of concentration and new developments?
It's an environmental engineering consulting firm that specializes in "rust belt" issues including smokestack pollution, water pollution and toxic waste. It uses cutting edge technology in these three areas, and it's increasing its business in Mexico and Eastern Europe by about 20 percent a year.

7. Does it seem to be community spirited and/or profess an interest in cultivating its employees?
While none of the articles I've read specifically mentioned this, ET does use humor in its ads by playing off the initials ET. A friend who lives in the Pittsburgh area told me he has seen a newspaper article that describes ET's pro bono work advising a few small towns about ways to dispose of their slag dumps.

8. What kinds of careers does it offer?
The careers that interest me the most are the engineering ones, particularly consulting assignments in Eastern Europe.

9. What specific experience, personality traits or skills do I have that might interest this company?
My parents have often talked about growing up in Poland, the natural beauty of the country, and the likely opportunities there now. I would like to use my environmental background and dual-language capability to get to know the country better and help residents make it beautiful and healthy again.

Writing the Direct-Mail Cover Letter

When you've done your research and selected 10 to 50 companies that interest you and may need your skills, write a tailored cover letter to each of them using the guidelines in Chapter 2. On page 74 is an example of a letter developed from the research form prepared on Environmental Technologies.

When reviewing this example, notice that:

☆ The inside address contains the name of a specific person. In a direct-mail cover letter, this is critical. The person to whom you address your letter should be the individual who has the power to hire you. Usually this will be your direct manager or the person to whom he reports. If the organization is small, writing to the president will attract attention. Whatever you do, don't send your letter to personnel unless you want a job in that department. Human resources screens applicants, but it doesn't make hiring decisions about anyone except its own staff.

   You can locate the name you need by calling the company's main number, reading its annual report, or reviewing directories of corporate managers including *Dun & Bradstreet Reference Book of Corporate Management, Encyclopedia of Associations,* and *Standard & Poor's Register of Corporations.* (For more information about each of these references, see Appendix.)

☆ The first two paragraphs of the letter provide information about why the candidate is specifically interested in the company. This approach not only pleases readers, it shows them that the writer does his homework.

☆ The third paragraph states compelling reasons for bringing this engineer on board. He has great experience, a personal commitment to helping Poland clean up its environment and a willingness to live there and use his relatives as contacts. How many American engineers gladly volunteer for such assignments or have a viable network of contacts in this part of the world?

☆ The final paragraph shows that the writer plans to continue taking the initiative in developing this relationship. This is the best approach for maintaining control of your job search and proving that you're willing to go after what you want. But be forewarned: If you say you'll follow up and then don't, your potential employer will view you more negatively than if you had never made the promise.

Direct-Mail Cover Letter

Wayne Saleski
223 Pinehurst Lane
Cleveland, OH 44129
216-682-3443

November 12, 1999

Mr. Gene Cunningham
President
Environmental Technologies Inc.
2222 Rimer Road
Irwin, PA 15146

Dear Mr. Cunningham:

For the past month, I've been doing research on the environmental consulting firms taking an initiative to work with countries in Eastern Europe. From the articles I've read in environmental trade journals and the documentaries I've seen on TV, there is a tremendous amount of work to be done in cleaning up the industrial pollution left from 40 years of Communist rule. I can also personally attest to this based on what I saw during a trip last year to visit relatives in Poland.

As I'm sure you know, many of the articles discussing efforts to tackle this multifaceted problem mention Environmental Technologies as a driving force in developing cost-effective solutions. I admire your organization's approach and the commitment you have made to helping these fledgling capitalists positively impact their environment's future.

I am writing to you because I think I might be of potential help to ET. I've spent the past ten years as an environmental engineer for Benchmark Steel and the Corrigan Group in both water pollution and solid waste management. I speak and write Polish fluently, understand the country's culture, and have family and contacts in Warsaw that might be useful in generating new business for ET. Most of all I would welcome the opportunity to live in Poland and play a role in creating a safe and healthy environment for its citizens.

I've enclosed a resume for your perusal and will call you next week to confirm your receipt of this letter and discuss whether scheduling a time to get together would be beneficial. I look forward to talking with you.

Sincerely yours,

Wayne Saleski

Enclosure

Other Cover Letters from Real People

Before-and-After Example

Nancy Leiberman worked for Estee Lauder for many years as a sales representative and a regional manager, specializing in conducting skin care and makeup clinics for her stores. She did an excellent job, but the company decided to eliminate positions such as hers because store revenues couldn't justify the marketing overhead for her services. Consequently, Nancy became a typical victim of downsizing—talented but traumatized.

Determined not to stake her future on a job with another large company, she decided to locate new and innovative players in the cosmetics industry and explore the possibility of landing a position with one of them. On page 76 is her first attempt at a direct-mail cover letter to one of these firms.

Before

2222 Mount Holyoke Circle
Houston, Texas 77017
October 20, 1999

Ms. Lena Tande
Juin Rachele Cosmetics Inc.
1300 Post Oak Road, Suite 1815
Houston, TX 77056

Dear Ms. Tande:

I'm writing to you concerning a potential management position with your firm.

As you can see, I've had quite a lot of experience in the cosmetic business and I would like to stress the fact that I "pioneered" a couple of positions such as the Account Executive job in Kansas City which, over the years, has become the basis for Estee Lauder's staying on top of their business.

Before Estee Lauder, I worked as a cosmetic sales and beauty consultant for several years in a department store in my home town (in Ohio).

I enjoy the challenge of working with *new* products and ideas and the excitement of watching them grow into successes.

Your new company interests me and I would like the opportunity of meeting with you to discuss the possibility of how my expertise could help your company grow and, in the process, start me on a new path in my career.

Looking forward to meeting you and seeing your products.

Sincerely,

Nancy Leiberman (name changed)
713-626-1934

Nancy included good information about herself in her letter, but she neglects to say why she's particularly interested in this cosmetic company. She also needs to take responsibility for following up on her resume.

In her second attempt, on page 78, Nancy "baits her hook" with a complimentary paragraph showing why this small firm intrigues her. She also has polished her language, which makes her letter easier to read, and stated her intention to follow up on her resume.

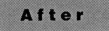

2222 Mount Holyoke Circle
Houston, Texas 77017
October 20, 1999

Ms. Lena Tande
Juin Rachele Cosmetics Inc.
1300 Post Oak Road, Suite 1815
Houston, TX 77056

Dear Ms. Tande:

Last week I read an article in the *Houston Post* about your cosmetics firm and its new approach to skin care for teenagers and young adults. I applaud your efforts in teaching young people "the basics" while they are just beginning to develop lifetime habits. Much of my work for Estee Lauder has been devoted to a similar mission.

As you can see from my resume, I've had quite a lot of experience in the cosmetic business. I would like to stress that I "pioneered" a couple of positions, such as the Account Executive job in Kansas City, which have become the basis for Estee Lauder's staying on top of its business. Also, before Estee Lauder, I worked as a cosmetic sales and beauty consultant for several years in a department store in my home town (in Ohio). I enjoy the challenge of marketing *new* products and thrive on the ideas and the excitement of watching them grow into successes.

Your new company interests me greatly. I would like the opportunity to discuss in person how my expertise could help your company grow and in the process, start me on a new career path.

I will call you next week to set up a time to meet with you and learn more about your products.

Sincerely,

Nancy Leiberman (name changed)
713-626-1934

The cover letter on page 80 was written by a person who (it seems) is a legend in her own mind. While she may have good reasons for saying these wonderful things about herself, what are they? What has she done to back up the statements in her letter? As they said in the popular TV commercial, "Where's the Beef?"

To make matters worse, she left space in the letter to insert addresses with a computer mail-merge program. This means she intends to use the same letter for who-knows-how-many people. Driving a final nail in the coffin, she suggests that potential employers call her if they're interested.

What's Wrong with This Cover Letter?

10336 Kingsley Road
Buena Vista, CA 90623

213-683-7220
June 22, 1999

Would your company benefit from increased sales? Increased profits? Professionally managed operations?

If you are interested in gaining a team player with a proven record of success as a Sales Manager and Marketing Representative, take a few minutes to look at the enclosed resume.

Your organization would be gaining a person with strengths that include:

Experience and expertise developed during 16 years in civic organizations . . .
seven solid years in sales.

Self-motivated . . . goal oriented . . . ability to generate income . . . reduce costs . . . increase profit margin. Excellent bilingual communication skills . . . effective listener . . . easily develops rapport . . . identify needs and problems . . . solutions oriented.

Understanding people . . . what motivates them . . . working with them to resolve problems . . . coordinate, delegate, supervise . . . to accomplish objectives.

Respected by peers . . . known for honesty, integrity . . . making things work . . . getting the job done.

If you are interested in knowing more about me and how my experience and accomplishments could benefit you and your organization, please contact me.

I look forward to hearing from you and meeting with you.

Sincerely,

Jane Doe

This candidate has a misguided approach to selling herself. Unfortunately, her grandiose, unproven claims will sabotage her chances of talking with a recruiter, unless she includes so many specific achievements on her resume that she manages to overcome this negative start.

ROBERT HALF'S RESUMANIA

A job hunter with an otherwise good resume added this note: "I simply can't afford to send one of these to everyone. Please feel free to make copies and distribute them to your branch offices, subsidiaries, and other potentially interested parties. Your cooperation in this matter is sincerely appreciated."

The Save-a-Tree Foundation should give him an award.

Here's a comment from another job seeker about his resume:

"Attached you will find six copies of my resume for your use. If you use them up, just let me know and I will send you lots more. If you have any use for ones that are old and out-of-date, I have tons of them, too."

Thanks for the offer.

Two Different Cover Letters, One Candidate

Larry Frantz was CFO of Graphics Tech when its parent company decided to split up the organization hoping that its parts were worth more individually than collectively. After thinking it over, Larry decided to start a consulting business specializing in investor relations and presentations for initial public offering (IPO) road shows, stockholder meetings, venture capital requests and other instances when complicated financial information must be explained in basic terms.

The following are two customized letters he prepared for a targeted direct-mail campaign. Larry knows never to send a cloned cover letter to anyone, especially presidents of companies. For this reason, each of his letters mentions when he heard or read about an organization.

LAWRENCE G. FRANTZ
6535 Southwestern Drive
Dallas, Texas 75248
214-233-1321

January 10, 1999

Mr. Charles M. Hansen, Jr.
President
Technotex Corp.
4111 Mint Way
Dallas, TX 75237

Dear Mr. Hansen:

I was reading about your recent IPO in the *Dallas Business Journal* and felt compelled to write and warn you of a potential pitfall on the rocky road of public offerings.

The biggest mistake we made after we went public in 1997 was not installing a proactive investor relations program immediately. We realized the error and hired an investor relations professional a year later. We spent most of the next year meeting individually with 100 analysts. These efforts were very effective in attracting interest in our stock, but by then the stock price bottomed at less than half the IPO price, and the majority owner decided to exit the industry by liquidating the company.

The company was Graphics Tech,* headquartered in Dallas and traded on the NYSE, and I was the CFO. When I started my investor relations consulting business, I decided to help newly public companies avoid the same mistake Graphics Tech made. We will never know, of course, whether we could have altered the course of events had we aggressively pursued the analyst community right after our IPO. A good investor relations program cannot compensate for lousy business conditions nor poor company performance. But every day there are investors who, for various reasons, want to sell their shares in your company. If you are not actively attracting new investors, your stock price may decline even if your company and your industry do well.

I would like to discuss Graphics Tech's story with you and offer feedback on your investor relations efforts. I will call next week to see when we might get together.

Sincerely,

Larry Frantz

Enclosure: Biographical Summary

*(Not a real company)

LAWRENCE G. FRANTZ
6535 Southwestern Drive
Dallas, Texas 75248
214-233-1321

November 12, 1999

Mr. Robert A. Bishop, II
President & CEO
CBI Healthcare Systems Inc.
802 East Street
Garland, TX 75042

Dear Mr. Bishop:

I enjoyed your November 10 presentation at the Southwest Venture Forum. The concept behind your company is a fascinating one and your opening line, "Ozone gas is the most powerful oxidizer known to mankind," certainly got our attention from the very beginning.

Your speech and handout material obviously took considerable time to prepare. Wouldn't it be convenient to have a well-designed presentation "on the shelf" to be pulled down and used whenever the opportunity arises? If you had such a preprepared presentation that you were confident would be well received, it would make the presentation a lot easier to give and the more it's given, the easier it is to raise new capital.

Such a presentation would include:

1. An outline of a speech that hits all the highlights of your business in a way that is most meaningful to potential investors or lenders.
2. Clear, concise presentation graphics that keep the audience interested and help them understand and remember your message (80% of us are visual learners).
3. Handouts that include the key facts and ideas you want the audience to remember or pass on to others.

As a former CFO, I know how to communicate with investors and lenders, and I'm good at explaining the key life-and-death factors of a business to people who are unfamiliar with it. That's one of the things I did for many years for my employer. Now I have my own business doing the same thing for small businesses like yours.

But I need your help. I need a track record of satisfied clients, and until I develop that record, you can take advantage of my expertise for a nominal cost. If you will ever again have to give a presentation to potential investors, then you will want to take my call next week.

Sincerely,

Larry Frantz

Enclosure: Biographical Summary

Human Resources Cover Letter

Ilona J. Torraca seems to have broken the rules by writing to the recruiting co-ordinator for Upjohn Company, until you realize that she's pursuing a human resources position. Her needs/benefits approach is an excellent example of a technique called "counselor selling." Regardless of the method you use—phone, letter, e-mail or personal call—the best way to sell a customer a product, idea or person is to state his needs and how you can accommodate them. Just be sure that you identify needs that are pertinent to your reader. If they aren't, you'll sound patronizing or out of your league.

P. O. Box 3306
Lake Allegheny, NY 11779
January 22, 1999

Ms. Carol McClure
Recruiting Coordinator
The Upjohn Company
7000 Portage Road
Kalamazoo, MI 49004

Dear Ms. McClure:

In doing library research on health-care issues, I found an article in the *Detroit Free Press* on the rising costs of employee benefits in large Michigan corporations. Naturally, Upjohn was among this group. Based on your steeply rising costs and my success in holding the line on health-care expenses, I think I might be of service to your organization by substantially improving the overall efficiency and effectiveness of your employee benefit plan.

The following are a few examples of how The Upjohn Company can benefit from my skills and knowledge.

What Your Company Needs

- An efficient and organized benefit plan that reduces costs and increases profits.
- Employee benefit planning seminars, especially retirement planning.
- Foreign language expertise to create and/or maintain international business relations.
- Establishment of new company policies from government health care reform.

What I Can Do for You

- Create a cost reduction employee benefit plan to satisfy the requirements of current business laws and increase employee motivation.
- Establish and conduct seminars, using excellent written and oral communication skills.
- Provide German language skills and cultural experience.
- Interpret complex government regulations into language that is understandable to your employees.

As you can see by the enclosed resume, I hold a degree in Business Administration and have six years of intensive experience with an international corporation.

I believe my background can be useful to your company, and I would welcome the opportunity to present my qualifications in a personal interview. I plan to travel to Michigan March 8–13, 1999. Perhaps we can schedule a meeting during that time. I will call you before my trip to see if getting together would be useful.

Sincerely,

Ilona J. Torraca
515-242-7355

More Direct-Mail Cover Letters

Five great examples of cover letters written for direct-mail campaigns follow. The first is by a graduate student in architecture looking for a postsecondary teaching position. Have you any doubt that Dean Ripley will be interested in this obviously intelligent young man who takes the time to read about fellow colleagues in pertinent journals?

Thomas Lamb

Armbruster Boulevard   **Denver, Colorado 80219**   **303-371-6677**

January 30, 1999

Dr. Melba Ripley
Dean of the School of Architecture
University of Louisiana
1000 Webber Hall
Baton Rouge, LA 70814

Dear Dean Ripley:

As someone who has devoted nearly five years to the study of how inexpensive housing can be made of native materials in Third World countries, I was more than intrigued by the recent accomplishments of you and your students in designing and providing "instant" housing to victims of the recent hurricane in Central America.

My purpose in writing is to inquire about whether you might have any positions available in developing new structures and working with students in this area. I have just finished serving on a committee that designed a four-semester curriculum on housing citizens of the Third World for the University of Denver. While the topography there is beautiful, I've decided that I would like to head for warmer weather and be part of the premiere effort to eradicate homelessness wherever possible.

During the past four years, I have been a Graduate Assistant to Dr. Graham Benson who has shared the rostrum with you at many academic and global conferences on housing. Together we, along with a group of high school and college students, have spent the past several summers showing people in south central Africa how to mix a specially prepared binder developed by our research lab with local materials to make durable homes in a matter of days. I would truly enjoy merging my knowledge of construction techniques with those of your colleagues to continue advancing the state-of-the-art in this innovative and humanitarian endeavor.

Enclosed you will find my vita. I plan to vacation in Louisiana this spring and would appreciate the opportunity to talk with you then about my career objectives and your need for new faculty. I will call you next week to ascertain a mutually convenient time for us to meet.

Sincerely yours,

Thomas Lamb

Enclosure

Josh A. Whitley
4131 Fawnhollow
Dallas, TX 75238
214-866-4990

April 8, 1999

Mr. Galen Crouch
Senior Vice President
Southern Company
1200 Peachtree Street
Atlanta, GA 30070

Dear Mr. Crouch:

A recent *Wall Street Journal* article quoted your description of the new "general asso-ciates" program for liberal arts graduates "from superior schools who have outstand-ing academic and leadership credentials." I believe I am one of those students and would like to be considered for your program.

As you can see from my enclosed resume, I've held several management positions, most notably president of my 165-member fraternity, which included managing a $20,000 budget as well as supervising six committees. I've also had extensive busi-ness experience, having financed 50 percent of my college education through a combi-nation of work study and summer jobs.

You will also notice that I am an English major with a Psychology minor. Through my English courses, I have learned to both think clearly and communicate effectively, qualities prized by corporations such as Southern Company, but often missing in more narrowly trained students. My psychology background helps me work with and super-vise people effectively, which is so necessary in business today.

I will be in Atlanta the week of May 5–10 and would enjoy meeting with you to discuss how I might fit into your program. I believe my immediate goal of entering a manage-ment training program with a progressive *Fortune 500* company matches your goal of hiring students with "high-quality academic and leadership experience." I will call your secretary later this week to schedule an appointment.

Sincerely,

Josh Whitley

Enclosure

Carrie E. French
717 Williamsburg Terrace
Evanston, IL 60203
708-234-6631

October 29, 1999

Ms. Colleen Gramacki
Recruiting Administrator
McKeith & Company, Inc.
One Preston Park Plaza
Suite 2000
Chicago, IL 60603

Dear Ms. Gramacki:

I want to make a difference!

Recently, I attended a presentation on your company's Business Analyst Program. I am very impressed with the program and McKeith & Company as a whole. Particularly appealing is the range of your industries and clients served, and the firm's ability to forge lasting partnerships. Equally impressive is the strong team structure and cooperation within the firm. It is clear that McKeith & Company is making a difference in the business world.

I feel my skills can make a difference to the McKeith team. Throughout my academic career, I have demonstrated superior achievement and developed strong quantitative and analytic skills. However, my skills extend far beyond the classroom. My extracurricular activities include positions of leadership as well as work on teams and committees. Through campus organizations and volunteer work, I have also made an effort to contribute both to the university and to the surrounding community. I can offer McKeith these abilities as well as my dedication, energy and willingness to learn new skills.

I am seeking a position in the McKeith & Company, Inc., Business Analyst Program at the Chicago office. I would like the opportunity to meet with you to explain more fully my qualifications and the ways in which I can contribute to the McKeith team. Thank you for your time.

Sincerely,

Carrie E. French

Randall T. Jones
4326 Hunter Avenue
Orange City, FL 32725

April 23, 1999

Mr. Barry Noggle
Flight Attendant Recruitment
Delta Airlines
Dallas, TX 75202

Dear Mr. Noggle:

Enclosed is my application for a flight attendant position with Delta. Delta is my favorite airline because of the camaraderie among its employees, its exceptional reputation in the industry and the commitment to quality services for its passengers.

I understand that Delta has many successful routes to Europe. Your hub in Frankfurt particularly interests me because I was born in Germany and understand its people and culture. Having been raised in both Germany and the United States, I am equally comfortable in either country. Flying with Delta would give me the opportunity to use my bicontinental experience in a career I can really be proud of.

In the past few years, I've been searching for the right niche. Being an international flight attendant seems to be an excellent match for my background and interests. My experience as a skycap reinforces my feeling that making people feel comfortable and cared for is very satisfying.

I would be proud to be part of your organization. I will call next week to confirm that you received my application and to answer any questions you might have.

Sincerely yours,

Randy Jones
407-299-7884

5625 Stamford Street—Apt. 12
Philadelphia, PA 19152
215-682-4127

January 21, 1999

Mr. Art Robb, Vice President
Baker Environmental Inc.
420 Rouser Road
Coraopolis, PA 15108

Dear Mr. Robb:

This past December, I graduated from the University of Pittsburgh with a B.S. in Civil Engineering that included an environmental course concentration. In my search for employment, I have selected companies that offer career opportunities, professional development, a challenging work environment and the potential for advancement. Baker Environmental is such a company.

I also want to be part of an organization that is dedicated to the improvement of our environment. As the corporation's fastest growing division in 1998, Baker Environmental has shown such dedication. Your work with OXY USA and CONOCO to capture coalbed methane gas is an example of the type of innovative solutions necessary to solve today's complex industrial problems. I was introduced to this method of resource recovery through a critique of an Environmental Impact Statement that dealt with the development of natural gas and coal deposits in Colorado.

In addition to the environmental impact statement process, I have been introduced to aspects of site remediation. The analysis of a fictitious hazardous waste landfill as part of my senior design project became a reality as I tracked project revenues and costs for a landfill remediation project in Ohio. I am also familiar with many of the different treatment systems available through work on an environmental products database and a quarterly publication that highlights innovative environmental technologies.

I have enclosed my resume for your review. I will contact you during the week of February 7 to discuss the professional opportunities that exist with Baker Environmental. Thank you for your consideration.

Sincerely,

Lorna M. Stuart

Enclosure

"I see here that you left your previous position because of insufficient vacation time."

5

Cover Letters for Help-Wanted Ads and Job Hot Lines

Ask any garden variety job seeker to tell you the first thing he would do to begin job hunting and he'll probably say, "Turn to the want ads in the city newspaper." Ask a savvier candidate where she started and she'll likely say, "I subscribed to the *National Business Employment Weekly* and began reading job ads and articles."

But ask a true job-search guru what he'd do to locate an ideal position, he'll reply, "First I'd make a list of all my contacts to inform them about my desire to change companies. Then I'd subscribe to the *National Business Employment Weekly* to ensure I was on top of the job openings in my field and level around the country. I would call a few executive search firms where I knew someone. Then I'd create a list of potential employers for a selective direct-mail campaign."

Ads play a role in every candidate's campaign. However, instead of assuming the classified section of a newspaper is the key to uncovering the best opportunities, enlightened candidates think of this resource as one of several in their arsenal of job-search techniques.

If you plan to make want ads a part of your job hunt, you'll need to tailor your cover letters and resumes to what each employer requires. While this may seem obvious, relatively few people bother to make this effort. It's likely that many of your friends and colleagues have complained about never receiving replies to their resumes. Perhaps you, too, have grumbled about rude employers who don't bother to acknowledge your correspondence. Yet before you become too indignant, ask yourself if you adhered to the job seeker's golden rule. Have you dealt with prospective employers as you expect them to deal with you? If you want the courtesy of an individualized reply, you must be thoughtful enough to craft a customized letter yourself.

Many want ads generate hundreds of replies, the majority of which have little in common with the requirements requested. You don't have to be a member of Mensa to realize that the only responses that will capture an employer's attention and generate interview appointments are those that speak specifically to the company's needs. This is doubly true if your resume is screened by a computer programmed to search for "key" words.

Do the potential employer—and yourself—a favor by replying only to those ads that are closely aligned with what you want and have to offer. Papering the world with semirelevant cover letters and resumes annoys recruiters and wastes time, energy and money you could be spending more productively taking contacts to lunch.

Interpreting an Ad

To ensure that your cover letter and resume contain what your screener (human or otherwise) is seeking, carefully comb want ads for key words and phrases that shout, "Use me or die [ignominiously in the round file]!" These words and phrases are pretty easy to spot, even for novice job seekers. For instance, review the following ad. Can you identify the "open sesame" words that your cover letter and resume must contain?

Fortunately, this ad begins with a short description of the company, which makes it relatively easy for you to do some research about the organization to customize your first paragraph. The company is a subsidiary of Wal-Mart Stores

McLane Company, one of the fastest growing companies in the U.S., is one of the largest distributors of food products and general merchandise to convenience stores, mass merchandisers and quick-serve restaurants and is a wholly-owned subsidiary of Wal-Mart. This position will be based at our Kissimmee, FL, distribution center.

HUMAN RESOURCES MANAGER

This position reports to the Division President and is responsible for employment, salary and benefit administration, safety and training, employee relations, employee enhancement programs, and other HR related duties.

Qualified candidate will have an undergraduate degree and 4 years' progressive experience as a Human Resource professional, as well as a primary focus on controlling health insurance through plan design and administration.

Our competitive salaries are complemented by an excellent benefits package including medical, dental and life coverage, 401(K) plan, stock purchase program, and more. For confidential consideration, forward your resume with salary requirements to: **Employment Manager, P.O. Box 6115, Temple, TX 76503-6115. Fax: (254) 771-7500.**

Inc., and references in most libraries and online computer services should provide plenty of background on it.

The McLane Company is one of the fastest growing firms in the U.S. This statement indicates that the recruiter will be interested in a human resources (HR) person with experience in a fast-paced company developing systems to accommodate growth, dealing with changing organizational structures and recruiting good people. If you have this type of background, you'll have an edge over candidates from companies that are already at the top of their market curve.

It is one of the largest distributors of food products and general merchandise to convenience stores, mass merchandisers and quick-serve restaurants. If you have HR experience in wholesaling or distribution to retail stores, especially large chains or franchise operations, McLane will be particularly interested in you.

This position reports to the Division President. This company takes its HR function seriously. Reporting to the president would make you a member of the executive committee. If you want high visibility and the opportunity to affect long-term corporate strategy, this job is for you.

This person is responsible for employment, salary and benefit administration, safety and training, employee relations, employee enhancement programs and other HR-related duties. McLane is looking for an HR generalist. If you're a specialist in one of these areas, but have little or no experience in any of the others, the recruiter probably won't recognize you as a qualified candidate. A person from a smaller organization who has had her fingers in all of these pies probably has the best chance of getting an interview.

The company wants someone with *an undergraduate degree and four years of progressive experience in HR.* Unlike many potential employers, McLane isn't hung up on specific or advanced degrees. If your degree is in anthropology but your experience is relevant, the company will be interested in you. How refreshing!

Consider this next statement carefully, because it deals with a hot issue. McLane particularly wants someone who'll *primarily focus on controlling health insurance through plan design and administration.* If you've developed a quality management program, explored or instituted self-insurance, negotiated successfully with a health-care provider or found another innovative solution to holding down health-care costs, be sure to mention it in both your cover letter and resume.

Tailoring Your Cover Letter

Now that we've dissected the ad and interpreted its pieces, let's put together a cover letter that speaks directly to its requirements.

Instructions on where to mail or fax your response are provided in the last paragraph of the ad. While faxing is fast, it spoils the appearance of your correspondence. By all means, fax your letter and resume if the ad says reply ASAP, you want to make a quick response or you think relatively few people will use this option (so you'll stand out from the crowd). Otherwise, mail your correspondence to highlight your use of a high quality printer and stationery. You'll present a professional image and perhaps stand out even more if you reply after the initial crush.

ROBERT HALF'S RESUMANIA

This recently appeared in a cover letter: "Please disregard my attached resume as it is woefully out of date."

Hardly destined to capture the attention of a prospective employer.

Inside Address

The address on the ad includes the title—but not the name—of the recipient of your letter. If you want to capture his attention, do some sleuthing to find it. In this case, you may only have to call information for Temple, Texas, ascertain the McLane Company's phone number, and ask the company's receptionist for the name of the employment manager. If this technique doesn't work, visit the library to review the references on U.S. company managers listed in the Appendix. Ideally, your inside address should look like this:

> Jane Rutledge (falsified name)
> Employment Manager
> McLane Company Inc.
> P.O. Box 6115
> Temple, TX 76503-6115

Greeting

Now that you know the employment manager's name, use it:

> Dear Ms. Rutledge:

First Paragraph

As mentioned in Chapter 4, a variety of library and online information sources carry extensive background data on many employers, such as:

1. McLane serves more than 34,500 convenience stores, mass merchandisers and quick-serve restaurants in the United States.
2. McLane has an established, highly automated distribution center to cut shipping costs and time, and has implemented an advanced computer system to track inventory and speed up checkout and reordering.
3. Wal-Mart bought McLane in 1990.
4. McLane's CEO/President is Grady Rosier.

Using this data, plus the short description in the ad, your first paragraph stating why McLane interests you might resemble the following example:

> I have been an ardent admirer of Sam Walton for many years. Watching Wal-Mart open a store in my hometown and offer us local citizens an array of merchandise beyond our imagination opened my eyes to the wonders of mass distribution, discount prices and retail innovation. In fact, it made such an

---

ROBERT HALF'S RESUMANIA

From a cover letter written by a New York-based job seeker: "My birthday is 9/25/94. I have extensive experience in administration and bookkeeping."

Talk about precocious; he'll be a CEO before he's shaving.

"While my work experience is scantiness, I am hard-working and highly movitated."

Actually, we were looking for someone more well-suited to the position.

"My talent is at an inordinately high level and my ability to maintain accurate figures and meet deadlines is unspeakable."

At these extremes, some things are best left unsaid.

"In closing, let me outline the previous bookkeeping experience I've been able to endure."

A riveting story about man versus numbers.

---

impression on me, I pursued a career in retail. I see by your ad in the *National Business Employment Weekly* that the McLane Company, one of Wal-Mart's subsidiaries, is looking for a Human Resources Manager to help it grow beyond the more than 34,500 convenience stores, mass merchandisers and quick-serve restaurants it currently serves. Because of my admiration for your organization and my highly relevant experience, I think I am an excellent candidate for the position.

Second Paragraph

As noted in earlier chapters, your second paragraph should state specifically why you think a potential employer would want to interview you. Taking the information highlighted in the ad and combining it with a summary of a viable candidate's parallel accomplishments, you can make a compelling case, as shown in the following paragraph:

> For the past six years, I've held increasingly responsible positions as a human resources professional. I began my career as an assistant personnel manager at a large Sears store and was promoted to manager after 18 months. Three years ago, I accepted a position as Director of HR for Valucom (not a real company), another rapidly growing distributor of food products supplying large restaurant chains and franchises. At both Sears and Valucom, I served as an HR generalist and am consequently very familiar with all aspects of personnel functions including recruiting exempt and nonexempt employees, working with unions, selecting and/or designing technical and professional development training, employee relations and enhancement programs, organizational development and salary and benefits programs.
>
> Last year I chaired a task force reporting to the president whose mandate was to find the optimal approach for maintaining Valucom's current level of health benefits while decreasing its rate of increase in premium costs. To date, we have held the increase to two percent, a substantial improvement over the past three years' seven percent annual increment.

At this point in your cover letter, you should have addressed the most important requirements in the ad. Let's check to see if our letter has accomplished this objective:

✓ *The McLane Company is one of the fastest growing firms in the United States.*

✓ *It is one of the largest distributors of food products and general merchandise to convenience stores, mass merchandisers and quick-serve restaurants in the United States.*

✓ *This position reports to the division president.*

✓ *This person is responsible for employment, salary and benefits administration, safety and training, employee relations, employee enhancement programs, and other HR-related duties.*

✓ *An undergraduate degree and four years of progressive experience in HR is required.*

✓ *There is a primary focus in controlling health insurance through plan design and administration.*

Yes, we've hit all of the high points except for the degree, which will automatically be included in the resume.

Third Paragraph

Keeping in mind that you want to remain in the driver's seat, your third paragraph will look something like this:

> I'm very enthusiastic about having an opportunity to discuss your management team's plans for the future and the human resources department's role in making those goals a reality. I will call you next week to confirm receipt of my resume and schedule a mutually convenient time for us to get together.

Copy to the President

You know from your research that Grady Rosier is president and CEO of McLane. Why not send a cover letter and resume to him too? After all, he's the person who'll be making the final hiring decision. Just be sure to indicate on your original that you're sending a copy to the president. You don't want to alienate the employment manager—she may be reporting to you in the not-too-distant future.

Here's the letter in its entirety.

38 Ridge Road
Tuscaloosa, AL 35486
205-455-9976
July 6, 1999

Jane Rutledge (falsified name)
Employment Manager
McLane Company
P. O. Box 6115
Temple, TX 76503-6115

Dear Ms. Rutledge:

I have been an ardent admirer of Sam Walton for many years. Watching Wal-Mart open a store in my hometown and offer us local citizens an array of merchandise beyond our imagination opened my eyes to the wonders of mass distribution, discount prices and retail innovation. In fact, it made such an impression on me, I pursued a career in retail. I see by your ad in the *National Business Employment Weekly* that the McLane Company, one of Wal-Mart's subsidiaries, is looking for an Human Resources Manager to help it grow beyond the more than 34,500 convenience stores, mass merchandisers and quick-serve restaurants it currently serves. Because of my admiration for your organization and my highly relevant experience, I think I am an excellent candidate for the position.

For the past six years, I've held increasingly responsible positions as a human resources professional. I began my career as an assistant personnel manager at a large Sears store and was promoted to manager after 18 months. Three years ago I accepted a position as Director of HR for Valucom (not a real company), another rapidly growing distributor of food products supplying large restaurant chains and franchisers. At both Sears and Valucom, I served as an HR generalist and am consequently very familiar with all aspects of personnel functions including recruiting exempt and nonexempt employees, working with unions, selecting and/or designing technical and professional development training, employee relations and enhancement programs, organizational development and salary and benefit programs.

Last year I chaired a task force reporting to the President whose mandate was to find the optimal approach for maintaining Valucom's current level of health benefits while decreasing its rate of increase in premium costs. To date, we have held the increase to two percent, a substantial improvement over the past three years' seven percent annual increment.

I am very enthusiastic about having an opportunity to discuss your management team's plans for the future and the human resources department's role in making these goals a reality. I will call you next week to confirm receipt of my resume and schedule a mutually convenient time for us to get together.

Sincerely yours,

Bill Smithers

Enclosure
cc: Grady Rosier

Interpreting a Tougher Ad

The ad from McLane was quite easy to answer because it gave us lots of good information for a targeted cover letter. Unfortunately many ads aren't this forthcoming. The following ad from the *National Business Employment Weekly* purposely neglects to mention much of the pertinent data required to construct a really compelling letter.

This ad may not mention the employer's name because:

☆ The current CFO doesn't know he is about to be replaced.

☆ The human resources department doesn't want to be deluged with calls.

☆ An executive search firm is soliciting potential candidates and will screen responses before selecting some to present to its client company.

☆ A search firm or corporation is testing the waters to survey the available candidates for positions similar to the one described, making this a bogus ad.

When you come across an ad like this one, think carefully before you answer it. Since it lacks so much important information, you won't be able to

---

CFO / VICE PRESIDENT

Exciting and challenging opportunity for an open-minded, creative, and people-oriented financial executive. Your ability to use financial information as a strong management tool company-wide will make you a candidate of choice. Opportunity to work in a totally integrated new generation computer environment. While you will be managing all financial aspects of a Texas-based corporation, you will also be responsible for financial control of Latin American subsidiaries.

Typically, you will have had 4+ years training at a major public accounting firm and 7+ years as a senior financial officer of a major consumer goods manufacturing corporation. Experience in a high speed assembly-type operation and accounting/reporting for a publicly-owned company a plus. Must have command of Spanish and have significant experience in financial control of sales and marketing subsidiaries in Latin America. You will have had 5+ years experience working in a totally integrated/computerized financial environment.

Our company is part of a rapidly growing international group, dedicated to manufacturing and marketing of high valued, fast moving consumer goods. A modern manufacturing operation of 250+ employees.

Our candidate of choice will earn $75-100K annually plus perks, depending on his/her ability to contribute.

Box YD773,The Wall Street Journal
1233 Regal Row, Dallas, TX 75247
Equal Opportunity Employer

develop an ideal cover letter. And not being able to produce your best effort will reduce your chances for landing an interview. However, if your experience closely matches the requirements stated, and the job sounds really enticing, go for it. You may not generate a reply, but a truly exciting opportunity merits taking some risks.

To show how you might respond to this blind ad, look at the underlined key phrases.

CFO / VICE PRESIDENT

Exciting and challenging opportunity for an open-minded, creative, and people-oriented financial executive. Your ability to use financial information as a strong management tool company-wide will make you a candidate of choice. Opportunity to work in a totally integrated new generation computer environment. While you will be managing all financial aspects of a Texas-based corporation, you will also be responsible for financial control of Latin American subsidiaries.

Typically, you will have had 4+ years training at a major public accounting firm and 7+ years as a senior financial officer of a major consumer goods manufacturing corporation. Experience in a high speed assembly-type operation and accounting/reporting for a publicly-owned company a plus. Must have command of Spanish and have significant experience in financial control of sales and marketing subsidiaries in Latin America. You will have had 5+ years experience working in a totally integrated/computerized financial environment.

Our company is part of a rapidly growing international group, dedicated to manufacturing and marketing of high valued, fast moving consumer goods. A modern manufacturing operation of 250+ employees.

Our candidate of choice will earn $75-100K annually plus perks, depending on his/her ability to contribute.

Box YD773, The Wall Street Journal
1233 Regal Row, Dallas, TX 75247
Equal Opportunity Employer

Reading between the Lines

This organization wants a charismatic, big-picture leader who's good at building and motivating a successful team to "go where no one has gone before" using state-of-the-art systems. Only Starship officers need apply!

Not only is this person in charge of the company's overall financial aspects, but he'll also be responsible for making sure the Latin America subsidiaries stay in tune and in touch. If you speak Spanish fluently and have been a financial executive in a multinational corporation, present this information prominently in your cover letter. This firm wants a heavy hitter with global savvy. Those with a

January 2, 1999

John Dillinger
2212 Braton Court
Tanglewood, NC 27361

The Wall Street Journal
Box YD773
1223 Regal Row
Dallas, TX 75247

Good Morning:

As an entrepreneurial financial manager who believes in using the most advanced systems available, I am intrigued by your ad for a CFO, particularly because your company is rapidly expanding in the global marketplace.

After graduating with a degree in accounting, I started my career with Ernst & Young in its Houston, Texas office. Because many of our clients were already making business inroads in Mexico, I acquired my MBA in International Business and eventually accepted an offer I couldn't refuse to be a controller for one of my client corporations, a manufacturer of heavy equipment parts with many customers in Latin America. During my tenure with Congdon International (not a real company), I have spearheaded the upgrade of our financial systems twice, developed more sophisticated reporting methods for our sales offices in Mexico, and encouraged the Executive Committee to reengineer our manufacturing and distribution processes.

At this point, I feel that I've accomplished my goals at Congdon and I'm ready for a new challenge. If your organization is looking for a financial pro with extensive Latin American experience and a penchant for high-tech systems, I think we should talk. I look forward to getting together with you to discuss how I can be of benefit to your organization.

Sincerely yours,

John Dillinger

Enclosure

rusty recollection of Spanish from high school or college who've never ventured beyond U.S. borders needn't apply.

While it's not specifically stated, this corporation probably plans to hire a CPA, because it's seeking candidates who have cut their financial teeth in a public accounting environment (4+ years). It's also looking for someone with considerable experience in a publicly-owned manufacturing firm that uses state-of-the-art equipment. Because it only has about 250 employees and the CFO's compensation is a meager $85–100K, it may be a young company staffed by young, dedicated executives who love working long hours.

This company prides itself on its high-tech, high-touch culture. To be successful, you'll have to be more than comfortable with computers—you must bond with them. And to become a valued member of the executive team, you'll probably have to spend "golden hours" bonding with your colleagues as well. So if your fingers have never touched a keyboard or you feel you've already put in too many 60-hour weeks, forget this job.

But if you're a hard-charging, team-building, computer-loving financial genius, here's a cover letter that should grab the screener's attention.

Comments on This Letter

When you're replying to an ad that includes only a newspaper box number, there's no way to learn the name of the company to whom you're sending your resume. Consequently, if you want to stand out from the competition without benefit of saying something nice about the company or unearthing the reader's name, you'll have to be creative. For instance, instead of saying "Dear Sir or Madam," "To Whom It May Concern" or "Dear Recruiter," try "Good Morning." It sounds chipper, friendly and professional, and gives the reader the impression you deserve his attention.

Since you can't use research information in your first paragraph, find something else from the ad that intrigues you. In this case, John makes a point of showing how his experience, personality and career interests mesh with the firm's culture and long-term marketing strategy.

His second paragraph includes background information that hits all the key characteristics the firm wants in its new CFO. Actually, John doesn't have as many years' experience as the ad requests so he purposely omitted time frames from his cover letter. He isn't too concerned about this discrepancy, though, because it's unlikely that the company's stated compensation will attract candidates with the specified amount of experience.

Since he doesn't have a name, there is no one he can call to follow up on his letter. Consequently, in his third paragraph, John has to suggest that the potential employer contact him. However, he strengthens his position by summarizing how his experience parallels the company's needs.

Assistant Premiums/Promotions Manager
New York Metro Area Based

In this game, you've got to use your head and be on your toes.

It takes a special calibre individual to excel in the fast-paced game of corporate promotions. And, as a major, well-known Fortune 100 multi-national marketer, our World Trade Group is comprised of sharp individuals who focus on the effective manufacturing, marketing, and distribution of premium and promotional items and related businesses.

Assisting our Promotions Manager, you will be at the forefront of this Group's efforts to develop new markets and clients for our premiums/promotions business. This will involve traveling extensively to Asia, principally China, to identify manufacturing facilities as well as marketing our capabilities to major quick service restaurant chains in the U.S.

To qualify, you must have solid experience in the premium/promotions business spanning 5 years as well as backgound in sales and marketing. We also require customer orientation, the ability to work systematically as a team player or independently, and good business judgment. Knowledge of every phase of complex promotional projects, with tight quality and delivery requirements, involving a few million USD to huge quantities would be a plus. Creativity strategic relationships in the premium and toy markets, as well as an understanding of toy safety regulations in the U.S. and EEC would also be desirable.

We offer an outstanding compensation and benefits package attuned to our experience and anticipated contributions to our global success.

No resume is needed to apply. For confidential consideration, call toll free, 24 hours/day, 7 days/week: 1 (800) 221-3333, ext. Q17. We are an equal opportunity employer m/f.

Ads Requesting Call-In Responses

The ad above gives a phone number that candidates can call 24 hours a day rather than sending written replies. Increasingly, companies are using this approach to prescreen candidates through a voice-mail system. If you respond to such an ad, have all your ducks in a row before you place your call. As with an automated computer system that scans cover letters and resumes, these phone systems are coded to recognize specific words candidates use. For you to propel yourself into the return call group, you must identify the important words and phrases, then use them liberally when answering the machine or person asking the questions.

I asked Larry Spivack, owner of Seeco Specialty Advertising, to call the number provided and report what happened. This is what he said: "When I placed the call, a person answered the phone and asked me which ad I was responding to. She obviously had a script in front of her with a specific set of questions for everyone inquiring about the ad. This prescreening process went as follows:

1. How many years of experience do you have?
2. Were you buying or selling specialty items?
3. Are you willing to travel to China?
4. What is your current company and title?
5. Do you have a prior employer?
6. What is your highest level academic degree and its major?
7. What is your salary range?
8. What is your phone number? Alternate phone number?

"The questioner then ended the conversation by saying, 'Thank you for calling. If your basic information meets the needs of our search committee, we will get back to you.'"

When asked what he thought of this process, Larry said it was effective, but cold. There was no opportunity for him to personalize his replies or ask questions. He said the committee probably looks for key words and eliminates anyone whose replies don't include them. His observation was astute for someone who hasn't looked for a job in years. Before you answer an ad by phone, review the copy carefully, then anticipate basic questions you may be asked. If it appears that your background wouldn't be a good fit, don't waste yours or the employer's time by placing the call.

Job Hot Lines

Many large employers, especially those in the public sector, have phone-in job lines that provide updated information on available openings. A good source of some of these leads is *Job Hotlines USA* on the Internet (www.careerbookstore.com), published by Career Communications Inc. of Harleysville, Pennsylvania, which lists information on more than 2,000 organizations throughout the country.

To give you a better feel for what to expect when calling a hot line, I phoned the numbers for five companies in various U.S. regions. Each had a different approach to handling its calls. These are the responses I got:

Rice University, Houston, Texas   Rice had a recording that began with demographic data about the university and where the employment office is located. It went on to say that you can call or mail your cover letter, resume and a list of references to a suggested address, or visit their home page on the Web at employment.rice.edu to access postings and application forms. A list of assorted job openings followed, but none were described. If callers want more information, they must phone a certain number during regular business hours.

Doubletree Hotels   This hotel chain offers a job hot line for each city where it has hotels. A friendly voice names each of the hotels and general areas where positions are available, such as kitchen, dining room, front desk, administrative. If you're interested in any of the possibilities mentioned, you must call the appropriate hotel for specifics.

Carnival Cruise Lines, Miami, Florida   From the sound of the recording, Carnival Cruise Lines lists only entry-level positions on its hot line. There is one number for shore jobs and another for those on ships. Each job is described in detail, and callers who are interested in any of them are asked to leave their names and numbers for return calls.

Rex Healthcare, Raleigh, North Carolina   This hot line, on the other hand, provided no descriptions but does break down positions by listings. It suggested sending a resume to Human Resources and gave the address for this purpose. It also offered a phone number to obtain an application.

If you decide to use hot lines as resources for job openings, think of them as verbal ads that deserve the same attention to detail as their written counterparts. When you call, be sure to have pen and paper handy for jotting down phone numbers, addresses, job titles and position descriptions. If you're given another number to call for more information, phone it as well to gather as much data as you can before writing a cover letter and resume.

Cover-Letter Examples from Real People

Before-and-After Example

Karen Allen is a professional volunteer who's now ready to make the transition to the paid workforce. For many years, she has been the premier fund raiser for a variety of organizations in her area. Because she holds a special place in her heart for women who have had breast cancer, she's particularly interested in pursuing a position with the Komen Foundation, a nonprofit group that raises money to fund breast cancer research and screening. She wrote the cover letter on page 109 in response to its ad for a development professional.

Before

KAREN E. ALLEN
1445 Rosemeade Parkway
Carrollton, TX 75006

January 20, 1999

Linda Cadigan, President
Susan G. Komen Foundation
6820 LBJ Freeway, #130
Dallas, TX 75240

Dear Ms. Cadigan:

I want to thank you for returning my call last week. Enclosed is the resume you requested.

My marketable strengths include an ability to network effectively within the business and social community, expertise in the consultative sales process, and understanding of nonprofit and volunteer management.

During my 20 years' experience in development, I have consistently raised the largest amount of funds for every committee on which I've served. My background includes public relations responsibility for the Dallas Junior League, Cerebral Palsy and the Society for Cystic Fibrosis.

I look forward to meeting you and will call next week to be sure you received my resume and answer any questions you may have concerning it.

Sincerely yours,

Karen Allen (name changed)

Karen's letter includes only two of the three key elements of a good cover letter, and she needs to add some sizzle to her verbiage.

In a great beginning for her improved cover letter, Karen explains why the Foundation's mission is so important to her. Now that she has refined her opening paragraph, her letter on page 111 is everything a good cover letter should be.

KAREN E. ALLEN
1445 Rosemeade Parkway
Carrollton, TX 75006

January 20, 1999

Linda Cadigan, President
Susan G. Komen Foundation
6820 LBJ Freeway, #130
Dallas, TX 75240

Dear Ms. Cadigan:

Thank you for returning my call last week to tell me about the Susan G. Komen Foundation and its goals for the future. When I saw your ad in the paper, I was pleased that you plan to increase your development program and may be able to use someone with my background. I am particularly interested in the Foundation because its work has the potential to positively affect millions of women and their families.

My marketable strengths include an ability to network effectively within the business and social community, expertise in the consultative sales process, and understanding of nonprofit and volunteer management.

During my 20 years' experience in development I have consistently raised the largest amounts of funds for every committee on which I've served. My background includes public relations responsibility for the Dallas Junior League, Cerebral Palsy, and the Society for Cystic Fibrosis.

I look forward to meeting you and will call next week to be sure you received my resume and answer any questions you may have concerning it.

Sincerely yours,

Karen Allen (name changed)

A Newcomer in Town

Joe Rodriguez is a liberated man who left a lucrative advertising business in Kansas to move to Dallas when his wife's company relocated her there. In his 50s and with excellent design skills, Joe worked hard to find a new position. He began his new career in Dallas doing both design and sales for a small, fast-growing publishing firm, then eventually started his own business, keeping his former employer as a major client.

January 14, 1999

Mr. Mike Jarvis
Blue Cross/Blue Shield of Texas, Inc.
PO Box 655730
Dallas, TX 75265-5730

Dear Mr. Jarvis:

Having recently moved to Dallas, I was pleased to see a familiar name in the want ads. I've been a Blue Cross/Blue Shield customer for years and I admire your high standard of service and your multifaceted marketing program.

I have a thorough knowledge of design, photography, type specs, photo cropping, make-ready art, paper stock, color keys, and negatives. I am a self-starter, capable and accustomed to working with marketing directors, secretaries, photographers, clients, paper merchants and printers.

Assuming this resume will take several days to reach you, I will call late next week to ascertain if you have received it and to discuss scheduling an interview.

Sincerely yours,

Joe Rodriguez

Enclosure

Breaking the Rules

Robert Bolton's cover letter on page 115 breaks the rule about using the first paragraph to say something that really intrigues him about Horizon Software, the company advertising the job opening. However, he accomplishes the same purpose in paragraphs three and four. Exceptions are Okay, as long as they get the job done.

350 Ocean View Drive
Fort Lauderdale, FL 33311
August 28, 1999

Mr. Glen Campbell
Chief Operating Officer
Horizon Software, Inc.
1500 Carver Road, Suite 200
Boca Raton, FL 33431

Dear Mr. Campbell:

Please accept this letter as my application for the position of VP of R&D as advertised in the August 2 edition of the *Boca Raton Business Journal.*

As Director of R&D for three years with Troubadour Software, my staff and I developed a series of CD ROM programs for use in grades K through 12. By soliciting input from both teachers and students, we were able to design a variety of educational and fun programs that were exceptionally well received and won several national awards, especially in the areas of mathematics and science.

Considering that your organization is highly respected, but a new player in the CD ROM arena, I think my experience and reputation in this form of interactive education would be a real plus for you. While I have truly enjoyed my tenure at Troubadour, I am excited by the prospect of working with an organization that is both an unquestioned leader in its programming niche and an enthusiastic risk taker in an entirely new frontier.

I understand from your secretary that you will be at the National Education Association Conference in Miami next month. I plan to be there too, checking out the latest CD ROM software in both science and the arts and enhancing my contacts in the educational community. Judging from the convention program, it looks like Friday, September 10 at 1:30 P.M. would be a good time for me to stop by your booth to get acquainted and possibly schedule another, less public, meeting. Please let me know if this time is inconvenient. Otherwise, I will plan to see you then.

Sincerely,

Robert Bolton

Enclosure

"You-Want-I-Have"

Nancy Symons sent a great cover letter for a blind ad. While the newspaper reply box kept her from locating information about the company, she really zeroed in on the specific qualifications this large commercial real estate firm wants in its senior real estate manager. The you-want-I-have format on page 117 is a good way to tell potential employers that you know and have the background they're seeking.

NANCY M. SYMONS
11327 David Way
San Bernadino, CA 92404
909-823-7376

May 9, 1999

Box 2222
The San Bernadino Gazette
3000 Communications Way
San Bernadino, CA 92404

Good Morning:

For more than 15 years, I have been working in the facility management and real estate field with one of the largest energy services companies in North America. For the last four years, I was the executive responsible for strategic business planning for their headquarters' facilities, encompassing over three million square feet. My most recent strategy is now saving the company over $20 million annually. In addition to my success in managing real estate assets, directing relocation and tenant improvement projects, and negotiating office leases, my leadership of a number of labor-management teams was a major contributing factor in changing the facilities organization to a more efficient, customer-focused enterprise. I have relocated to Los Angeles and now have my work permit.

Here is a list of my qualifications as they relate to your requirements for the position of Senior Manager, Real Estate.

Your Requirements	*My Qualifications*
5–7 years of related managerial experience.	Over 9 years of managerial experience in real estate and facilities, including project management of tenant improvements such as telecom.
Strong negotiation skills.	Experience negotiating office leases, sales, leases and licenses of corporate properties, meeting or exceeding targets for cost savings or increasing revenues.
Degree in a related field.	M.Sc. in Urban and Regional Planning.

Enclosed is my resume which outlines my skills, key achievements, experience and education. I left Ontario Hydro on very good terms and can provide excellent references from several of their senior executives. I look forward to meeting with you to discuss how I can make a very strong contribution to your organization.

Sincerely,

Nancy M. Symons

Other Good Cover Letters Responding to Ads

The authors of these cover letters clearly state how their abilities and interests match the available openings. Do you feel their replies would survive the first cut by a designated resume screener?

DANA HERMAN
202 Rolling Hills Lane
Green Bay, Wisconsin 54301
414-687-3345

February 12, 1999

Ruth Scholl
Universe Oaks, A Psychiatric Hospital
7808 Fields Drive
Tampa, FL 33607

Dear Ms. Scholl:

Having read your brochure, I was most impressed by your programs, particularly ROPES and Youth Directions. I feel with my background and dedication, I would be an asset to your treatment center. When your ad appeared in last week's paper, I decided to apply.

I recently graduated from the University of Wisconsin with a B.S. in Family Studies. Both my activities on campus: Panhellenic Rush Counselor, APEX, Eating Advocacy Team, Assistant Pledge Trainer and Standards Board member, and my required courses: in relationships, counseling techniques, psychology and drug abuse, have given me some experience to fulfill the positions of Mental Health Worker or Mental Health Specialist. In addition, I am currently training with Contact Green Bay to volunteer for their crisis intervention hot line.

I have enclosed a copy of my resume to supply additional information. I feel these credentials make me a strong candidate for these positions. I look forward to getting together with you for an interview soon.

Sincerely,

Dana Herman

Enclosure

JAMES B. HENRY
312 SHORECREST DRIVE
EULESS, TX 76039

September 2, 1999

Mr. Edward G. Smith
Digital Matrix Systems
2302 North Stemmons Freeway
Suite 2100
Dallas, TX 75245

Dear Mr. Smith:

As you recently said to Diana Kunde of the *Dallas Morning News,* "Quality control and safety will be of critical importance in the 1990s as DMS seeks to maintain a competitive edge at home and abroad." I saw your ad in the paper and I decided to reply.

With 19 years of work experience in quality control, safety and management, I can offer your company a unique and valuable set of skills. In 1997, I received the highest performance rating from my employer, reserved exclusively for employees who save the company at least $150,000 per year through quality control and other cost-reducing methods.

I am confident I can make a big difference in helping your organization work safely as well as maintain its quality edge over competitors. I will call you in the near future to explore our mutual interests and arrange for a meeting convenient to your schedule.

Sincerely,

James B. Henry

Enclosure

Ms. Shannon P. Moore
115 Red Oak Trail Drive
Oak Leaf, TX 75154-3617
214-617-0570

February 9, 1999

John Eldon
Manager, Human Resources
HDI
1919 South Shiloh Road, LB13
Garland, TX 75042

Dear Mr. Eldon:

Please accept this letter and resume for the position of trainer/facilitator with HDI. They are in response to your newspaper advertisement.

You require:	*I offer:*
Excellent interactive training skills	A well used, excellent combination of counseling, education, business skills emphasizing experiential participation.
Highly skilled in group facilitation	Over 15 years in counseling, training, and teaching: very effectively using diverse, potent facilitation/processing skills.
Dynamic, expressive, enthusiastic personality	Yes! I'm an energetic, personable, articulate, good humored, enjoys-work-and-laughter, lively, balanced professional.
8–12 years' experience in corporate training and facilitation	11 years' experience in training and facilitation at universities, 3 years' private practice.
BA, Master's preferred	2 Master's: 1) counseling; 2) education administration (including MBA courses: organizational behavior, management).

I believe that I am well qualified for the trainer/facilitator position, and I hope you agree with me. I will call you next week to see if our scheduling an interview would be worthwhile. Thank you for your consideration.

Sincerely,

Shannon P. Moore

Enclosure

Dan Umbarger
6015 Lincoln Trail
Minneapolis, MN 55421
214-888-9900

December 10, 1999

Box ZW182
The Wall Street Journal
Dallas, TX 75247

Good Morning:

My 13 years of experience as a PC Trainer would enable me to make a significant contribution to your organization in the role of Technical Trainer, a position you are currently advertising. The job description closely mirrors my work experience and portrays a position that would be exciting and interesting for me!

- I have the required degree work cited in your job description.

- I have developed communication skills by teaching computer programming, introductory DOS, data structures, and computer applications at both the secondary and community college level.

- I have, of necessity, had to create my own materials as existing materials were too difficult for many of my students.

- My supervisors have repeatedly cited me as being enthusiastic, team-oriented and hard-working, and I possess a strong work ethic, integrity, and a dedication to quality work.

I would welcome the opportunity to meet with you to explore how I could be an asset to your company. I can make myself available for an interview at your convenience.

Sincerely yours,

Dan Umbarger

Enclosure

October 16, 1998

AT&T Resume Center
Room 7075
Promenade I
1200 Peachtree St. NE
Atlanta, GA 30309
Ad Code# IN81001915

Dear AT&T:

As a second-year student at the Yale School of Management, I look forward to joining a company after graduation that offers a challenging and rewarding career opportunity. Consequently, I am very interested in the prospect of working for AT&T as a Client Business Manager.

I find the dynamic environment in which AT&T operates to be very exciting, particularly given the rapid evolution in communication services. AT&T's strategy to be the leader in providing new and innovative solutions, such as those over the Internet, is indicative of its progressive company culture. Forward thinking is a crucial characteristic I am looking for in an employer. Given my strong interest in customer service, I am impressed by AT&T's known industry leadership in this area. Its Malcolm Baldrige National Quality Service Awards and ranking as "a top ten service industry icon" are clear indications of AT&T's commitment to customers. Without question, the overall environment of your company very closely matches my profile of an ideal place to work.

I believe I would make a significant contribution to the continued success of AT&T. I have worked directly with a telecommunications company and understand the importance of excellent customer service. As a result of previous work experience, I have cultivated the interpersonal skills needed to collaborate with customers to find value-added solutions to meet their needs. I have a strong sense of integrity and commitment to exceeding client expectations. And, I thrive on teamwork and developing relationships with others. Finally, I truly relish the challenge of working in a demanding environment and turning complex situations into success stories.

I would enjoy the opportunity to meet with you to explore the possibility of a full-time position at AT&T Corporation. I look forward to talking with you.

Sincerely,

Amber Jones

"You have outstanding references, an excellent academic record, choice experience and you're fully qualified. Now, let's discuss this speck of lint on your cover letter."

6

Cover Letters for Search Firms, Temporary Agencies and College Career Centers

While search firms, temporary agencies and college career centers work with a variety of individuals, from seasoned executives to inexperienced high school and college students, they all have a common mission. Each matches qualified candidates to compatible job openings, and except for a few organizations that charge applicants a fee to place them, each tries to find the right people for employers, not vice versa.

Because of the diversity of candidates they serve, these employment brokers have varying preferences regarding cover letters and resumes. While retained executive recruiters have almost no interest in cover letters, college career centers strongly recommend them. Let's take a look at how these organizations work and how you can tailor your cover letters to meet their needs.

Executive Search Firms That Work on Retainer

When job seekers think of headhunters, they often picture a group of arrogant, somewhat mysterious professionals who know of many great opportunities, but guard them like proverbial dogs in a manger. This stereotype is particularly prevalent among job seekers who assume recruiters are in business to find candidates jobs. If everyone understood the executive recruiter's true purpose—locating the best person to fill a search assignment—far fewer people would get angry and frustrated when their unsolicited resumes and calls go unanswered.

To learn more about how search firms on retainers operate, I spoke with these professionals in the field:

1. David Westberry, Managing Director in Dallas for Korn/Ferry International, the world's largest executive search firm conducting searches worldwide for senior-level executives.
2. Robert Morrison, owner of Quetico, an HR-consulting firm in Texas that concentrates on search assignments in the hospitality and food service industries.

Knowing how search firms find individuals who match the requirements of their corporate clients will help you understand why sending unsolicited cover letters and resumes to recruiters isn't likely to get you a job.

According to David Westberry, corporate clients pay retainer search firms a fee even if they don't find a qualified candidate. This fee is typically one-third of the position's annual compensation (salary plus bonuses) and is paid in three installments: one upon signing the search contract, another a month or so later, and the third 60 days later regardless of the success or failure of the search. As

Westberry says, "When you have paid me one-third of my fee up front, you've got my time and attention. Your problem is my problem."

To find the best candidates, these firms initiate a sophisticated research project that often lasts several months and typically includes the following components:

- ☆ *An Organizational Assessment.* A comprehensive study of the client company to understand its philosophy, management style and culture, and learn the professional and personal attributes of its ideal candidate.

- ☆ *Preparation of a Position Specification.* A document describing the organization's characteristics and mission, and the position's duties and responsibilities, including reporting relationships, education, experience and desired personality traits. This document is approved by the client company and used as a benchmark when interviewing candidates.

- ☆ *Search Strategy.* A research process that determines which local, regional, national and international companies, organizations and professionals in the firm's database might yield an initial 75 to 100 potential candidates.

- ☆ *Recruitment.* Phone calls to individuals in the candidate pool to ascertain their interest in the position or to get referrals. These calls usually yield about 10 to 15 professionals who are interested in and qualified for the position. They are asked to send a resume.

- ☆ *Candidate Interviews.* In-depth personal interviews to gain an understanding of each candidate's background and determine his suitability for the position.

- ☆ *Presentation of Candidates.* Detailed written biographical and interview summaries of approximately five people who are all interested in the position and fit its requirements. The search firm then arranges client-candidate meetings to identify the best person for the job.

- ☆ *Reference Check.* Contacting the final candidate's managers, peers and subordinates at current and past employers to verify factual data and achievements, explore strengths and weaknesses and learn about his personal and professional style. This information is submitted to the client in a written report.

Given the time and effort search executives put into this process, you can understand why they aren't interested in the unsolicited calls, cover letters and resumes they're deluged with daily.

Three Cover-Letter Attention Getters

Most retained search professionals sift through their correspondence to ensure they don't overlook an interesting prospect. (This is especially true at new or small recruiting firms.) Your cover letter is more likely to capture a recruiter's attention if it includes one of these three items:

1. The name of a familiar person who referred you. The main reason executive search firms are so effective is that they use networking extensively. Even high-powered search professionals feel more comfortable working with people they already know or who are recommended to them. If you have a contact who knows a recruiter you're writing to, use his name as soon as possible in your first paragraph.

2. Experience that fits a current assignment. Unfortunately, when you first write to a search firm, you don't know its immediate needs (unless you were contacted as a potential candidate for a search). Consequently, the best approach when sending an unsolicited letter is to spotlight your most marketable achievements and experience and hope for the best. But if a recruiter asks you to mail a resume after a preliminary discussion, use the inside information she gave you to summarize the relevant skills and experience you'd bring to the position.

3. An unusually strong background in the career or industry in which a recruiter specializes, or where there's a shortage of qualified candidates. For instance, if you have years of experience in developing managed health-care programs or consortiums, a health-care search firm probably would want you in its database.

Cover-Letter Components for Retained Search Firms

Cover letters for search firms don't follow the same format as those sent directly to employers. Certain components may be identical, but headhunters want information up front that you typically wouldn't reveal to a company. For instance, while you'd still include your referral's name in the first paragraph and your most relevant experience in the second, your third paragraph should contain your geographic preferences and current compensation. All recruiters want to know this information before they talk to you. Providing it in your cover letter makes their job easier and gives you a leg up on candidates who choose not to divulge it.

While most cover letters should state your intention to follow up with a phone call, search firms are the exception to this rule. Retained headhunters don't welcome calls, unless you're a bona fide candidate for a specific search. If they aren't pursuing you, your call will be viewed as a waste of time. They will neither take nor return it.

Example Cover Letters to Retained Search Firms

These cover letters were sent to search firms that do assignments on retainer. The first, by George Kloppenberg, shows how to write an unsolicited letter to attract a headhunter's attention. Larry Frantz wrote the other to Heidrick and Struggles after he was asked for a resume for a CFO slot.

GEORGE C. KLOPPENBERG

6123 Green Manor Drive   **502-387-6857 (H)**
Louisville, KY 40219   **502-481-0777x242 (W)**

November 17, 1999

Mr. David Roser
Availability of Hartford
566 New Britain Avenue
Newington, CT 06111

Dear Mr. Roser:

Vince Vascati, who served me well as an Engineering Manager, suggested I write to you.

Until recently, I was **Division Manager with $10 million annual sales P&L responsibility** at Lindstrom Manufacturing in Pohatan, New York. This major precision sheet metal contract fabricator lost its primary customer and has downsized rapidly to survive. I am in "outplacement" and hoping to transition to a much smaller operation.

Please review my resume in light of your current assignments. The following profile may be helpful:

1. *Desired Positions*
   President, Vice President or General/Division/Plant Manager of a small (50 to 200 employees) manufacturing company in a "low-tech" industry such as sheet metal, wood, wire, or related products.

2. *Location*
   Willing to relocate. Preference is for New England or Mid-Atlantic area, coastal Mid-South or Chicago.

3. *Compensation*
   $75–$100,000 base plus performance bonus and applicable package.

My resume is enclosed. I am seeking a challenging leadership position where my open, participatory management style, coupled with the ability to make significant operational and financial improvements, will be welcomed. Thank you for considering my situation.

Sincerely,

George C. Kloppenberg

Enclosure

LAWRENCE G. FRANTZ
6535 Northpoint Drive
Dallas, TX 75248

July 1, 1999

Mr. Charles Leman
Heidrick & Struggles
2000 Seascape Drive
Boca Raton, FL 33427

Dear Charles:

Thanks for the call on Tuesday about the CFO assignment you are working on for Triple Drilling. They are a direct competitor, especially in deep drilling, to one of Hope Energy's subsidiaries, Hope Drilling, so I am very familiar with them. Though they are smaller than Hope Energy, I would be very interested in this opportunity, because I am a believer in the return to profitability for the domestic drilling business. Also, my experience fits in well with what they require.

1. I have been through a recent IPO so I know what to expect.

2. I have dealt with the situation of a majority owner (Muswalt, 51%) and minority (49%) public ownership.

3. I know not only the land and offshore drilling business, but also their customers' business (through Hope Energy's E&P businesses and ownership of HOMCO).

4. I handled not only the CFO duties, but also the investor relations activities, and that experience is very important to newly public companies.

I am looking forward to talking further with you and the company about this opportunity. Meanwhile, say hello to David for me.

Sincerely,

Lawrence G. Frantz

Enclosure

WORDS OF WISDOM FROM THE EXPERTS

Along with their advice on cover letters, Mssrs. Westberry and Morrison volunteered these observations about retained search firms and their preferences. Some of their insights may surprise you.

Mr. Westberry:

"Don't spend a lot of your job search courting headhunters. Unsolicited resumes have about as much chance of getting someone a job as unsolicited manuscripts have of being published."

"Don't start trying to get my attention when you begin your job search. It's too late by then. To increase your visibility to search firms, excel in your position and be actively involved in professional organizations and/or your community."

"Tell me the truth when I ask you about your salary, experience, personality traits and skills. No one is perfect, so I don't expect you to be. However, if I find out you've embellished upon your accomplishments, etc., I can't recommend you to my client."

Mr. Morrison:

"I work with both employed and unemployed candidates, as long as they are qualified to do the job. Most search professionals realize there are many unemployed persons who are out of work through no fault of their own. In fact, I often call outplacement firms looking for good candidates for current search assignments. However, there are still some recruiters in business a long time who discriminate against people without jobs."

Both:

"Age is no barrier. I find the best person for the job, whatever his age."

"Specialized skills are important, but I also consider a candidate's personality traits, management style and philosophy in determining the best match for a position."

"Don't look to me for job-search salvation. Rely on networking to find the position you want."

Search Firms That Work on Contingency

Like retainer firms, contingency recruiters also are paid by employer clients, not job applicants. However, they collect a fee only if they find the candidate who's hired for the position. Generally, contingency firms fill professional and supervisory positions salaried at less than $75,000 a year. While they strive to find good matches for available openings, their efforts aren't as rigorous as those of a typical retained search firm.

Valerie Freeman, president of Imprimis Group, an umbrella organization for several permanent and temporary agencies, says that contingency and temporary firms constantly solicit candidates by:

☆ Networking with people and organizations.

☆ Running ads in newspapers.

☆ Speaking to groups on job-search or hiring techniques.

☆ Soliciting databases from churches and other clubs whose members might be interested in changing jobs.

☆ Maintaining job hot lines.

☆ Promoting referral programs that offer incentives to individuals who send excellent applicants their way.

They usually maintain extensive databases of high-caliber candidates that are updated with solicited and unsolicited cover letters and resumes. While these firms don't find many candidates among the stacks of unrequested resumes that arrive daily, they appreciate it when individuals take the initiative to contact them. If they're working on a search for someone with your background or have clients who constantly need people with your skills, you'll probably be contacted for a phone interview.

Components of Cover Letters to Contingency Search Firms

Cover letters to contingency firms should contain the same information as those to retained recruiters. In the first paragraph, explain why you sent a particular firm your resume. To attract special attention, you might mention:

☆   A referral from a mutual acquaintance.

☆   An article you read about the agency.

☆   A recommendation you saw about their firm on the Internet.

☆   A point of mutual interest. For instance, in Ms. Freeman's case, you could say that you've always enjoyed working with women-owned businesses.

The second paragraph should discuss your most marketable background and skills. Because you have neither a specific job description nor information about a particular employer to guide you, you won't have the tools to tailor your letter. Instead, you'll have to decide which skills and experience your industry and field deems important and highlight your achievements in these areas.

Contingency firms also want to know your geographic preferences and most recent salary, so include them as well.

Like retained recruiters, contingency headhunters prefer not to receive follow-up phone calls. They're more likely to respond to an unsolicited resume than a retained search firm, but they share the don't-call-us-we'll-call-you mind-set.

Tips on Cover Letters for Contingency Recruiters

To augment my research on contingency search firms, I contacted David Lord, former editor of Kennedy Publications, which publishes *The Directory of Executive Recruiters* and *Kennedy's Pocket Guide to Working with Executive Recruiters* (1998, Kennedy Publications, Fitzwilliam, NH). The following are his and Valerie Freeman's tips for composing cover letters that get results:

☆   Make your cover letters short and to the point. More than one page is too long.

☆   Cover letters that contain typos, poor grammar or nonsensical language will hurt your candidacy. Recruiters expect resumes to be perfect since most candidates mail the same version to many firms. But since cover letters are individually prepared, they're more likely to have gaffes that you might not catch. If you aren't a stickler for detail, ask a nitpicking friend to review your cover letters before mailing them.

☆   Talk about achievements and results, not personality traits and be-
liefs. Recruiters are more interested in tangible accomplishments than
philosophical dissertations.

☆   Use your cover letter as a vehicle to stand out from the competition and
form a personal connection with its readers. Along with mentioning
why you're contacting a particular agency, suggest ways you can help
them with current assignments. Discuss rare or highly marketable experience or offer to provide names of qualified candidates for certain
openings.

☆   According to Ms. Freeman, candidates often badger agencies, complain-
ing that they haven't found suitable job matches for them. Talk about
biting the hand that feeds you! No matter how frustrating your search
becomes, don't take your feelings out on the people who can refer you to
an employer. If they have openings that parallel your experience,
they'll call you. If they don't, don't expect them to hunt for one. It's
your mission to find a new job, not theirs.

Deciding Which Executive
Search Firms to Contact

Experts differ on how to select which recruiting firms to contact. Some say to
concentrate on firms where you know someone or have been referred by friends.
Others suggest mounting a major direct-mail campaign and sending your credentials to every search firm that might have an opening for someone with your
experience. I favor networking over resume blitzes, so I agree with the selective
approach. However, if you're leaning toward a direct-mail campaign, refer to
Chapter 4 for advice on how to organize it, and use either *The Directory of Executive Recruiters* (1998, Kennedy Publications, Fitzwilliam, NH) or *Executive
Recruiters of North America* (1998, Hunt Scanlon Publications, Greenwich, CT)
as resource directories.

Before-and-After Cover Letters for a Contingency Search Firm

It's important to be honest in your correspondence with search firms, but don't bludgeon readers with the truth. Concentrate on your positive experience and achievements. Squelch the compulsion to apologize or dwell on negative information. At some point, you'll have to explain employment gaps or reasons for leaving to a search professional. However, it's better to do so face-to-face.

The following "before" letter, which Angelina Garcia sent unsolicited to Valerie Freeman, is pretty good, except that it repeatedly mentions her unemployment (I've italicized these notations to make my point). The revised cover letter omits the sentences stressing her joblessness. If you were a recruiter, which one would you prefer?

Before

ANGELINA M. GARCIA
291 Schyler Ave.
Hamilton, Ohio 45011
513-872-9493

4 April 1999

Valerie Freeman
Freeman and Associates
5550 LBJ Freeway, Suite 150
Dallas, Texas 75240

RE: Possible Employment

Dear Ms. Freeman:

I am an *unemployed technical writer* looking for work in either Texas or Oklahoma. I grew up in North Houston, and attended both the University of Houston and Texas Tech University. I lived in Irving before moving to Ohio in 1987. I would like to return to Texas to be closer to my family and friends and I am hoping you can help.

I have been *unemployed for the last six months;* however, last year, I worked for Envirotech Inc., an environmental consulting firm, as a Technical Editor/Project Information Analyst on a DOE Emergency Response Program. My primary responsibility was editing documents. I was also responsible for using the correct format for publication and distribution of documents to the client from our particular office. My latest and largest document was a Site-wide Quality Assurance Project Plan which was distributed to both the U.S. and Ohio EPA, the DOE, and the client.

With Envirotech, I gained a broad knowledge of environmental issues and problems along with an understanding of what is required to edit and produce multivolume documents. Now I am looking for a position that will allow me an opportunity to expand my editing skills. I have been told by many of my co-workers that I am a take-charge person who is multitask oriented and demands quality.

I realize that I have spent a great deal of time unemployed which is reflected on my resume. After graduation from Miami University in December, 1991, I took a job where my husband worked to help them with the huge increase in work that occurred when the interest rates fell. *In May 1992, I spent several months in Texas looking for employment but was unsuccessful.* I returned to Ohio and almost immediately found work with Envirotech. *I resigned in September because of a change in management which occurred in April.*

I would welcome an opportunity to discuss my professional experience and qualifications with you in person.

Sincerely,

Angelina M. Garcia

Enclosure

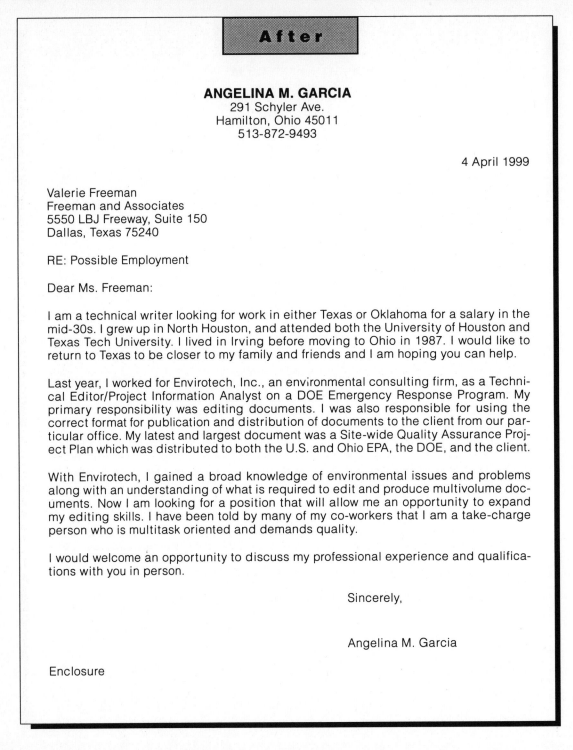

After

ANGELINA M. GARCIA
291 Schyler Ave.
Hamilton, Ohio 45011
513-872-9493

4 April 1999

Valerie Freeman
Freeman and Associates
5550 LBJ Freeway, Suite 150
Dallas, Texas 75240

RE: Possible Employment

Dear Ms. Freeman:

I am a technical writer looking for work in either Texas or Oklahoma for a salary in the mid-30s. I grew up in North Houston, and attended both the University of Houston and Texas Tech University. I lived in Irving before moving to Ohio in 1987. I would like to return to Texas to be closer to my family and friends and I am hoping you can help.

Last year, I worked for Envirotech, Inc., an environmental consulting firm, as a Technical Editor/Project Information Analyst on a DOE Emergency Response Program. My primary responsibility was editing documents. I was also responsible for using the correct format for publication and distribution of documents to the client from our particular office. My latest and largest document was a Site-wide Quality Assurance Project Plan which was distributed to both the U.S. and Ohio EPA, the DOE, and the client.

With Envirotech, I gained a broad knowledge of environmental issues and problems along with an understanding of what is required to edit and produce multivolume documents. Now I am looking for a position that will allow me an opportunity to expand my editing skills. I have been told by many of my co-workers that I am a take-charge person who is multitask oriented and demands quality.

I would welcome an opportunity to discuss my professional experience and qualifications with you in person.

Sincerely,

Angelina M. Garcia

Enclosure

Another Contingency Search Cover Letter

PAULA MATTHEWS
2060 Bryn Mawr Circle
Atlanta, GA 30327

March 18, 1999

Ms. Valerie Freeman
President
Wordtemps, Inc.
5550 LBJ Freeway, Suite 150
Dallas, TX 75240

Dear Valerie:

I was referred to you by Jack Spein as a contact for a job search I've recently undertaken in the Dallas area. I'm currently in the process of relocating from Atlanta to Dallas with my husband, who accepted a position in January with Southern Telecom.

Jack Spein and I met last year in Atlanta as a result of a consulting assignment he had there. I assisted him with several human resource and management development projects for Lodi Building Products Inc., a building materials retailer headquartered in the Atlanta area. Jack suggested that you would be an excellent contact for pursuing job opportunities in North Dallas.

I have more than 11 years' experience in the field of human resources. Although I would like to focus primarily on positions in training and development or compensation, I'm open to any opportunities in human resources, including generalist positions. During the past two years, I've worked from my home as a Field Trainer. While there are definite advantages to working at home, I've missed the stimulation and friendship that co-workers provide. As a result, I'm looking for a position which offers that element of a working environment. My salary requirement is in the mid-60s.

I'd enjoy meeting with you or someone from your firm to discuss the job market in North Dallas. During the week of March 22nd, I will be completing my last assignments for Hart-field National in Atlanta. My phone number is 404-316-7912. After March 26th, I will be permanently residing in Dallas and can be reached at 972-305-2348.

I look forward to meeting with you in the near future.

Sincerely,

Paula Matthews

Cover Letters for Temporary Agencies

Temporary agencies are placement firms that match applicants to temporary assignments. They may work with people with specialized technical skills, such as desktop publishing, accounting, law, bilingual interpretation or translation, computer programming, or general skills required in offices or light industry. A few such as Imcor, even concentrate on filling temporary positions for executive-level projects. Temporary firms solicit job assignments from companies, then fill them from a constantly changing pool of qualified candidates. Because their work often requires a quick turnaround, they need available applicants who can cover a variety of assignments. Since they're always seeking and soliciting new applicants, they're pleased when candidates take the initiative to approach them. Temp agencies will always take and return calls.

In fact, you can probably be listed in a temporary firm's database by completing a test to determine your skill level and providing your name, address, phone number, preferred fee per hour and availability. You also can send a cover letter and resume and follow up by phone. If you decide to initiate contact in writing, find out in advance which skills and experience the firm's clients need most, then tailor your correspondence to match.

Since the firms are constantly filling temporary positions, applicants have about a 50 percent chance of being hired, according to Ms. Freeman. You can increase the likelihood of gaining temporary employment by registering with several agencies simultaneously.

In the past few years, the role of temporary agencies has evolved far beyond its stereotype. Four major trends are transforming the industry and increasing employment opportunities for job seekers:

☆ More companies are using a temporary-to-permanent approach to fill job openings. To avoid the costs and legal problems involved with terminating employees who don't work out, many employers pay temporary agency fees and evaluate new hires for several months instead of placing them on the permanent payroll immediately. This method cuts unemployment expenses, allows more flexibility and saves face for everyone if the situation doesn't work. It also makes temp work a more likely source of permanent jobs than in the past.

☆ While the term seems contradictory, many employers are arranging for work to be performed on a *long-term temporary basis*. This helps them to maintain flexible staffs that don't have to be hired and fired as business ebbs and flows. Since benefits aren't provided, this approach helps keep overhead low. Remember this method if you apply for temporary work. If you don't want to be a long-term temporary, mention it in your cover letter along with your preferred fee per hour and work schedule.

☆ Many temporary firms are doing outsourcing work for corporations that want to reduce the number of employees not involved in their core business. For instance, functions such as delivering internal mail, making copies, bookkeeping, running MIS, training and recruiting may be delegated to temporary agencies that take over the staffing and payroll for these areas. If you send a cover letter and resume to a temp firm, don't be surprised if you're offered a permanent position working directly for the agency instead of one of its clients.

☆ Corporate interest in using high-level candidates for short-term projects has increased significantly. By putting highly compensated professionals on the payroll only as needed, companies can cut overhead. The firm also can "try out" an executive before making the decision to bring him on board. This new recruiting function calls for candidates who aren't accustomed to pursuing temporary employment. If you are a CFO, VP of marketing, director of human resources or have other high-level executive experience, you may want to research "interim executive" firms that specialize in placing people like you.

The manufacturing executive who wrote the following cover letter is a prime candidate for a project or temp-to-perm position available through an interim firm. His resume is included since it provides an understanding of his excellent qualifications and lengthy experience. If he began his career in 1955, he's currently in his 60s. Even though age discrimination is illegal, his age will make it hard for him to find a permanent management position with a new employer. On the other hand, his many years of experience make him a great candidate for a consulting assignment. If he starts as an independent contractor and dazzles the executive committee with his uncanny solutions to intractable problems, he may be offered a permanent job or, at least, another assignment to keep him on board.

Cover Letter and Resume for a Temporary Agency

DAVID C. PALMER
13204 Coronado Court
Manassas, Virginia 22111
804-763-2301

5 May 1999

Ms. Elaine Preminger
ChemSearch, Inc.
20348 Rockefeller Center Drive
New York, NY 10020

Dear Ms. Preminger:

Do you have opportunities for a mature professional with nearly 40 years of successful management experience? Your recent *Wall Street Journal* advertisement indicates you may have clients who could use my expertise.

I built on my chemistry degree with assignments in manufacturing, pharmaceutical, household and personal products. I designed and installed blending and packaging systems and trained key employees on these systems, resulting in an 18 percent improvement in average output. I also formulated numerous successful products.

I upgraded laboratory staff, streamlined procedures, and developed new analytical methods for better process control, which allowed a nearly 50 percent reduction in laboratory staff. I led employees in analyzing work flow and designing their stations for maximum efficiency, which reduced compounding waste nearly 60 percent. I converted manual scheduling systems to PC-based forecasting and scheduling programs and negotiated and managed manufacturing contracts, resulting in a 25 percent savings in product costs.

During my career, I have prepared and published manufacturing specifications, quality assurance manuals, HAZCOM handbooks, and hundreds of technical articles in trade and consumer publications, and edited SAE papers, technical brochures, and advertising copy.

This varied experience qualifies me to coordinate operations and technical support for small or medium-size companies. I can be valuable to those firms that need expertise in several technical areas without hiring specialists for each. I have a good understanding of process and product optimization. My operations, QA, and sales experience strengthen my interaction with team members at all levels of management. I am dedicated to producing top quality while maintaining profitability.

I moved to Virginia after completing a consulting assignment in Boston last September. I am seeking opportunities in the Southeast to put my skills to productive use. May I put them to work for your clients?

Sincerely,

David C. Palmer

DAVID C. PALMER
13204 Coronado Court
Manassas, Virginia 22111
804-763-2301

A broad-based, well-balanced career encompassing technical and operations management . . . a strong manager and skilled communicator experienced in product formulation, packaging operations, and quality assurance . . . seeking to apply my expertise in manufacturing quality products through . . .

OPERATIONS MANAGEMENT

D. C. Palmer & Associates, Ltd.   **1995–1999**
Contract Management, Consulting and Technical Writing

The Recovery Group   **1994**
Bankruptcy Trustee for Piedmont Molecular Corporation

Consultant
- Maintained PMC operations and accounts
- Advised Trustee on PMC technology

Piedmont Molecular Corporation   **1988–1993**
Developer and Manufacturer of fuel additives

Director of Technical Services; Director of Public Relations
- Directed manufacture of PMC's products
- Developed cost analyses and pricing schedules
- Prepared technical literature, brochures, annual reports, newsletters, and SAE papers
- Assisted sales force with customer's technical questions
- Negotiated motorsports sponsorships; represented the Company at motorsport events and trade shows
- Prepared and published Company Quality Assurance manual
- Prepared and published Company HAZCOM manual
- Maintained mixed Macintosh and DOS PC computer network

XI Industries   **1983–1988**
Contract packager of automotive products and adhesives

Director of Technical Services
- Designed a $2.5 MM highly flexible sanitary XP emulsion blending system, bulk storage facility, and accessory tanks and equipment
- Earned a Ford Q rating and established XI as a Ford vendor
- Prepared and published Company Quality Assurance manual
- Prepared and published Company HAZCOM manual
- Converted from a manual scheduling system to PC-based forecasting and scheduling programs.
- Assisted sales increase from $4.8 MM to $16MM in 3 years
- Supervised disposal of hazardous waste materials

David C. Palmer   Page 2

Barr Company   **1975–1982**
Manufacturer of household and cosmetic products

Sales Manager   **1980–1982**
• Developed new business accounting for 33% of sales volume
• Maintained accounts in excess of $150 million annually

Plant Manager   **1978–1980**
• Installed a $2.5MM production system on time and under budget
• Trained key employees in start-up and troubleshooting this new production system.
  Output reached 70,000 units per shift, twice the original projection
• Supervised 250 people manufacturing 80 products in runs from 50,000 to
  12,000,000 units annually
• Increased output per shift by 18% while reducing average down-time by 15%

Technical Director   **1975–1978**
• Reduced compounding waste by over 60%
• Reduced laboratory staff 50% while improving quality standards
• Supervised 2 compounding and 4 laboratory personnel

MSL Industries, Aerosol and Plastics Division   **1965–1967**
Contract manufacturer of household and cosmetic products

Technical Director
• Supervised 6 laboratory personnel
• Developed several new aerosol propellant systems

Rochester Aerosol Corporation   **1961–1965**
Contract manufacturer of household and cosmetic products

Peterson Filling and Packaging Corporation   **1958–1961**
Contract manufacturer of household and cosmetic products

Allied Chemical Corporation   **1955–1958**
Basic chemical manufacturer

B. A. Chemistry   **University of Pennsylvania**   **1955**

Additional Studies: William and Mary   Purdue University
                     Oakland University   Washington University

SUMMARY
My experience includes steadily increasing responsibility in operations and support management. In meeting a wide range of challenges, I developed market awareness, product knowledge, personnel perspectives, and communications skills which contributed to my growth. Let me put these skills to work for you.

Cover Letters for College Placement Centers

Career or placement centers at colleges and universities help students find internships or full-time employment. They typically assist their constituents in identifying career choices, networking, writing resumes and cover letters, interviewing and developing relationships with potential employers.

Good career centers pursue corporate recruiters and coach their students on the best techniques to attract employers. According to Catherine Halvorson, campus relations manager for Electronic Data Systems Corp., most centers try to schedule either open or closed recruiting sessions. For open recruiting, companies schedule on-campus interviews with any students who sign up for them. With closed recruiting, companies preselect candidates whom they want to meet. You may not need to provide cover letters and resumes to companies conducting open recruiting visits. However, these documents are recommended for companies doing closed recruiting because they are used in selecting interviewees.

To improve your chances of being chosen for on-campus interviews, you should tailor your cover letters and resumes to each opening that interests you. Start the process by getting a copy of the job description from your career center, then highlight the position's key qualifications and buzz words and match your cover letter and resume to these requirements.

According to the career center at Southern Methodist University in Dallas, students' biggest challenge when preparing cover letters is to avoid a bland fill-in-the-blanks formula and to breathe life into their writing. If you think about it, composing a cover letter is similar to writing a thank-you note. Few people

---

ROBERT HALF'S RESUMANIA

In a cover letter, a Texas college graduate listed the 10 subjects she enjoyed most during her college career, followed by the subjects she liked least: "1. Ethics; 2. Physical Science; 3. U.S. Government."

This type of information really shouldn't be included in a cover letter. But in her case, there was an even better reason to leave it out. She applied to a company whose corporate motto is "Ethics First."

relish either task, so they take the path of least resistance and finish the distasteful chore as quickly as possible. A get-it-out-of-the-way thank-you note looks something like this:

> Dear Aunt Kate,
> Thank you for the new outfit. I really like it.
> Love,
> Heather

While Aunt Kate may be grateful to get any kind of thank-you note, she's probably disappointed that Heather didn't say anything about the outfit's color or style, where she plans to wear it or whether it coordinates with other items in her wardrobe.

Suppose Heather had written the following letter. Wouldn't it give her aunt the feeling Heather really appreciates her gift?

> Dear Aunt Kate,
> When I opened your birthday present, I couldn't wait to put it on. Its teal color (my personal favorite, as you know) goes really well with my red hair and coordinates with many of the shoes and belts I already have. It should be just perfect for my interview with JCPenney next week. Thank you so much for finding me such a wonderful and useful gift.
> Love,
> Heather

Granted, cover letters written to corporations aren't as personal as thank-you notes to loved ones, but tailored correspondence can give corporate recipients the same satisfaction nonetheless *and* make a strong case for your enthusiasm and qualifications for the job.

Karen Andrews from Kennesaw State University (KSU) in Kennesaw, Georgia, sent me a copy of the cover-letter guidelines that she gives all students visiting her career center. I'm passing them along since they're right on target.

KSU Cover-Letter Rules

1. Send typed originals with all resumes, not copied form letters.
2. Use quality paper, preferably the same as your resume.
3. Address it to a specific person whenever possible.
4. Emphasize achievements that are relevant to a particular position.

5. Be brief and concise. Keep your letter to one page with three to five short paragraphs, so it will be easy to skim.

6. Your letter should be both professional and personal. The words you choose will speak volumes about you and serve as a deciding factor in whether you are selected for an interview or not.

KSU Cover-Letter Components

1. *Opening.* State why you are writing. Mention the position and how you learned about it. Express some knowledge of the company and why you are interested in it.

2. *Body.* This is your chance to tell the employer why you are the best person for the position. Highlight your education and the achievements that qualify you. Be sure to research the company and the opening so you'll know what sells.

3. *Closing.* Reemphasize your interest in the position and what your next step will be: I will call you next week; I look forward to our interview on April 20; and so on.

Cover-Letter Examples from Graduating Students

The following cover letters were written by students graduating from Northwestern University, University of Pittsburgh and Southern Methodist University. These letters showcase the students' academic backgrounds, extracurricular activities and part-time jobs and provide excellent reasons for hiring the applicants—despite their limited paid experience.

CARRIE E. FISCHER
717 University Street North
Rockford, Illinois 61606

January 28, 1999

Ms. Marlene McKasberg
Merrill Lynch & Company
Investment Banking Group
5500 Sears Tower
Chicago, IL 60606

Dear Ms. McKasberg:

Your financial analyst position at Merrill Lynch offers everything I am looking for in a first job, including the opportunity to work in investment banking while staying in Chicago. I won't waste time discussing details of the job since you are well aware of them but I would like to share with you something you will find more interesting: What I can offer Merrill Lynch.

I feel I would be a valuable addition to the Merrill Lynch team. During my academic career, I have striven for excellence in all areas. Through my economics coursework and related classes, I have developed strong quantitative and analytic capabilities as well as written and verbal abilities. Through my summer internships at Detroit Diesel Corporation, I learned to apply these skills in financial and business settings. I also acquired some new skills, including computer applications and an introduction to financial reporting and accounting. I have also been involved in extracurricular activities, both as a leader and as a member of a team or committee. Through campus organizations and volunteer work, I have tried to do my part to make the university and the surrounding community better places to live and work. I can offer Merrill Lynch these skills as well as my dedication, motivation and desire to learn new skills.

I am seeking a position as an Investment Banking Analyst with Merrill Lynch & Company's Chicago Industrial Corporate Finance Group. I would like the opportunity to meet with you and share more about my qualifications and the ways in which I can contribute to the Merrill Lynch team. Thank you for your time and consideration.

Sincerely,

Carrie Fischer

Mark A. Bohanon
SMU P. O. Box 753853
Dallas, TX 75275-3853
214-239-4455

January 18, 1999

Ms. Melissa Stephenson
Recruiting Coordinator
Freeman Consulting
602 Main Street, Suite 212
Dallas, TX 75202

Dear Ms. Stephenson:

I am writing in reference to your advertisement for a staff consultant as listed in the Southern Methodist University Career Center. I will be graduating in May 1999 with a Bachelor of Science degree in Electrical Engineering and I believe my qualifications to be consistent with those desired by your firm.

Throughout my collegiate career, I have attempted to stay well-rounded combining academic excellence with leadership and work experience. By majoring in Electrical Engineering with a concentration in Biomedical Engineering, I have been exposed to all facets of scientific and analytic disciplines from mathematics to circuit analysis to Fortran. Beginning with my appointment to the President's Developing Leadership for Tomorrow freshman year, I have chosen to actively participate and take on responsibility in community service and campus activities during my four years at SMU. I have also worked continuously while in college. I am currently working at MJ Skyline in Dallas, a technology management company, generating reports and updating their database. My previous work experience has provided me with a strong exposure to both corporate and technical environments and has taught me the importance of team work and open communication with clients and co-workers.

I look forward to meeting with you on January 28 to further discuss my qualifications with you. Thank you for your consideration.

Sincerely,

Mark A. Bohanon

Enclosures

PAUL MCWHORTER
UNIVERSITY OF PITTSBURGH
P. O. Box 2131J
Pittsburgh, Pennsylvania 15214

February 7, 1999

Mr. Jeffrey Scanlon
Manager, Executive Recruitment
Marshall's
400 Fifth Avenue
Pittsburgh, PA 15219

Dear Mr. Scanlon:

I would like to interview with Marshall's during your February 21 recruiting visit to the University of Pittsburgh. I am particularly interested in a career with your organization because of your excellent reputation as having one of the ten best executive training programs in your industry. As a candidate, I can offer your company strong interpersonal skills, organizational ability and retail sales experience.

As a sales executive at Lantrip's, I developed effective selling techniques, resulting in consistently exceeding my store's quotas. Through extensive contact with customers, assisting in merchandising and performance of daily store operations, I gained valuable experience.

My internship at WKPA Radio and my work-study position at the University of Pittsburgh have provided me with an opportunity to develop oral and written communication skills, as well as experience in researching and analyzing data. I am confident that these skills have provided me with the background for a successful and productive career at Marshall's.

I have enclosed my resume for your review. I am very interested in further discussing my qualifications with you. I will contact your office on February 14 to arrange a mutually convenient time for a meeting. Thank you in advance for your consideration.

Sincerely,

Paul McWhorter
412-639-4800

Enclosure

SMU P. O. Box 753853   March 18, 1999
Dallas, TX 75275-3853

Ms. Melissa Stephenson
Recruiting Coordinator
Freeman Consulting
602 Main Street, Suite 212
Dallas, TX 75202

Dear Ms. Stephenson:

Your position in Change Management Services, which I learned about through the Career Center at Southern Methodist University, intrigued me. I am honored to write to you to request an interview. I will be graduating in May with a Bachelor of Arts degree in Psychology with Departmental Distinction and a double minor in English and Women's Studies. My current major GPA is 3.88/4.00 scale and my cumulative GPA is 3.66/4.00.

I am excited about the possibility of working with Freeman Consulting because this position is an opportunity for me to combine my skills, interest and experience in a career I would truly enjoy. My ideal job description would include utilizing my psychology degree while working on a team in a business setting, but most important, serving others. Your position provides the perfect fit to realize each of these ideals.

As my resume reveals, several of my personal qualities meet your needs as I understand them:

- Consistent teamwork and leadership ability demonstrated through positions held in numerous extracurricular activities including overseeing editorial policy while serving on the Student Media Company Board of Directors composed of professors, peers, and staff.

- Advanced critical thinking and effective writing obtained through extensive coursework and psychological research including an honors thesis written for departmental distinction analyzing data collected at the Dallas Juvenile Detention Center concerning family variables of violent juveniles.

- Creative planning and efficient delegation skills demonstrated by coordinating and participating in successful programming including serving as New Programs Coordinator and Talent Show Props Director for SMU Student Foundation Parents' Weekend Committee, planning two successful events attended by over 2,500 students and parents.

- Effective interpersonal and communication skills developed through working on numerous committees with administration, professors, and peers to revise and expand the Academic Orientation conducted for 1,300 incoming freshmen.

I am eager to meet with you to further discuss this opportunity. Although I prefer the Dallas area, I am not limited by geographic location. Thank you very much for your consideration.

Sincerely,

Allen Robinson

Enclosure

"We'll be in touch . . . and thanks for coming in on such short notice."

7

Cover Letters for Networking Contacts

By now you've probably noticed my bias concerning how you should uncover job opportunities. So far, I've suggested that direct-mail campaigns, answering want ads and contacting executive search firms are useful job-hunting techniques, but my lukewarm endorsement damns these methods with faint praise. Yes, I have a bias, and it's toward networking. In my view, it's the one method that merits most of a job hunter's energy and time.

Why Network?

Talking to people is how most job openings are filled. This should be no great surprise for a variety of reasons. From the potential employer's point of view:

☆ It's basic human nature for employers to want to hire people they know and trust or who have been recommended. For this reason, talking with an employer face-to-face or on the phone before applying for a position will build more rapport than sending a resume.

☆ It's a relatively hassle-free process. Most employers hate to slog through a pile of resumes to unearth a few truly qualified candidates. But they can quickly find great applicants through employees and friends, who won't risk damaging a valued relationship by referring people who can't handle the position or who have poor attitudes.

☆ It's inexpensive. We're talking a few phone calls, maybe a lunch or two, rather than running costly ads or paying possibly gut-wrenching executive search fees.

From the job seeker's perspective:

☆ Networking can provide information about a position or company that can help you interview more effectively than more out-of-the-loop competitors.

☆ Networking can give you a feel for whether you want to work for a potential employer.

☆ Being recommended by a mutual friend or trusted colleague gives you an aura of credibility that responding to an ad, sending direct-mail letters or working through a search firm can never duplicate.

How to Use Contacts

There are two ways to use contacts when job hunting: a direct referral for a job opening or a networking appointment. Generally, a direct referral will result in your sending an employer a cover letter and resume tailored to a specific position, while a networking appointment or information interview allows you to explore various possibilities with no particular job in mind. Here's how to create cover letters and resumes based on both types of networking assistance.

Start networking by listing current contacts who are likely to be valuable sources of information, whether their careers interest you or not. Relatives, friends, friends of friends, colleagues, fellow members of professional organizations, alumni of your college or fraternity, people in your church, health club, softball team or continuing education class all can provide helpful insights about their companies or industries and suggest names of other contacts as well.

These people know you, like you and have your best interests at heart. While you may feel uncomfortable asking them for advice and contacts, your willingness to request help shows that you trust them enough to risk being in their debt. The old cliché, "The best way to solidify a relationship is to ask for help," is only too true during a job search. So give your friends a chance to nurture you, and everyone will benefit from the experience.

A variety of other contacts whom you don't already know can provide excellent information on companies, industries and jobs. Professors at local colleges and universities, continuing education course instructors, professionals in state employment offices, exhibitors and speakers at conventions—even potential employers that you contact directly—have insights and advice to offer if you're willing to ask for their input.

A relatively new and highly active job-search network has developed on the Internet via a variety of specialty bulletin boards and user groups. If you have a computer and a modem, give them a try. You may be amazed at the number of jobs listed and the amount of information you can glean from fellow board buddies as you "surf" through cyberspace. (See Chapter 8 for more information on how to access these online resources.)

Cover-Letter Information from Networking Appointments

Information interviews are helpful in determining what a potential employer might require in a job candidate. Use these networking appointments to learn about different industries and companies and uncover positions not typically advertised or filled through executive search firms. These interviews differ from employment interviews in several important ways:

☆ They're less stressful because you're asking for information, not a job.

☆ You're the interviewer, researching the job market during these meetings, while the company representative is the interviewee.

☆ You take the initiative to set up the appointment, not the employer.

Because this interview is a friendly conversation, not a mutual sales discussion, it doesn't carry the expectation of a job offer. Without this pressure, both parties needn't worry about revealing the "skeleton in the closet" and can be candid about their requirements, expectations, strengths and challenges.

Why would potential contacts be open to spending their valuable time with someone they don't know? There are at least three good reasons:

1. They like talking about themselves and expressing their opinions while basking in your undivided attention. How often can any of us play the expert to a genuinely appreciative audience?

2. It may not always be evident, but most people have a streak of altruism. If you're honestly asking for information—and not covertly seeking a job—potential interviewers will probably empathize with your situation.

3. Meeting with you is a low-risk way to find a potentially excellent candidate. Few employers enjoy the process of finding a new employee. It's time consuming, expensive, and fraught with potential misjudgment. With networking, you do all the work and they get all the credit. You set up the appointment, do preliminary research, prepare a list of questions in advance, take the interviewing lead and send an enthusiastic thank-you note. The two of you build a relationship without the stress accompanying a typical employment interview. It's hard for potential employers not to admire your approach. Should they or a friend have an opening that matches your background, it's in their best interest to take advantage of your availability. If they hire you, they've saved themselves the angst and expense of an ad or executive search firm. And if they discover you for a friend, they may be rewarded with a favor or two down the line.

When scheduling an information interview, remember that your primary goal is getting information, not a job. But even though you're pursuing knowledge, not a position, it makes sense to contact the person who can provide both. It's doubtful you'll find this individual in the human resources department, unless you specifically want an HR job. Your best bet is to contact the person who would logically be your manager. He knows what's happening in his department, and he's in a position to hire you if there's mutual interest in bringing you on board.

When you call to schedule your appointment, your half of the conversation should go something like this: "This is Taunee Besson. Jim Beverly suggested I give you a call. [If you have a referral, mention his name as quickly as possible. You gain credibility because your contact knows that Jim wouldn't recommend a

ROBERT HALF'S RESUMANIA

In a recent cover letter, a New York candidate came up with an interesting reason for being willing to relocate: "Because my wife and I are newlyweds, we suffer the sort of pressure from both families that all young, recently married people experience. For that reason, a move away from New York would not only alleviate this pressure on us, it would force us to forge a closer bond as we stand together in a strange and new environment."

I wonder how many members of both families got to see his resume?

real loser.] I'm leaving Sears after a 15-year stint, and I'm trying to find out if the types of projects I handled there are relevant to the world at large. Jim thought you would be an excellent person for me to talk to because you left the company several years ago and forged a successful career in an entirely different industry. If you're willing, I would like to meet you in your office for about 30 minutes, and ask you some key questions. I know your answers will provide important insights concerning my potential long-term career options. I'm free Wednesday, Thursday or Friday afternoon. Would any of those times be convenient for you?"

After you make the appointment, head to the library to do some research on your interviewee's company and industry using the techniques mentioned in Chapter 4. Then prepare a list of questions based on your research and your contact's professional experience. You might address some of the following issues:

☆ How did your interviewee make the transition from one industry to another?

☆ What have his career path and educational background been to date?

☆ Where does he hope to go from here?

☆ What does he most enjoy and dislike about his job, company, industry?

☆ What does he think are his greatest challenges, now and in the future?

☆ What are the skills, personality traits and backgrounds needed to be successful in his department, company, industry?

☆ Where does he envision his department, company, industry heading in the future?

☆   Who else does he think you should contact? Usually interviewees enjoy serving as referral sources. In fact, if you network wisely, there's a good chance you won't have to cold-call or write letters to strangers. This is an advantage because correspondence sent to someone who knows you isn't likely to go into the round file. You'll also be able to tailor your queries to the specific needs of your recipients.

After you've developed rapport with your interviewee by asking questions, tell him about your background, goals, skills and values. Keep your description concise and clear. It may help to practice your statement about your ideal job ahead of time. This way, you'll have your two- to three-minute "commercial" ready to go. After describing your goals, ask your contact for any ideas he might have about compensation, people and companies you should target. He may even consider the possibility of hiring you himself.

As you talk with your interviewee, consider taking notes. Jotting down his perspective of your qualifications, industry or company trends, correctly spelled contact names, compensation estimates and position requirements for available openings might be useful as your job search progresses. It's a lot easier to be accurate if you have this information on paper rather than in the remote recesses of your already overloaded brain.

As quickly as possible after the interview, write down the more subjective knowledge you gathered from the meeting. Include how you felt about the interviewee, the company and its policies, and your potential for landing a satisfying position there. Also, note the best way to follow up on this appointment. Store these notes in a binder, on cards or in your computer for future reference. If you conduct the 20 to 30 networking discussions typical of most job seekers, you'll need this informal record to remind you of each of your interviewee's specifications. A completed contact form should look like the example on page 159.

It's easy to see how the information gained from a networking appointment can be used as background material in a tailored cover letter. If you and your interviewee have discussed an available position, you already know which experience, skills and personality traits to include in your cover letter and resume. In fact, you've probably already noted these requirements on your Information Interview Evaluation Form. Should your contact want to review your resume for an opening at his company or a friend's, send it with a thank-you note/cover letter that matches your most useful experience with the requirements of the job(s). The inside information you've gathered and the rapport you've developed will allow you to outdistance your competition and put you in the "interview" line up.

Information Interview Evaluation Form

Person interviewed: John Hirsch
Title: VP of Marketing
Name of company: Global Information Systems
Address: 663 Burlington Drive
                             Chicago, IL 60605
Phone number: 312-287-2242
Secretary's name: Heather McCracken
Name of person who can hire: John Hirsch
Date of interview: July 26, 1999

General Feeling about the Interview
John was very accommodating. He took me on a tour of Global's recently expanded offices and suggested we get together again Tuesday. The people at Global seem to enjoy themselves. I heard occasional laughter and lots of spirited discussion in a variety of languages. The atmosphere was upbeat and full of enthusiasm. I felt comfortable there.

How Did the Interviewee Respond to Questions about Himself?
John was very candid about his transition from a large multinational company to a smaller one. He said the cultures and perks were very different, so it took him a while to adjust. However, he also mentioned that his connections in the Pacific Rim and his understanding of how to negotiate with Asians has served him well, even though he is marketing a different line of products. He seemed very open to answering questions about his company's past and future and musing over the explosive growth that NAFTA is generating in information services throughout the Western Hemisphere.

How Do I Feel about the Company and Its Policies?
Global is a very entrepreneurial company. The success of the individual is predicated on his ability and willingness to adapt to global demands and cultural idiosyncrasies while providing a benchmark quality product and a high level of customer service. I like that. Individual ideas are encouraged. Teamwork and empowerment are not just clichés.

While Global prefers to promote from within, its fast and steady growth necessitates hiring people from other companies as well. The company looks for individuals who genuinely believe in serving the customer, even if it means sacrificing the immediate bottom line. Previous industry experience isn't as important as personality, transferable skills and a passion for taking Global's products and services worldwide.

How Do My Skills, Personality Traits and Experience Mesh with What This Company Needs and Wants?
Obviously I have the commitment to customer service and the desire to serve the client even if my quota suffers for it this quarter. I like the fact that Global doesn't require specific industry experience, because I consider myself to be more of an international sales generalist than a specialist in a particular product. It seems my

constant "ideaphoria" will serve me well here, where it has caused me problems in the past. I particularly enjoy working with international businesses, which are a major target market for Global.

Can I Fit into the Current Structure? Can I Create a New Job for Myself? Does This Company Have Opportunities That Meet My Requirements?
Much to my pleasant surprise, John wants to hire two experienced sales pros as soon as possible to concentrate on Latin America. Given what I've seen of the company so far, I think this job would suit my skills, personality and goals. While John won't be leaving his job anytime in the foreseeable future, he says there will be opportunities to expand sales territories or become a regional sales manager as the company continues to stretch across the globe. I speak Spanish and the chance to live in a foreign country is very appealing.

What Should I Do to Follow Up on This Information Interview?
Of course, I will send a thank-you note and resume immediately to confirm our employment interview appointment, and tell John why I am especially enthusiastic about the company and think I could help expand its information technology worldwide.

Thank-You Note/Cover-Letter Example

Using the information gleaned from John Hirsch at Global Information Systems, you could develop a combination cover-letter/thank-you-for-the-appointment note much like the following one.

July 28, 1999

Mr. John Hirsch
Vice President of Marketing
Global Information Systems
663 Burlington Drive
Chicago, IL 60605

Dear John,

Thank you for getting together to talk with me about your perspective on the global opportunities in information technologies, and especially about your goals and plans at Global. It's exciting to hear about how the field is exploding with growth and how your company is cultivating its own important niche (or would lane be a better word?) on the worldwide information highway. It was also wonderful to talk with a business pro who honestly believes that exceptional customer service and a creative, flexible approach to developing new markets will always generate greater sales in the long run, even if the immediate bottom line isn't as good this quarter.

I was particularly gratified to hear that my international business background and my desire to be a part of the communications revolution are key attributes for moving into your organization. And, based on our discussion, my understanding of business mores in other countries, enthusiasm for information technology, and proven ability to sell sophisticated products and services should be beneficial to any international organization in the high-tech arena.

Discovering you have a sales position open in Mexico was a most fortuitous surprise and an opportunity I want to explore more thoroughly. I look forward to seeing you again on Tuesday to discuss the job more specifically and how I might be of benefit to Global should you hire me for your new "south of the border" venture. Enclosed is a resume that will give you some relevant information on my background in light of the role I would be playing in Latin America.

Sincerely yours,

Joseph Lopez

Enclosure

Cover Letter for a Direct Referral

Networking contacts that you talk with by phone or in person often won't have openings at their own companies but will know of someone who does. When you uncover this type of job lead, ask your referral source for the name of the hiring authority and other pertinent information. Use the Information Interview Evaluation Form or the Company/Agency Research Form (see pages 71–72) to document your discussion, then visit the library to locate other important information. If appropriate, call the hiring authority, mention that "Jean Johnson" suggested you call concerning "XYZ position," and ask about the position's job description, salary range and required background, traits and skills. Then offer to send a cover letter and resume explaining how your experience might be an excellent fit for the opening.

A typical cover letter in this situation might look something like the following example. Note that the first paragraph of this letter mentions the name of the person who provided the referral. This reinforces your relationship and gives you an aura of credibility. Also notice that the letter alludes to the personality traits, lovable idiosyncrasies and philosophy that the parties involved have in common. This is a powerful way to build rapport; in fact, it serves as a partial substitute for not meeting face-to-face. The more you tailor your letter to the available opening *and* its reader's mind-set, the more likely you are to secure an interview.

200 Bristol Court
Short Hills, NJ 07078
201-676-2233

January 22, 1999

Dr. Jim Mantock
Vice President of Research and Development
Medtech Group
65 Oak Road
Durham, NC 27701

Dear Dr. Mantock:

   Last week I was talking to Rudy Williams, who was my college roommate at MIT. As we were catching up on each other's lives, I mentioned to him that I was finishing up a three-year project at work and was feeling ready for a new challenge. Well, you know Rudy. He launched into his famous (infamous?) brainstorming mode and began listing a variety of possibilities he was certain would intrigue me. While not every idea was a blue ribbon candidate, your research on developing a nonintrusive system for diabetic testing really captured my attention, especially when he said you were looking for another biomedical engineer to round out your team.

   I am a biomedical engineer with ten years of experience in designing nonintrusive methods for diagnosing a variety of medical conditions. I was one of the team that developed and tested the MRI at Southwestern Medical School. I've also studied and improved the effects of electrical stimulation to heal bone and muscle tissue. Most recently, I've been the lead engineer working on a system for improving mammography techniques. While these may seem to be diverse experiences, they all have one thing in common: They reduce the need for poking, prodding and otherwise distressing the body when we can devise a kinder, gentler approach to achieve the same or better results. From what Rudy tells me, you and I have a common philosophy on this issue.

   I've enclosed my resume for your perusal. I'll call you next week to confirm its receipt and discuss if we should set a date to explore the possibility of working together on a way to make the lives of diabetics a lot easier.

Sincerely yours,

Tom Yoo

Enclosure

Networking Cover Letters from Real People

Before-and-After Example

Lisa Brady Gill was an elementary school teacher for 10 years before deciding to switch to a career that would allow her to interact more with adults. Because she still had a strong desire to serve people, she opted to look at careers in the nonprofit area, particularly those linking business with education. The following cover letter is in response to a need for an Adopt-a-School coordinator.

Since then Lisa has spent several years as the education coordinator for *The Dallas Morning News* and *The Dallas Times Herald*. In 1995, Lisa joined Randy Best in getting the Voyager Expanded Learning program up and running. Voyager is designed to motivate students to learn after school and during the summer. The firm partners with public schools, community colleges and universities to provide extended-time programs for K-6 children. While it started in Dallas, Voyager now employs several hundred individuals and works with educators across the country. As regional director, Lisa collaborates with school administrators to sell, develop and implement programs in their districts.

You'll note her cover letter continues to be closely aligned with her evolving career.

October 12, 1999

Ms. Constance Burch
Director of Education
Dallas Chamber of Commerce
1507 Pacific Avenue
Dallas, TX 75201-3481

Dear Ms. Burch:

I was pleased to learn that the Adopt-a-School position at the Dallas Chamber of Commerce is open. Please accept my attached resume.

After 10 years of teaching elementary school in the Richardson Independent School District, I resigned to pursue a new career. For the past six months, I have gathered information by interviewing numerous members of the corporate, academic and social service communities. I learned about the Adopt-a-School program from involved businesspeople as well as from former Dallas Chamber employees. I was so impressed that I proposed a similar program to administrators of the Richardson Independent School District as well as the Director of the Richardson Chamber of Commerce. Although the timing is not right for such a program in RISD, I remain interested in the Dallas Adopt-a-School position.

I am confident that my skills and knowledge qualify me for this position. I look forward to talking with you about this exciting program.

Sincerely,

Lisa Brady Gill
2930 Antares Circle
Garland, TX 75042
972-495-7796

In her first cover letter, Lisa includes an excellent paragraph on why she's interested in the Adopt-a-School program sponsored by the local chamber of commerce. However, she doesn't summarize her relevant experience or mention that she'll follow up on her resume.

In her improved letter, her second paragraph becomes her first, and she adds an excellent summary of why she would make an ideal Adopt-a-School coordinator. She also keeps the ball in her court by volunteering to call to schedule an appointment.

After

October 12, 1999

Ms. Constance Burch
Director of Education
Dallas Chamber of Commerce
1507 Pacific Avenue
Dallas, TX 75201-3481

Dear Ms. Burch:

I appreciate your getting together with me to discuss the Dallas Chamber of Commerce Adopt-a-School program. As I mentioned in our discussion, I first learned about the Adopt-a-School program from involved businesspeople as well as former Dallas Chamber employees. I was so impressed that I proposed a similar program to administrators of the Richardson Independent School District and to the Director of the Richardson Chamber of Commerce. Although the timing is not right for starting this project in RISD, it seems serendipitous that your program has developed an opening.

After 10 years of teaching elementary school in the Richardson Independent School District, I am ready to pursue a new career using the community contacts, project management, and PR skills that I have honed through interaction with parents, colleagues, administrators, business executives and fellow volunteers. It seems that working for the Adopt-a-School program would provide the ideal opportunity to combine my teaching experience with my background in volunteer coordination and fund raising.

Attached is the resume you requested. I will call next week to make sure you received it and see if we can schedule an interview.

Sincerely,

Lisa Brady Gill
2930 Antares Circle
Garland, TX 75042
972-495-7796

Claudia Dixon

Claudia Dixon was the office manager for three professional practices during a 12-year period. She enjoyed her jobs because the work was interesting and her schedule allowed her to spend time with her children and do volunteer work. When her girls went off to college, she realized she was ready for a more challenging career.

To expand her horizons, Claudia signed up for mediation training at Cincinnati's Dispute Mediation Service and earned a Masters in Conflict Resolution. While she was training, she learned that the service needed a part-time office manager to handle its business activities. Claudia applied and got the job. Now she works half days in the office and mediates family cases as well.

6154 Grandberry   513-224-7637
Cincinnati, OH 45219   513-939-9990

June 12, 1999

Herbert V. Cooke
Executive Director
Dispute Mediation Service of Cincinnati Inc.
3400 Carlisle, #240, LB-9
Cincinnati, OH 45216

Dear Herb:

Since receiving my DMS mediation training and becoming a volunteer mediator last year, I have been very impressed with the service DMS provides. I value your management approach and the professionalism of the DMS staff, and would like to take a more active role in the growth of DMS and mediation in Cincinnati.

My background in office management, nonprofit associations and education all seem to point me in the direction of this position. I'm grateful for the opportunity to apply and hope you will give my resume serious consideration.

I will be out of town July 3–11, but would be available to meet with you or clarify any questions relevant to my application before or after those dates.

Sincerely yours,

Claudia Dixon

Enclosure

Other Good Networking Cover Letters

These next letters are good examples of the effort dedicated networkers make to pursue leads through referrals or make contacts with new people who might provide assistance. For instance, after attending a professional association meeting, Nancy Symons seized the chance to introduce herself to the guest speaker in hopes that he will suggest names of others she can contact.

NANCY M. SYMONS

11327 David Way   **San Bernardino, CA 92404**   **(909) 823-7376**

May 9, 1999

Mr. Bruce Jordan
AST Research Inc.
602 Val Mar Drive
Suite 500
San Bernardino, CA 92404

Dear Mr. Jordan:

I was present at the IFMA meeting last night and was very impressed with your presentation on computer applications for business. Having moved from Canada and secured my work permit, I am networking to explore industries and companies that could utilize my background in strategic facilities planning and real estate.

I am a new member of the San Bernardino IFMA Chapter. I was active in the Toronto, Canada, chapter and most recently was editor of the Utilities Council newsletter in which I contributed to the professional development of the association's members. I am writing to you because I realize that your knowledge of the industry is extensive and I would like to ask for your help.

For over 15 years, I have been in the facility management and real estate field with one of the largest energy services companies in North America. For the past four years, I was the executive responsible for strategic business planning for their headquarters facilities, encompassing over 3 million square feet. My most recent strategy is now saving the company over $20 million annually. I was intrigued by your comment about your building's floorplates being over 40,000 square feet in size. The headquarters that I managed is over 50,000 square feet and curved in shape which, as you know, presents some interesting challenges.

In corresponding with you, my hope is that the name of a few particular individuals or companies may come to mind as possible target opportunities. I expect your insight could prove beneficial in helping me sort out likely prospects for further investigation and networking. For your convenience, enclosed is a copy of my resume which details my skills, experience, key achievements and education.

I realize you are busy so I will call you next week to arrange a convenient time for us to meet briefly. At that time, I can introduce myself more fully, listen to your advice, and discuss ideas which could be of benefit. Thank you in advance for your help. I look forward to speaking with you.

Sincerely,

Nancy M. Symons

Enclosure

7723 Chalkstone   314-490-9684
St. Louis, MO 63558   314-491-7777

June 21, 1999

Todd Meier (name changed)
1385 Club View Court
El Cerrito, CA 94530

Dear Todd,

Thank you for the information you gave me over the phone today about your CEO position with the Berkeley Youth Club. When Tom Bennett called to tell me your Executive
Director was leaving, I was very interested in finding out more about your agency. As
you will note from my resume, I graduated from Syracuse University, and I would
welcome the opportunity to move back to New York where I have friends and family.
Having served on Youth Club staffs around the country for more than 12 years, I know
the agency's philosophy and culture very well.

On December 31, I left my position as Downtown Executive Director/Metropolitan
Vice-President of the St. Louis Youth Club to pursue an interest in professional fund
raising. I spent two years as a professional consultant with a nationally recognized
fund-raising company. Additionally, I have served for two years as Executive Director
for a very large home health agency in Dallas. I feel very confident that my high
energy level and my management experiences, both inside and outside the Youth Club,
will enable me to be a very effective, successful, and contributing Chief Executive
Officer for Berkeley.

I am personally challenged by Youth Club Boards, lay leadership and staff who are
engaged in planning for future growth and development in operations budgets and
long-range plans.

I will call you next week to confirm your receipt of my resume and ascertain whether I
am the type of candidate you are seeking.

Sincerely yours,

Charles H. Brown (name changed)

Glenda Martin

11 College Road   Commerce, TX 75428   903-262-0088

December 7, 1999

Glenn W. Maloney
Campus Activities Office
UNB 4.304
Austin, TX 78713-7338

Dear Mr. Maloney:

Dr. Ruth Ann White, a professor of counseling and guidance at East Texas State University, suggested I contact you concerning the position of student Development Specialist III. I am particularly interested in your opening because I would like to continue my career in student services at a larger institution of the caliber of the University of Texas.

My masters in guidance and counseling and four years of experience working with students, their organizations and faculty should serve as an excellent background for the position.

As this resume is due by December 9, I will call you the week of December 19 to be sure you have received it, answer any preliminary questions and ascertain your interview schedule.

Sincerely yours,

Glenda Martin

Enclosure

7 Park Lane
Oklahoma City, OK 73101
405-789-5454
March 26, 1999

Mr. Harland Stauffer
Vice President—Engineering
Frito-Lay Inc.
PO Box 660634
Dallas, TX 75266-0634

Dear Mr. Stauffer:

John Hill, the president of Logisticon and an old friend, called me today and said he had discussed my job search with you. You suggested to John that I send you my resume and then follow up with a call.

Frito-Lay might be in need of a senior-level executive with a background of accomplishment who has worked on both the user and the vendor side of the fence in implementing system solutions.

I was recently a Vice President with Rath & Strong, a well-known national consulting firm in Boston. I resigned to pursue a senior management position with a company in the Dallas area.

My managerial career has been a diversified one.

- In my last position, I was responsible for highly successful projects that generated millions of dollars of increased revenue and/or cost reduction for client companies.
- As COO of a software company I managed the company through a severe cash crisis to its successful acquisition by a Fortune 200 company.
- As CFO of a $200+ million manufacturing company I was responsible for the restructuring of the financial function and the implementation of MRP, distribution and financial systems which provided for the reduction of costs and inventories, resulting in savings of millions of dollars while, at the same time, optimizing resources and increasing revenues.

I have marketed and sold Computer-Aided Process Planning and MRP II software.

My greatest strengths are my leadership skills and the ability to motivate the people with whom I work. In over 25 years of management experience, I have been very successful in meeting ambitious objectives on time and within budget.

I would like the opportunity to discuss my background and experience in more detail in a personal interview. I will call you in the next week to follow up.

Sincerely,

William F. Cunniff

Enclosure

Connie Littlefoot
66 Brookside Way
Carson City, NV 89701
702-565-2348

August 2, 1999

Mr. Don Stiver
Vice President of Human Resources
Austin Industries
P.O. Box 1590
Las Vegas, NV 89030

Dear Mr. Stiver:

Doris Thompson's husband, a former student of mine, stopped by after class one day last week to tell me that Doris knew of "the perfect job for me!" Naturally, this piqued my curiosity, so I gave her a call. After discussing the job description for manager-developer and the company's philosophy with her, I have decided to submit my resume for consideration.

Judging from Doris's comments, Austin Industries would provide me with a wonderful opportunity to use my 16 years of human-resource development experience in a flexible atmosphere, among people who really care about the organization and each other.

I look forward to discussing your training department and its future development at our soonest mutual convenience. As I am out of town teaching most of the week, I will call you on Friday, August 9, to assure you have received my resume and to schedule a time for us to get together.

Sincerely yours,

Connie Littlefoot (name changed)

Enclosure

BONNIE THOMPSON
4915 Windmere Drive East
Phoenix, AZ 85044
602-424-8647

February 3, 1999

Ms. Sharon McGovern
Human Resources
Camco Inc.
11333 Palm Canyon Drive
Phoenix, AZ 85018

Dear Ms. McGovern:

I am a client of Taunee Besson, having just moved to Phoenix from Kansas as a relocating spouse. When Taunee called me about your senior administrative assistant position, I was really enthusiastic about the opportunity it represented. Consequently, I am sending my resume for your consideration.

For the past six years, I have served as a "jack of all trades" office and human resource manager for two organizations. During that time, I:

- Hired, trained and terminated employees
- Wrote employee handbooks and training manuals
- Conducted and monitored performance appraisals
- Justified promotions, transfers and raises to upper management
- Wrote employment ads and job descriptions
- Maintained employee benefit and other HR records.

While human resources was only one of the many functions of my job, I particularly enjoyed it because it required me to use my people, planning and resourcing skills.

I am looking forward to discussing how the position and my background might be a good match. I will call you next week to confirm receipt of my resume and schedule an appointment.

Sincerely yours,

Bonnie Thompson

BT:ds

Enclosure

JEFFREY SAMUELS
921 Northlake Parkway
Atlanta, GA 30345
404-221-7904

January 15, 1999

Ms. Laura Montclair
Manager, Professional Employment
Charter Medical Corp.
1 Main Street
Macon, GA 12346

Dear Ms. Montclair:

At a recent meeting of the Regional Sales Association, I met James Smith, a Charter marketing representative, who suggested I contact you about employment possibilities in the South.

Through my conversation with Mr. Smith and the article on Charter in the December issue of *Atlanta Business Chronicle,* I understand that you are expanding the Southern territory into Tennessee and Alabama. Having attended school at the University of Tennessee-Knoxville, I would welcome the chance to live in that area again.

My education and experience have prepared me well for a position as sales representative. My degree program in Professional Selling included courses in Consumer Behavior, Buying and Selling, Marketing Management and Sales Promotion. Through these and other courses, I have developed strong skills in verbal and written communications as well as organizational and analytical abilities.

During the past three years, I have chosen summer jobs that allowed me to test out my interest in sales and marketing. At Rich's I had extensive contact with customers and enjoyed assisting them in merchandise selection. My work at UPS helped me realize that I can effectively handle a job which involves traveling and meeting a variety of people in different locations.

I would appreciate the opportunity to speak with you during my spring vacation (March 12–19), if that would be convenient. I will call next week to discuss when we might get together.

Thank you for your time and consideration.

Sincerely,

Jeffrey Samuels

Enclosure

8

Using the Internet in Your Job Search

Unless you've been living without electricity in a cabin in the wilds, you have been bombarded with media reports about how the information superhighway is revolutionizing global communication and commerce. If you're already surfing the Net, you have probably formed your own opinion about what this emerging resource is capable of doing. However, if you're like many U.S. professionals, you're probably mystified about what cyberspace has to offer and how you can access useful online information while seeking your next career opportunity.

As you might imagine, one chapter can't possibly provide everything you need to know about the Internet or even complete instructions on how to use it as a job-search tool. But if you want to develop a basic understanding of the Internet and visit some key job-search sites, this chapter is for you.

The True State of the Net

Despite all the hype about cyberspace, the Internet is still in its infancy. It's maturing very rapidly, however, and more and more Americans of all ages, occupations and backgrounds are taking their first tentative step onto the information superhighway. They are arriving via a large and growing number of Internet Service Providers (ISPs), companies that offer access to the Internet with a local telephone call. ISPs range from industry giants, such as America Online (AOL) or AT&T's Worldnet, to smaller operations like Megalocity.com in Cleveland and Erols.com in northern Virginia. They connect offices and homes, public libraries and schools, government agencies and airports, even phone booths and highway rest stops to the Internet. Indeed, those of us who have been exploring its possibilities regularly experience gridlock on the information superhighway because its "under construction" infrastructure can't handle the constantly increasing traffic.

Some Intriguing Statistics

☆ In mid-1995, there were 35 million people in 80 countries were using the Internet. By mid-1998, that figure had increased to 73 million and by 2002, it's expected to top 116 million. To put it another way, the Internet is coming into our lives at a far more rapid pace than did the now ubiquitous television set.

☆ Monster.com, one of the premier employment sites on the World Wide Web, records over 5 million unique visits per month! The site has only been in operation since April 1993.

☆ The first day Texas Instruments, a multibillion dollar Texas-based high-tech corporation, went online with its home page (another name for a World Wide Web site or destination), it had 10,000 hits.

☆ In 1996, one of the early leaders in online employment services, a Web site called E.Span (now JobOptions), posted 2,000 new job listings per week. In 1998, another leading firm in the field, HeadHunter.NET, routinely posts 1,400 new jobs every day.

While the Internet may be in its formative stages, it already has the global clout to list more available positions and generate more responses in any given time period than *The Wall Street Journal.*

User Perspectives

Opinions about the Internet run the gamut from "a communications tool that will revolutionize our world" to "an incredibly frustrating, hard-to-use, over-hyped boondoggle." The reactions I've gathered from talking with employers, service providers and job seekers who use the Internet are illuminating.

According to Gary Baum, general manager of CareerWeb, "The Internet presents job seekers with a kit bag of new and powerful tools to aid their job search. Information about companies and extensive job databases with powerful search engines are now only a couple of keystrokes away. Job seekers can even use automated job-search agents to continue the search process when they're offline. However, the fundamentals of job seeking still apply—nothing replaces a targeted job search coupled with diligent follow through."

The bottom line is connecting the right person with the right job, and there's growing evidence that the Internet makes such connections happen. Kristin Synder, a recruiter at a PepsiCo Inc. plant in Witchita, Kansas, worked with Nation-Job Network, another leading Internet employment site, to fill an accounting position. She comments, "We have recruiters all over the country looking for CPAs, but through NationJob we found one right here locally and landed her right away! NationJob also has been great for customer service and information technology positions, and we're recommending it to other PepsiCo locations."

Peter Weddle publishes "WEDDLE's," a newsletter about the online employment world. He says, "The Internet is the most important development in employment since the creation of the resume. But, as with the resume, it has its own special rules and conventions which job seekers must master if they want to put the Internet to work for them."

Don Seaquist, a Net-savvy job seeker, says, "If I were in the $60 to 80K range, I would be spending about 60 percent of my job-search time online, especially if I were in the high-tech or health-care industries."

In fact, the Internet can be a valuable tool, even for senior-level managers and executives. It's a particularly good resource for research and networking and can also be helpful with certain aspects of their personal development, including on-going education through distance-learning programs.

I think of the Internet as a multilane superhighway, which can take you anywhere on the globe at lightning speed or subject you to an uncompromising gridlock that rivals The Big Apple during rush hour. Indeed one job seeker has likened it to "Rome without the traffic cops, utter anarchy!" Should you choose to use it at peak periods, you'll have to creep up the on-ramp, endure stop-and-go traffic, and risk finding a full parking lot when you finally reach your destination. And yet, cyberspace has such a wealth of resources that most surfers (people who use the Internet regularly) are willing to put up with the hassle to get to the goodies.

Using the Internet for Employment Purposes

Three groups use the Internet to make employment or contractual connections: companies seeking to hire people; third-party or independent recruiters, and job seekers or professionals pursuing project or contract work. A variety of online options can help each of these groups find the right match.

Companies

Company home pages on the World Wide Web can be useful to job seekers who want to tailor cover letters to reflect an organization's unique culture and job possibilities.

☆ Corporations often put their annual reports on their home pages or on an employment Web site, such as CareerWeb, which they pay to list job postings. These reports are gold mines of information about products, services, new technology and trends, financial data, names of high-level executives and charitable projects. While you can dig for a company's annual report in your local library, the Internet allows you to access it in the comfort of your home.

☆ Many companies target college graduates via the Internet. For instance, Texas Instruments (TI) invites college recruits to e-mail requests for a computer disk describing its entry-level openings and what it's like to work there. It also provides an online multiquestion profile to help potential candidates decide if they would enjoy working at TI.

☆ Firms also may post magazine and newspaper articles about themselves and literature about product launches on their home pages. For instance, TI's home page provides sophisticated videotapes and interactive opportunities for learning more about what it sells.

☆ From a job seeker's viewpoint, job openings are probably the most important items companies can post on their home pages or career sites. While there's currently a preponderance of positions listed for engineers, information technologists and other technically-oriented professionals, you'll now find a broad range of career opportunities in fields such as finance and accounting, sales and marketing, human resources and operations and in industries ranging from healthcare and transportation to communications and manufacturing. You'll also find jobs posted for administrators, account managers, linguists, teachers, insurance professionals, repair technicians, retail sales clerks, morticians, actors and actresses, radio announcers, and more.

Increasingly, employers like the responses they're getting from job ads posted in cyberspace. As John Blakely, who hires computer experts for Magnet Interactive Studios, says, "As an employer, I'm looking for people who keep up with the most current information in their profession. As far as I'm concerned, these people are the ones who are networking online with peers, asking questions and looking for the latest trends."

Every employer we interviewed who uses the Internet agrees that it's a tremendously efficient, cost-effective vehicle for attracting responses from talented, intelligent candidates worldwide. They agree that online recruiting efforts are in the beginning stages, but expect to expand and refine their techniques and strategies as they explore the Internet's possibilities.

Third-Party and Independent Recruiters

For years, employment agencies and independent recruiters have used networking in person and by phone to identify qualified candidates for client openings. When necessary, they've also run ads in national publications such as *The Wall Street Journal* and in local newspapers.

The Internet merges these two strategies into a new kind of networking— networking electronically. It enables third-party and independent recruiters to post job openings worldwide 24 hours a day, 7 days a week at a fraction of the cost of traditional print advertising. In essence, these recruiters can now reach out and connect with prospective candidates at any time and anywhere in the world.

Some post their opportunities at commercial employment Web sites; others create and use their own recruiting Web sites. Still more recruiters do both. These postings provide longer and broader visibility, which increases the chances that the ads will be seen by large numbers of job hunters. They also offer more in-depth information about the positions than print ads, enabling the recruiters to "sell" them to the candidates passing by.

In addition, many third-party and independent recruiters use the Internet to search for candidates proactively. Many believe that Net surfers tend to be more intelligent, better educated and more likely to adapt to new trends and technology than peers who stick with more conventional ways to advertise themselves to employers. To find these high-caliber candidates, recruiters routinely scour online communities called newsgroups, public and private resume databases operated by commercial employment Web sites, databases of prospective college graduates and alumni maintained by college placement centers, personal Web sites created by individual job seekers and myriad other locations. In the process, they've transformed the nature of networking from a face-to-face exercise to an electronic interaction in cyberspace.

Job Seekers and Independent Contractors

With practice, a how-to book about the Internet and, ideally, a friendly mentor who can answer initial questions, job seekers will find an incredible array of resources online.

☆ A plethora of information is available about companies, careers, industries and cities where you might want to relocate, if you know how to access it. Many publications, such as the *NBEW, Business Week, Fortune* and *The Wall Street Journal,* offer current issues or databases of past articles through proprietary home pages or at the Web site of one of the major search engines online such as Yahoo! (http://www.yahoo.com) and Excite (http://www.excite.com). As mentioned, corporate annual reports and product/service data also can be found on the Net. In fact, there's so much information on employment and economic issues, you'll never be able to research everything that interests you. Fortunately, you only need to discover a small portion of it to gather enough background material for a successful job search.

Further, directories are available online to help you find exactly the kind of information you need. These include Hoovers Online (http://www.hoovers.com), where you can research companies at no charge and acquire their URLs, operating locations, officer's names, sales figures and more. Additional information is available for a fee. Similarly, at Companies Online (http://www.companiesonline.com), you'll find free information on 100,000 public and private companies, including their annual sales, workforce size, trade names, and corporate structure. At the EDGAR database of the U.S. Securities and Exchange Commission (http://www.sec.gov), you'll have free access to the SEC filings of all companies.

If you're unsure about a future career path, online services can also help you assess your skills and identify jobs that are likely to fit your interests and capabilities.

Many colleges and universities use the Net to connect directly to the home pages of employers who recruit students. Entry-level job seekers can read about a company's culture, products/services and opportunities, then send a resume or schedule an interview via e-mail. Some progressive corporations have set up hyper-links (direct electronic connections) to recruiters who will answer student questions in real time (at the moment) or by return e-mail.

Perusing job listings on the Internet can become a full-time occupation because of the proliferation of employers who use it to search for candidates. If you browse for a while, you'll find specific Web job-related sites or career centers suited to your employment or contract needs to bookmark for easy future access. Later in this chapter, I list some of the sites most admired by the employers, candidates and service providers I interviewed.

Because the Internet is a populist communication tool, you can easily post your resume on it to attract the attention of employers who need your particular background and skills. To maximize your Internet exposure, you can even create your own home page, or you can put others' sites to work for you. There are a variety of online resume services that allow job seekers to list their credentials for free or a nominal fee.

For instance, OnLine Solutions Inc. in Morrisonville, New York, provides a service called ResumeXPRESS!. This service will:

☆ E-mail the full text of your resume to more than 2,400 companies and recruiting organizations seeking candidates, and

☆ Promote your credentials to thousands of employers and recruiters who visit the service's online resume database.

OnLine Solutions is just one of the many services that can help you tell the world you're seeking a new opportunity.

In fact, as noted earlier, the term networking takes on a whole new meaning when it's done in cyberspace. Participating in online Usenet groups or bulletin boards allows job seekers to ask fellow Net surfers about careers, companies, industries and contacts. These online forums enable people with common interests to congregate and chat or send e-mail messages to one another. While this revolutionary method for meeting fellow professionals may sound impersonal, it's actually in tune with the "high tech, high touch" trend John Naisbitt described in his best-selling book *Megatrends*. In fact, according to communications researchers at Northwestern University, project teams that collaborate via computer actually develop greater camaraderie and work more efficiently than counterparts who meet face-to-face. Given this finding, cyberspace can be a terrific venue for building rapport with people who can provide insider information applicable to your job search.

Candidates willing to venture onto the information superhighway will find it an invaluable way to access global contacts, visibility and previously unheard of amounts of useful information—all while tapping at the keyboards of their home computers. However, because it's still relatively new, the Net isn't the utopia that ads and the media would lead you to believe. It can be frustratingly slow, convoluted and arbitrary. But like any precocious child, its good moments make the bad ones seem worthwhile.

How to Hook Up

To use the Internet in your job search, you'll need to do some advance preparation. You must have the right equipment and a reliable Internet service provider, so investigate available options to determine what best suits you.

Equipment

First, you'll need a computer. The Internet is accessible to either PCs or Macs, although new advances in Internet software tend to come out for PCs first. That's not surprising since the Internet was originally developed to support the academic research community and the federal government, where DOS, the Disk Operating System used in PCs, was predominant.

Surfing the Net takes more than basic equipment. You'll need at least 16 megabytes of RAM, and, if you plan to download many application or text files, the bigger your hard drive the better. In fact, one veteran cybernaut says you can't even be in the game without at least 500 megabytes of memory on your hard disk, and many Net travelers now use a one gigabyte or more hard drive. You'll also need a modem, but don't buy anything slower than 28.8 bits-per-second (bps). (Bill Warren, president of the Online Career Center, says 28.8 is marginal at best. He recommends 56.6 bps.)

You'll also need a telephone line. If possible, pay to have a second line installed, since calls on a home line can disrupt your computer's Internet connection and cause no end of frustration. Call waiting can play havoc with your connection as well. With a separate, dedicated Internet line, you can send and receive e-mail messages, participate in newsgroups, visit employment Web sites, fax information to employers and become "a real player" in cyberspace.

The Connection Provider

Many people begin their exploration of cyberspace by becoming a member of one of the commercial providers on the Internet. The best known is America Online (AOL), but similar services are also offered by the Microsoft Network (MSN), AT&T Worldnet and MCI. Typically, these services provide members with an array of information and activities (called "content" in Net jargon) on their own Web sites as well as a hypertext link to the Internet and World Wide Web. For example, on AOL, content areas deal with news, sports, entertainment, travel, personal finance, computing, employment, games, shopping, health and more. There's plenty to see and do, but if you plan to use the Internet a lot, such services can become very expensive at the per hour rate. Moreover, in some cases, their connections to the Internet are slower and more fraught with problems than those offered by an Internet Service Provider (ISP).

Should your job search turn you into an Internet junkie (this can happen more easily than you think), you're much better off subscribing to a local or national service provider that specializes in direct Internet connections. Look for one that charges a fixed monthly fee so you can spend unlimited time on the Net without incurring a per-hour surcharge. Installment fees, monthly charges, number and bps rates of data lines, accessibility of application software, technical support for using the Net and a variety of other issues will vary tremendously from provider to provider. To find the best provider for you, ask friends in your local area which service they use or visit Jay Barker's Online Connection (http://www.barkers.org/online) to find a comparison of the major commercial providers and national ISPs.

A less expensive alternative is to access the Net through a university or the National Public Telecomputing Network available in many large communities. These connections are free to individual users or covered by tuition or taxes, but their accessibility varies widely. You may be able to connect to a system from a computer in your dorm room or have to wait your turn for a computer at a centralized location, such as a large public library or other city building.

The Difference between the Internet and the World Wide Web

The Internet is comprised of thousands of separately administered computer networks of many sizes and types that link millions of computers belonging to educational institutions, businesses, governments, nonprofits and individuals. This incredible supernetwork provides data transmission through phone lines, fiber optic cables and microwave and satellite links around the globe.

The World Wide Web, on the other hand, is a tool for navigating throughout the Internet to sites of greatest interest to the public, including ones that job seekers typically use. (For instance, the Department of Defense has many computers on the Internet, but you can't get in touch with them through your connection, unless you're an accomplished hacker.) You'll note that many of the addresses in this chapter begin with "www," which designates a World Wide Web site.

Netiquette

As with any civilized communication method, the Internet has its own rules of etiquette. If you're a neophyte on the Net, it's a good idea to observe these rules, since your messages are a reflection of your "computerized" identity. Below are important guidelines to remember, especially if you're involved in a bulletin-board group or sending e-mail.

☆ *Be polite.* Remember, you're communicating with other human beings. Your message may be read by one or hundreds of people from varying backgrounds, cultures and positions. Some may be executive recruiters and potential employers.

☆ *Describe the subject of your message well enough so that readers don't have to wade through the entire text to know what it's about.* This saves readers time and reminds others to be succinct as well.

☆ *Edit your messages before you send them.* They should be well organized and to the point. Check for spelling and grammar errors and avoid using all capital letters, which can be construed as obnoxious. (All caps is the online equivalent of shouting.) Avoid using abbreviations, such as IMO, which people may not realize stands for "in my opinion."

☆ *Direct your message to a relevant group.* Don't send it to multiple groups unless you're sure it applies to them as well.

☆ *Use one-on-one e-mailing when appropriate.* Don't waste others' time with messages that they don't need to see.

☆ *Familiarize yourself with a particular newsgroup or mailing list by reading some of its messages before participating.* You'll make a better first impression if your communication is in tune with the convention that everyone else is using.

☆ *Know that once a message is posted, it's usually considered in the public domain and not eligible for copyright protection.*

☆ *Being rude, inappropriate or "flaming" someone is an exercise in futility.* (See Spamming and Flaming in the Glossary.) It also can hurt your job search.

In other words, approach communicating on the Net as if you were writing letters or speaking personally with business colleagues.

The Best Resources on the Internet for Job Seekers

As the Internet keeps growing and changing, current sites will change or perhaps disappear relatively quickly. Therefore, suggesting the best sites for job seekers and career changers is risky. Nevertheless, several months of researching current sources and interviewing employers, job seekers and Internet service providers has produced a short list of sites that deserve your attention. They're excellent resources for finding information about companies and job opportunities, as well as for posting resumes or filling out credential forms for specific openings.

"Be sure to visit them as you surf the Net," says Bill Warren, president of Monster.com. "While you can't possibly find every applicable job opening on the Internet, going to these main sites is bound to put you in touch with the vast majority of them."

CareerMosaic   http://www.careermosaic.com

CareerMosaic is sponsored by Bernard Hodes Advertising, the largest purchaser of newspaper advertising in the United States. It was launched July 4, 1994, and today has more than 35 partnerships or co-branding alliances with industry-specific and other sites, including Healthopps (http://www.healthopps.com), the Insurance Career Center (http://www.insjobs.com), Finance and Accounting Jobs (http://www.accountingjobs.com), The EE Times and HR Plaza.

As with other sites described in this chapter, CareerMosaic provides a meeting ground for job seekers and recruiters representing employers with jobs to fill. According to Nielson/IPRO, an independent site auditor, CareerMosaic records more than 3.9 million visitors per month. It also posts 70,000 new job openings each month and averages an astonishing 350,000 + job searches every day . . . proof positive that the Internet and leading sites such as CareerMosaic are fast becoming a key part of every job seeker's strategy for success.

Indeed, Bruce Skillings, the executive vice president of CareerMosaic, says, "The Internet has been the 'killer app' for the global workforce. Companies and potential employees now have a powerful way to exchange information as they come together in a global job marketplace."

Careers.wsj.com   http://www.careers.wsj.com

Careers.wsj.com is a free site of *The Wall Street Journal* Interactive Edition, the largest subscriber-based newspaper on the Internet and relies heavily on content from *The National Business Employment Weekly.* It features columns and analysis of employment issues from The Journal, practical advice and salary data from *NBEW,* an exclusive directory of executive recruiters and a large database of job postings. Unlike what you'll find at many of the other employment Web sites on the Internet, the Careers.wsj.com database has an unusually high percentage of senior level and executive positions.

CareerWeb   http://www.cweb.com

CareerWeb is fast becoming one of the preeminent employment sites on the Web. CareerWeb is owned by Trader Publishing, which also publishes employment guides for the top 40 U.S. markets.

CareerWeb has focused on keeping its site easy to use, while providing a powerful search engine that can pinpoint jobs based on location, industry category and keyword. The site only takes jobs from employers who subscribe to its service so all positions in its database are current and available. The quality of these openings attracts many job seekers, who can either respond directly to the postings or contact employers about other available positions. For example, National Semiconductor has used CareerWeb for more than a year to recruit for an array of technical positions throughout the United States. Since the middle of 1997, the company has received 778 candidate resumes, including 31 resumes in response to specific job postings, and hired four individuals from among that group.

In addition, CareerWeb has a feature called Job Search which permits you to specify the type of job you want and receive e-mail if a matching position is listed on the site. Similarly, employers can use a CareerWeb feature called Resume Finder to notify them whenever a resume submitted to the site's database matches a specified candidate profile. These services and others at employment Web sites are taking much of the work—and hassle—out of matching the right person with the right skills to the right job in the right place.

HeadHunter.NET   http://headhunter.net

HeadHunter.NET is a popular, full-featured commercial employment Web site that is free to job seekers and to employers. You can post your resume in its resume database and look through its large database of job postings. Its search engine enables you to specify a wide range of criteria so that you can quickly find the particular openings you want to see. The positions are posted directly by employers and through other Web sites who have re-posted their listings on HeadHunter.NET to increase their exposure. In all cases, however, the positions are either updated or purged every 45 days.

Monster.com   http://www.monster.com

Monster.com was launched in January 1999 with the merger of two of the Web's leading sites: the Online Career Center and The Monster Board. Owned by TMP Interactive, an advertising agency, the combined site is positioned to be one of the largest and most visible employment destinations on the Internet.

For a reasonable fee, companies can list their own home pages, which include information about them and current job listings. You can find a company's job listings on its home page or use a keyword search engine developed by the site to locate position openings by job title or state. If you find an ad you like, you can either e-mail, fax or snail mail your cover letter and resume directly to the company.

Monster.com operates a special area called My Monster where you can enter, update, archive indefinitely and distribute your resume to employers worldwide, all at no charge. Those who are concerned about confidentiality may be reassured to know that these resumes are accessible only to member companies, not independent recruiters. Monster.com also has the additional advantage of accepting resumes in HTML as well as ASCII text. (Most resumes and cover letters sent via Internet connections have to be formatted in ASCII or they arrive at their destination as gibberish.)

NationJob Network   http://www.nationjob.com

Founded in 1995, NationJob Network has built a solid reputation supporting job seekers in the engineering, finance, medical, legal, education and other professions and in such industries as advertising, aerospace, biotech and hospitality. When you've got lots of other things to do, this site is one that can keep your job search moving ahead at full speed. It offers a free, confidential Personal Job Scout (or "P.J. Scout," the intrepid pioneer of the job frontier) which will review all new jobs posted at the site and notify you by e-mail whenever one meets your specifications. It's a great way to stay informed about what's going on in your career field, regardless of whether you're actively job-hunting.

What AOL Offers Job Seekers

Finally, although not a true employment Web site, America Online (AOL) provides a variety of resources for job seekers as well as access to the World Wide Web. You must join AOL to gain access to this content, which is organized into a channel called The Workplace. Within this channel, there are two subject areas:

☆ Your Business, which includes information on how to start and operate a business, and

☆ Your Career, which addresses how to find a job or manage your career.

The Your Career area includes four different and occasionally overlapping kinds of content:

☆ AOL posts employment classifieds acquired directly from employers and recruiters and, indirectly, from relationships with commercial recruitment Web sites;

☆ Gonyea & Associates provides career counseling, interactive discussion forums, examples of resumes and employment letters, and other services helpful to your job search process;

☆ AboutWork publishes career and employment information in an on line magazine format; and

☆ Ask the Headhunter answers individual questions about job search and recruiting.

In addition, AOL's site provides direct access to a variety of business information resources. Through its Internet connection, you can visit specific online career sites, newsgroups and mailing lists. Its business information falls into two major categories:

☆ Searchable databases for gathering information on companies, such as Hoover's Co. profiles. By using Hoover's, for instance, you can find detailed company profiles of thousands of the largest U.S. and international companies, as well as profiles of smaller high-growth U.S. companies, capsule descriptions on a broad range of public and private companies, facts and figures for hundreds of U.S. industries, rankings of the largest companies and sources of other business reference information.

☆ Searchable publications and magazines, such as *Business Week, Time, The New York Times,* and *The Chicago Tribune.*

Its Internet connection will lead you to:

☆ Specific online career sites including CareerMosaic, Monster.com, Careers.wsj.com, HeadHunter.NET, NationJob Network, CareerWeb and others,

☆ Newsgroups, some of which carry information and conversations about career issues, although you'll have to hunt for a while to locate the most useful ones, and

☆ Mailing lists that may assist you in your job search.

Usenet Newsgroups

One of the best resources for networking and gathering career and employment assistance on the Internet is Usenet newsgroups. These "virtual communities" are actually online bulletin boards where you can post questions or even your resume, communicate with other job seekers and acquire information, advice and support. Best of all, participation is free. Strict netiquette rules often apply, however, and I strongly recommend that you read a group's posted guidelines first or observe participants' interaction before leaping into the conversation.

There are more than 40,000 newsgroups operating on the Internet. Many of these bulletin boards deal directly with employment and careers and receive visits from recruiters seeking candidates for open positions. Moreover, even those groups dedicated to other topics (subjects range from archeology to zoology) will help a faithful participant deal with a job search or career issue by offering job-search tips and networking contacts. To find the best newsgroup for you, use the directories at DejaNews (www.dejanews.com) or Liszt (www.liszt.com).

If you're participating in a newsgroup for the first time, it's probably wise to find a group with a moderator, since they tend to be easier to follow and stay on the subject better than unmoderated groups. As Nancy Pelham says, "In the unmoderated groups I felt like I had wandered into a garage sale set up with little rhyme or reason, and walked away with no bargains." Once you get the hang of it, however, newsgroups are easy to join, fun to visit and can provide you with a competitive advantage in your job search.

Search Engines

The Web sites of most major search engines are another good source of career information and job opportunities. A search engine is an automated index of the information that's available at all or most of the sites online. Among the best known are Yahoo! at http://www.yahoo.com, Excite at http://www.excite.com and AltaVista at http://www.altavista.com. There now are more than 800 search engines, so you may want to consult the meta-list online at http://home .netscape.com/home/internet-search.html or the comparative table listed in Job Hunting on the Internet by Richard Nelson Bolles.

Search engines can help job seekers in at least two ways. First, many offer employment "channels" or special areas on their Web sites where they post jobs and provide other information related to job hunting. These areas are open to the public and can be used at no charge. Second, you can use a search engine to sort through its index of Internet sites using specific parameters—called "key words"—to describe the resources you're seeking. For example, you might instruct a search engine to use the nouns "engineer" and "jobs" to locate a site which posts engineering jobs.

The more precise your instructions, the more likely the computer will locate the sites you want. For this reason, the nouns used as search criteria are connected with other words—called Boolean operators—to specify their relationship. For example, if instructed to search using the phrase, "engineer jobs," a computer would look for any site which dealt with jobs (including those in any other field) or with engineer (including journals of engineer studies) or with both. However, if you tell the computer to look for engineer *and* jobs—the word "and" is the Boolean operator—it would look only for sites which referred to both terms. In other words, it would identify only sites which deal with engineer jobs.

The Boolean search logic that each search engine uses is usually described at its site, either in a special introduction or a section called Frequently Asked Questions (FAQs). Admittedly, the process may seem daunting at first, but with practice, using Boolean operators is no more difficult than speaking pig Latin.

Professional Sites

Finally, don't forget to check with your professional association and industry trade group. Many of these organizations have launched sites on the World Wide Web and now offer job-search and career management information and assistance online. Their services vary widely, but can include resume databases, job postings, salary surveys, continuing education, career counseling and electronic networking in chat areas and on bulletin boards.

Finding a Job on the Internet: A Short Illustration

The following vignette illustrates how one job seeker used Internet employment resources to find a new position. Although no two job-search campaigns are alike, his experience shows what can happen when you put the information superhighway to work for your career.

In late 1997, Bob McMillan, a senior call-center manager with a large U.S. financial services company, saw his job disappear in a corporate cost-cutting initiative. Unwilling to relocate from his home in Dallas, Texas, he accepted a separation package and, for the first time in his career, found himself involuntarily looking for a new job.

With years of experience using telecommunications systems under his belt, McMillan was determined to apply every possible technological advantage, including the Internet, in his job search. He'd been online only once, however, to visit his employer's home page, so he replaced an old modem that had been "fried in a storm" and began to explore the Internet's resources for job searching. Here's what he did:

1. Although he could have selected one or more of the free employment Web sites listed above, he decided to use a fee-based site called Exec-U-Net (http://www.execunet.com), located in Norwalk, Connecticut. He paid its subscription fee and began searching its private, online database of un-advertised senior-level jobs daily.

2. He visited the home pages of prospective employers to learn about their products and culture.

3. He used e-mail to respond to job openings and forward his resume to em-ployers advertising positions for which he was qualified.

4. He visited trade group Web sites to learn which companies in his indus-try were expanding, where key executives were moving and what new products were being developed and launched.

McMillan did not limit his efforts to the Internet, of course, and he spent con-siderable time on the more traditional components of a good job-search campaign. However, it was an opening posted in the Exec-U-Net database that led to an inter-view and ultimately to a new job. Today, he's director of customer service at Pearle Vision, a subsidiary of Cole National in Cleveland, Ohio. He says, "If I lost my job tomorrow, I'd be a lot more comfortable in my job search because of the Internet."

Future Trends

While it's said that nothing is certain except death and taxes, it's a pretty good bet that the Internet will continue to exert more influence on the job market. Surely it's bound to become more user friendly.

And, as more companies and applicants use cyberspace as a matchmaker, service providers will continue to enhance their offerings.

According to Jeff Taylor, CEO of TMP Interactive (which oversees Mon-ster.com), that means more "personalization and customization. You'll begin to see sites where you'll definitely sense that someone's home. There also will be considerably more interactivity."

For example, Monster.com expects to begin using new technology that will allow job hunters to use its services without having to input extensive data. Using your address, it will determine a reasonable commuting distance from your home to work, then notify you of all new job postings which fall within that range.

Further, the types and numbers of positions posted on the Internet will continue to expand. Already, you're seeing many more listings for higher level jobs as well as those not connected with high-tech industries.

As a populist vehicle, the Internet also has the potential to level the recruiting playing field among large and small companies. An employer doesn't have to be as large as Texas Instruments to have a constantly changing home page that attracts high-caliber candidates.

And job seekers will have a worldwide cornucopia of career possibilities they can access whenever and wherever they want with little more than the click of a mouse.

The Last Word

Yet for all the wealth of information and opportunities the Internet may hold, Bill Warren, Monster.com's president, offers a final, important word of advice. "Computers can't and will never do everything for everybody. Use the Internet as a wonderful new tool. But don't neglect the other proven methods that have found jobs for people over the years."

Glossary

It's easy to feel defeated before you start because of the deluge of buzz words about cyberspace that are totally foreign to everyday language. Here's a list of selected terms that will help you understand the esoteric jargon spouted by veteran cybernauts.

America OnLine—One of the major online service providers typically used by job seekers.

ASCII—Pronounced "askee"; acronym for American Standard Code for Information Interchange, which is a numeric code that computers use to communicate with one another. Sending or receiving files in ASCII means they are not document-formatted and are difficult for humans to read.

Attached file—A file that is sent as an addendum to an e-mail message when the file is downloaded separately from the message. A resume is often an attached file.

Baud rate—The speed at which a modem transmits information over a telephone line from one computer to another (the more accurate measurement is bps). Currently modems typically operate at 28,800 bps and 56,600 bps.

BBS or bulletin board system—A computer-based system that allows users to communicate through a modem over a telephone line. The creation of bulletin boards pre-dates the Internet. There are now more than 20,000 in operation in the United States.

Bookmark—A feature used to mark and save specific names of sites and/or menus in a "file" for future use.

Boolean operators—The terms ("and," "or," "and not") used to establish relationships between nouns and phrases that are used as criteria by a computerized search engine to explore the contents of an on-line database. (see Keyword below)

bps—Bits per second; eight bits equal one letter or character.

Browser—A software package which enables you to access the Internet (e.g., Netscape Navigator, Microsoft Internet Explorer).

Chat—The ability to hold online conversations with one or more people at the same time.

Client server or server—A computer which stores the information that is accessed by other computers (i.e., the clients) via the Internet.

CompuServe—One of the major, well-established online service providers typically used by job seekers.

Cyberspace—The vernacular term for the world of computers and, people who use them.

Database—A computerized file of information.

Discussion group—A group of people who share ideas and/or information through newsgroups or mailing lists.

Domain name—The individual Internet address for each host or user computer.

(Continued)

Download—To retrieve a file from another computer over a network.

E-mail—Electronic mail or e-mail is used to send messages on the Internet or to/from bulletin boards.

E-mail address—Address identifying the location of someone's computer "mailbox."

FAQs—Acronym for Frequently Asked Questions; a list of the most commonly asked questions and the answers used by most newsgroups, mailing lists, online service providers, companies with home pages, and so on.

File—Information stored in a computer using a unique name.

File transfer—To either receive (download) or send (upload) files.

Flaming or Flame—To retaliate rudely against inappropriate remarks during an Internet discussion, usually with a highly critical, sometimes crude statement (see Spamming below).

Free-Nets—Free bulletin board systems which specialize in giving a community computer access to the Internet. They are organized by the National Public Telecomputing Network and are available in many large communities.

FTP—Acronym for file transfer protocol; a program to transfer, copy or share files between computers.

Gateway—Hardware or software that allow computers that don't use TCP/IP communication protocol to connect to the Internet.

Hit—Used to describe a single visit to a World Wide Web page by an Internet user.

Home page—The first screen you see when you go to a World Wide Web site. It serves as an online table of contents for the contents of that site.

Host computer—Any mainframe, minicomputer or microcomputer (Macintosh or PC) that provides access to the Internet.

HTML—Hypertext Mark-up Language, the computer code that allows words and images to be posted on the World Wide Web and establishes electronic connections or links between those words and others that are posted at other sites on the Web.

HTTP—Acronym for HyperText Transfer Protocol, the method used to make documents readable on the World Wide Web.

Internet—Otherwise known as the Information Highway: a worldwide affiliation of millions of computers linked together by a network of computer networks.

Keyword—A word used in a search program such as Gopher or in a database to find specific information more quickly.

Mailing list—A type of discussion group to which you subscribe.

Message—The text of an e-mail communication.

Message board—The location where messages are listed, typically showing the message's recipient, date and subject.

Modem—Acronym for modulator/demodulator; the electronic device or part of your computer hardware that allows data to be transmitted from your computer to another computer over telephone lines.

Netiquette—The etiquette for communicating over the Internet, primarily applicable to discussions within newsgroups or on mailing lists.

Newsgroup—A forum for discussion on a specific topic. Unlike a mailing list, messages can be posted to a newsgroup without specifically subscribing to it. Some newsgroups are "moderated" which means that the newsgroup administrator reviews all messages before they are posted.

(Continued)

Online—To be connected to the Internet or a bulletin board by use of a modem.

Prodigy—One of the major online service providers typically used by job seekers.

Public domain—A file that hasn't been copyrighted and is typically available through on-line services for downloading at minimal cost.

Search—To look for files or entries such as a specific World Wide Web site.

Search engine—A program that allows people using the internet to find specific information by using keywords or other key criteria. Yahoo!, Excite and Alta Vista are search engines.

Site—A computer location accessed via the Internet.

Snail mail—Mail sent through the U.S. Postal Service.

Spamming or Spam—The communication of inappropriate messages (usually commercial or obscene) to a Usenet newsgroup.

Spider, robot, crawler—A term used to denote a software application which roams publicly accessible sites on the Internet to find certain pre-selected bits of information and then copy and bring them back to its home site.

Surf—To randomly search for information not readily apparent, commonly used in the term "surfing the Net."

TCP/IP—Acronym for Transmission Control Protocol/Internet Protocol; the set of rules, or protocols, that allow computers on the Internet to exchange information.

Telnet—A computer command that allows you to log on to another computer and browse its information via a Telnet interface used primarily by universities and governments.

Text file—A file that's easily read by humans vs. machines.

Unique users—The number of users, counted just once during a specified period of time, who visit a Web site.

Upload—To send a file from your computer to another one via a network.

URL—Acronym for Uniform Resource Locator, typically used as a way to find the Internet address for sites on the World Wide Web.

Usenet—A system on the Internet where messages can be posted and responded to; often referred to in conjunction with newsgroups.

World Wide Web—Also known as WWW or W3; a client/server system that allows users to jump from place to place on the Internet through the use of hypertext.

Yahoo!—Both a site and an extensive search engine arranged by subject in menus, which links you to a variety of sites in the World Wide Web. (http://www.yahoo.com).

Bibliography

CareerXroads, *The 1999 Directory,* by Gerry Crispin and Mark Mehler (1998, MMC Group).

Internet Resumes: Take the Net to Your Next Job, by Peter D. Weddle (1998, Impact Publications).

Internet Yellow Pages, by Harley Hahn (1998, Osborne McGraw Hill).

Job-Hunting on the Internet, by Richard Nelson Bolles (1998, Ten Speed Press).

Job Searching Online, by Pam Dixon (1998, IDG).

The Guide to Internet Job Searching, 1998–1999 Edition, by Margaret Riley Dikel, Frances Roehm and Steve Oserman (1998, NTC/Contemporary Publishing Group).

The Internet for Dummies, 5th Edition, by John Levine, Carol Baroudi and Margaret Levine Young, (1998, IDG).

WEDDLE's Wildly Useful, Up-to-the Minute Newsletter about Internet Resources for Successful Recruiting, by Peter D. Weddle, Old Greenwich, Connecticut.

"Not bad, not bad at all . . . sink one more and the promotion will include a 15 percent raise."

9

Cover Letters for Internal Corporate Use

I f you're restless in your current job or expect your company to go through a downsizing shortly, your first inclination may be to review the want ads. While staying in touch with the job market is always a good idea, you might want to check out opportunities at your own company before seeking a position elsewhere.

Reasons for Conducting an Internal Job Search

Moving to another position within your organization offers many advantages over leaving it altogether:

☆ You already know the ropes. You understand the formal and informal power structure, how things get done and whom to see when you need information. Building an internal network and developing relationships in a new company takes time and effort. If an alternative career path is available within your current corporation, you can learn it much more quickly than if you move somewhere else.

☆ You've developed a bond with other employees. If you've been a recognized contributor for a number of years, you're a known quantity with fans in many departments. You're considered reliable and trustworthy and will be readily accepted as a member of a new team.

☆ You have a track record with management. If you've excelled in your work, other company managers may be interested in taking you into their fold. People want to work with individuals they know and trust. That's why corporations hire from within whenever possible.

☆ Looking for a position outside your firm is a tricky proposition if you're still employed. Your manager may encourage your job search and give you time to make phone calls and go on interviews, but it's unlikely. Consequently, you may find yourself hunkering down in your cube when contacting potential employers and feeling guilty if you call in sick for networking appointments and interviews. Many bosses don't want to lose subordinates but are more accepting when the transfers are internal.

☆ It's a shame to give up the golden handcuffs (if you have one or more): a 401(k) plan, stock options, medical insurance that covers preexisting conditions, upcoming bonus, health-club membership and other goodies that bind you to your employer. If you stay with the firm, you get to keep them all.

☆ Most important, you can renew your commitment to your career and your company by seeking an internal position that uses your most satisfying skills. The employer/employee relationship is like a marriage. It takes work to keep it healthy, particularly when economic conditions and personal agendas create stress and disunity. When things aren't going well on the job, many professionals fix the problem by leaving it behind. Unfortunately, unless they've clearly identified the reasons for their unhappiness, they may trade one set of negatives for another.

Taking stock of yourself and looking for other options internally is like giving a once-happy marriage a second chance. Your renewed enthusiasm and initiative may reawaken management interest in you and generate some surprising possibilities. And if you ultimately move to another firm, you'll leave knowing it's the right choice.

If you decide to seek another position at your company, network internally to learn about other careers and departments. At the same time, respond to posted internal job openings that might allow you to learn new skills and increase your marketability. Just as in an external job search, you should learn as much as possible about suitable internal openings, then tailor your cover letters, resume and interview comments to meet their requirements.

How to Learn about
Internal Job Openings

There are two ways to identify other company positions you would enjoy: networking and job postings. Networking is an informal approach that requires initiating meetings with others and talking to them about jobs and departments, regardless of whether there's an opening. Responding to job postings is a reactive process that requires you to read about current openings (via a paper or electronic bulletin board), then prepare a cover letter, resume or application that parallels the job requirements. Let's review specific networking and posting techniques and how to write applicable cover letters.

Networking to Uncover Openings

The most popular networking approaches include:

- ☆ Initiating and building your own networking circle.
- ☆ Identifying other departments where you might like to work.
- ☆ Meeting with targeted managers to determine if your background, skills and interests match her group's mission.

As you might have noticed, this process is similar to the information interviewing techniques discussed in Chapter 7. You can use the same questions and evaluation form that is provided for talking with people outside your organization. Your thank-you note after the meeting replaces a cover letter and should include what you like about the department, how your skills and background compliment its purpose and why you'd appreciate being considered for any openings in the future.

A True Story

A sportswear department distribution planner at a New York company spent her days in a cubicle, developing assortment plans and sending merchandise to stores she'd never visited around the country. She worked closely with the buying department, where employees had window offices and left the building each day for lunch and business meetings with vendors anxious to gain their orders. While the distribution planner was paid as much as her buying colleagues, she knew they outranked her and enjoyed their work more. She wanted to be one of them but didn't know how to make a move.

One day, she left her cubicle for a rare trip to a regional store convention. She was excited about finally meeting some of the store managers to whom she had sent sportswear these many years.

Once settled in her seat on the plane, she was surprised to see the merchandise manager for the sportswear department coming down the aisle. This man was the head honcho, two levels up from the buyers whose jobs she envied. She could hardly contain her excitement when he took the seat beside her.

As the plane headed for Pittsburgh, they conversed about their jobs and the circumstances that had brought each of them to New York. Much to her surprise, she found him to be a nice person, not the hard-driving executive she expected.

Before long, the manager started asking her about her career and whether she had *ever considered going into buying*. She couldn't believe her ears! Mustering all her professional reserve, she said quietly but firmly that she had often thought about it, but didn't know how to make the move. He continued talking with her and had her accompany him to a dinner she wouldn't otherwise have attended with the managers of several large stores. Within two weeks, he requested her transfer to his department, where she stayed for several years, enjoying a window office and frequent lunches with vendors.

This young professional was a belated, but lucky, pawn of fate. If she had taken the initiative to talk to the manager sooner, she wouldn't have stayed so long in her cubicle. If her inaction seems uncomfortably familiar, start networking now. You don't need a plane trip to gain access to a senior executive.

☆ **Visit human resources.** This department is growing in clout because of technical and legal employment complexities and changing employee demographics. Due to its knowledge of the company's personnel needs, the HR department is in a unique position to help you locate satisfying career paths and opportunities. If necessary, ask for advice on the QT from a personnel professional whom you trust. An informed person may even serve as an intermediary with department heads you might like to meet.

If human resources calls you about a job opening in a department where you have been networking, ask your contact about the specific requirements of the position, then send the appropriate manager a cover letter and resume addressing those needs. This approach will give you an advantage over competitors who lack friends in personnel.

☆ **Talk to your manager.** When I advise job hunters to mention their interest in transferring to their boss or HR coordinator, they sometimes look at me in total disbelief. While some managers doggedly guard their best workers from the clutches of other departments, others want subordinates to move to more satisfying and challenging positions. These managers know that such moves reflect well on their ability to encourage and mentor their employees.

If your manager is a good networker, he can advise you on whom to call for information interviews. In fact, he may even make appointments for you. If you're going to leave his department, he'll want everyone to know it's with his blessing.

If one of his cronies should offer you a position, tell your boss about it and give him the credit. Write a thank-you note/cover letter to your potential manager singing your boss's praises. A genuine compliment is a rare and special gift. Your mentor will remember it if you ever need another favor from him.

☆ **Get to know people in task forces, company sports teams, professional seminars, United Way campaigns or other company-sponsored activities.** IBM offers a networking module during its career-planning workshops. The networking session follows a period devoted to brainstorming on potential careers in IBM's fast-changing environment, and with good reason. It's amazing to watch a diverse group offer each other leads on jobs throughout the company. Apparently, the adage "You're no more than seven people away from anyone in the world" is true. Within a company, even one the size of IBM, you're probably no more than two or three people away from your next job.

Example Cover Letters Derived from Networking

Here are two cover letters tailored to positions uncovered through networking. The first one is the result of approaching the hiring manager directly. The second comes from a contact initiated by the writer's supervisor.

Carrie Roberts
Technical Services
MS 330-2900
Phone 383-4441
January 23, 1999

Ms. Robin Courins
Vice President,
Marketing
MS 332-2880

Dear Robin,

Thank you for getting together with me to discuss the skills and personality traits needed to be a successful technical sales rep. As an engineer, I've always felt I was marching to the beat of a different drummer. Now that I've talked to you, I think I've found my true calling.

It seems that technical sales requires a combination of skills not typically needed in engineering. While I've enjoyed creating new products, I think I would be more effective applying my technical knowledge in a situation where I can explain to customers how the particular features of our hardware can benefit them. Until you pointed it out, I never realized that most engineers are neither adept nor interested in working with customers, but I am. No wonder I've felt like the ugly duckling.

I was particularly gratified when you suggested I apply for a sales opening you are currently trying to fill. As per your request, I've attached a resume that will give you a better idea of my experience and how I can use it to satisfy our clients' needs. I look forward to seeing you again next week to discuss why I am the right person for the job.

Sincerely yours,

Carrie Roberts

Enclosure

April 19, 1999

Tom Ling
GB-HR-2S
Phone: X 217

Raymond Abbruzio
GB-SM-3L
Phone: X 344

Dear Ray,

I understand from my manager, Rolanda Hoover, that you have an opening for a merchandise coordinator in the home furnishings area. When she recommended I contact you, I was really excited, because I'm looking for a new challenge. Based on what Rolanda tells me, your position may be it.

During my five years with Carpenters, I have worked in housewares and linens, investigating merchandise trends, accompanying buyers on buying trips, making recommendations for new lines and coordinating our spring fling promotion. You may have heard of the new group of pillows I developed, which added an extra $100,000 to our bottom line its first year.

I'm sending you my resume per Rolanda's suggestion. I'll call next week to see if you have any preliminary questions and schedule an interview if you think it's appropriate. Working for Rolanda has been a great experience, but I'm ready to try my hand at something new. She says that I couldn't find a better manager/mentor than you, other than herself, of course.

I look forward to talking with you soon.

Sincerely yours,

Tom Ling

Enclosure

Using Job Listings to Find Openings

Many companies give employees first crack at job openings before advertising them to the general public. Depending on the company and its technology or the HR department's preferences, the positions are put on bulletin boards in high-traffic areas, published in booklets distributed company-wide or listed on electronic mail systems. Employees might respond in several ways, from using official applications to hand carrying, mailing, e-mailing or faxing resumes and cover letters.

To learn more about job-posting systems and how to respond to them, I contacted HR professionals at the corporate offices of JCPenney Co. Inc., Electronic Data Systems Corp. and Raytheon Systems Company. Their posting systems are unique but have a lot in common. Here are typical ways these companies tell employees about internal opportunities.

Published Job Listings

Raytheon Systems disseminates more than 7,000 books of job listings a week worldwide. The books describe the company, its benefits and locations, and list the jobs by category and site. Each listing includes a job title, grade level, department, location, functions, required knowledge/skills/experience, education, years of related experience and useful comments. The listings are available to all employees. The following example is a listing from Raytheon's job-posting book.

A Raytheon Systems Published Job Listing

COST ACCOUNTANT   **Grade 26/28**   **Available: 6/20**

DEPARTMENT: Cost Accounting

Supervisor: Liberty Ford

Group Mission: Provide support to Cost Accounting in all areas of factory cost and production.

Job Purpose: Supports financial and accounting aspects of business unit.

JOB FUNCTIONS: Monthly close activity for production and development. R&D accounting, project tracking, various cost analysis, management reporting, inventory control, standard setting, implement activity-based costing, innovative approach to accounting requirements. Coordinate closely with financial analyst.

KNOWLEDGE/SKILLS/EXPERIENCE:

Current Proficiencies: General ledger, CMS, Modplan, Accounting/financial knowledge, analytical abilities. Lotus or Excel, Activity based accounting, Freelance or other graphic software, SMS, Previous accounting experience required.

Education: Bachelor degree in Accounting, Finance or other degree.

Years Related Experience: 3–5 years.

Other/Helpful: Proactive/innovative attitude. Teaming skills. Communication and presentation skills. Accounting in a manufacturing environment.

To respond to this ad, you should first determine the position's key requirements. If you have questions, you would clarify them by contacting the department supervisor directly or through your supervisor. The information you receive could help you develop a resume or application highlighting your relevant knowledge, skills, personality traits and education. You should also attach a cover letter that resembles the following one.

Cover Letter Responding to a Job Posting

6/22/99

From: William Moss
       Radar Division
       Accounting Department
       MS: 3A-333

To: Ms. Liberty Ford
       Manager, Cost Accounting
       MS: 2B-204

Dear Ms. Ford:

Yesterday, as I was reviewing our weekly job postings, I noticed your available cost accountant position. I am particularly interested in this area and I believe it offers a great future with Raytheon Systems. I am gratified to see our company emerging as a leader in the defense electronics business.

For the past three years, I have been an accountant in the Naval Radar Division in Balch Springs, performing the same functions mentioned in your job listing. During that time I was chosen team leader of my department's quality management effort, which resulted in our being able to cut reporting turnaround from seven to three days. As the spokesperson for my team, I also presented our suggestions on how to move toward a paperless office to other accountants and financial analysts throughout our area.

I enjoy trying new techniques that have the potential to provide more useful information in more understandable formats. Using suggestions from manufacturing managers, I recently developed a new report on just-in-time procurement that has been very popular with users.

I will call you next week to ascertain if my qualifications are a good match for your cost accounting needs. I look forward to finding out more about your department and its preference for proactive/innovative team players.

Sincerely yours,

Bill Moss

Enclosure

In most companies, the human resources department screens information from applicants for internal positions to make sure they meet the basic job requirements. HR then sends the applications from qualified candidates to hiring managers, who schedule interviews. While HR people aren't impressed by cover letters, hiring managers usually are; they like to see why you're interested in their position.

A hiring manager at JCPenney confirms this view. "A cover letter sets you apart from your competition," she says. "It gives you the opportunity to make a unique case for why you deserve the job." To help the hiring manager decide in your favor, include a cover letter with your resume or application whenever possible.

Electronic Bulletin Board Job Postings

Putting job openings on a computerized system requires technology that some companies lack and may never have. Still, it's important to know about these systems and how to use them, so you won't be shut out of this arena, particularly at large companies. For instance, EDS, JCPenney and Raytheon use online job postings, although the number and type of positions listed vary greatly. Here's a typical entry and how to respond to it with a cover letter.

An Online Job Posting

Send resumes to sgordon@softech.dc

FEDERAL ACCOUNT SALES MANAGER

Grade 28/29   **Available 7/25/99**

DEPARTMENT: FEDERAL   **Supervisor: Sara Gordon**

Group Mission: Sell products and services to federal agencies and contractors.

Job Purpose: Responsible for specific territory of federal government. Sales will be dependent upon effective communications with several levels of government management ranging up to very high executive personnel. Products to be sold are technical. A successful applicant must have experience in the application of advanced system techniques in varying government environments.

KNOWLEDGE/SKILLS/EXPERIENCE:

Current Proficiencies: Experience with prospecting and developing new territories. Minimum 5 years of major software sales experience ($100,000+) in presenting strategic solutions using high-ticket products. Proven track record of meeting or exceeding sales quota.

LEARN: 90 DAYS: Create a business plan for territory, develop and maintain strong client and prospect knowledge, sell complete solution software and service.

EDUCATION: BS in Business or Computer Science with 5–8 years related experience.

OTHER/HELPFUL: Experience selling to large government agencies/departments, software development or consulting experience, leadership or management experience.

Cover Letter Responding to an Online Job Posting

From: Tom Polanski
polanski@softech.la
Phone: 213-991-6600

7/30/99

To: Ms. Sara Gordon
sgordon@softech.dc
Re: Federal Sales Account Manager Position

Dear Ms. Gordon:

When I saw your opening for a high-level software sales professional on the ACCESS system yesterday, I decided to get in touch with you as soon as possible. As part of a dual-career couple, whose wife has just accepted a higher level position with the EPA in Washington, I am interested in finding employment in that part of the country.

However, my marriage isn't the only reason why I look forward to moving back to D.C. For several years I enjoyed selling software systems for Softech to government agencies in Washington and the surrounding states, where I still have many customer/friends. While I was there, I increased sales in my territory by 150 percent and opened six new key accounts along with a number of smaller ones.

Apparently word of my success spread to LA, where Softech sales were in massive decline. Bill Stevens, our Western Regional Manager, called to offer me a position on the West Coast working with our major accounts on the same large software systems your open position handles. Because I saw LA as a tremendous opportunity to sell our big ticket systems and turn a declining territory around, I accepted the offer. (My wife came along.)

In the three years I have been here, I've sold at least eight $100,000 systems annually, plus a number of smaller ones, to new clients who are testing the waters before they spend serious money. While I would be happy to continue growing my business here, I really prefer the Mid-Atlantic's topography and lack of fire, floods, droughts, earthquakes, mud slides, riots and assorted other disasters for which LA has become notorious. Besides, my wife is headed to DC in two weeks, and I don't want a 3,000-mile commuter marriage.

As time is of the essence, I will call you this week to have a preliminary discussion about my enclosed resume, your opening and your opinion of my qualifications. As you have probably guessed, I am confident I can do the job and enthusiastic about becoming a member of your nationally recognized team.

Sincerely yours,

Tom Polanski

P.S. Bill has given me his blessing if I want to transfer and asks that you call him for his feedback on my performance.

A Final Note on Cover Letters

As you can tell from the first eight chapters of this book, cover letters are an integral part of your job search, whether you're looking within your company or competing in the universal job market. These zesty pieces of correspondence give your readers a focus, add sizzle to your resume and tell potential managers why you want and deserve to work with them.

Never take a shortcut or try to save a few minutes by jotting a quick note to send with your resume. The temptation to substitute a brief, handwritten comment—especially if you know the person you're contacting—can be great. *Ignore it!*

"There, now that's out of the way . . . let's talk about
something besides your market letters."

10

Market and Broadcast Letters

Market Letters

Market letters resemble cover letters with one major exception. Their experience section is longer, which eliminates the need to attach a resume.

Why would anyone stray from the accepted cover letter/resume combination? There are several reasons. Employers are being deluged with resumes. Sending unsolicited correspondence to companies is a numbers game that requires uncommon ingenuity to produce a respectable response rate. One way to differentiate yourself is to write an arresting letter—without your resume. This document will stand out because it's shorter than a letter/resume combination and it offers more flexibility to discuss your experience than most resume formats.

The components of a market letter correspond with those of a typical cover letter:

☆   A first paragraph that says why you're particularly interested in the potential employer.

☆   A longer section about your experience that correlates your skills, personality traits and credentials with those the employer needs.

☆   A section explaining how you plan to follow up on your letter.

The following market letter was written by Lynne Dicker during her search for a regional management position with a national temporary firm. Because she wanted to submit her credentials quickly but lacked a prepared resume fitting the position's requirements, she chose to send a market letter.

Also take a look at Lynne's resume. Although she prepared it for another employer, notice how she extrapolated the most important information for her letter to *Today's Temporary.*

Market Letter and Resume

4131 Edgecreek Drive
Dallas, Texas 75227
February 14, 1999

Donna Allen
Today's Temporary
700 North Pearl Street
Dallas, Texas 75201

Dear Donna:

It was a pleasure talking with you on Tuesday. When I did some research on your company, I was excited to learn that Todays Temporary has been in business only since 1982, while its major competitors started in the 1940s. This indicates to me that your firm is an aggressive, savvy, fast-moving company with a clear mission. I am attracted to those qualities in an organization and view it as the kind of firm with which I want to be associated. I think you will understand why as you read about my past experience.

When I left New York City, where I serviced accounts such as Harry Winston, Macy's, A&S, Fortunoff, Zales, Kay's, Saks Fifth Avenue and Service Merchandise for ODI, I moved to Dallas to become manager of electronics with Macy's in the Dallas Galleria. After the fall season, I joined Finlay Fine Jewelry, a former account I reestablished at ODI. Finlay is the nation's largest fine jewelry leasing company with over 800 locations in fine department stores.

During my three years as Regional Coordinator for the 21 Foley's fine jewelry departments, we enjoyed double-digit increases every year. I developed happy, professional salespeople who executed beautiful displays in well-run departments and, most importantly, made the cash register "sing" by closing sales. My proudest accomplishments have been in helping managers cultivate the skills necessary to be successful. Because of my achievements, I was promoted to Assistant Group Manager in August 1998. I am responsible for the $10 million cost of merchandise and the advertising for our group, which exceeds $1 million. I supervise 3 buyers, 3 regional coordinators and an office of 13 highly motivated "go-getters."

This past Christmas season, we were the #1 group in our region, which was the #1 region in the country. We achieved our nine-week Christmas sales goal of more than $6,433,000. We sold more than $17,000,000 for the year. I am proud to have been a driving force in that effort. My planning and motivational talents made a difference.

I will call you next week to confirm receipt of my letter and schedule a time for us to get together. I really look forward to discussing how my skills and experience can benefit your organization.

Sincerely,

Lynne Dicker

LYNNE DICKER
4131 Edgecreek Drive
Dallas, Texas 75227
(214) 991-1524

OBJECTIVE: Vice President of Merchandising and Marketing at Melart Jewelers.

PROFESSIONAL SUMMARY:

- Adept at juggling many projects simultaneously, adjusting priorities as needed.
- Receive tremendous satisfaction from setting and achieving goals.
- Highly skilled at maximizing the potential of vendor relationships.
- Particularly enjoy training and mentoring staff to be the best they can be.
- Talented at finding solutions to problems, even if it requires swimming upstream.

EMPLOYMENT HISTORY:

Finlay Fine Jewelry, *the nation's largest fine jewelry leasing company with more than 800 department store locations.*

Assistant Group Manager, 1992–Present

- Manage 3 buyers, 3 regional supervisors and an office of 13 highly motivated staff. These people support 20 branches that produced annual sales of $18 million in 1995.
- Emphasize goal setting as a motivational tool. Create contests, awards and fun activities to encourage achievement in sales and operations.
- Select items for all catalog, ROP and direct mail advertising.
- Determine price points and key items to maximize gross margins.
- Recognized as the authority in customer service for my three-state group of Foley's Fine Jewelry departments.
- Train branch managers to use good judgment, develop creative options, and defuse problem situations.

Regional Coordinator, 1990–1992

- As the only Regional Coordinator for 21 branches, made goals for Christmas season in 1990, 1991 and 1992 with double-digit increases over previous years.
- Spearheaded the turnaround of several branches in a 21-store group.
- Worked closely with buyers to put the right merchandise in each branch.
- Fostered a climate where branch managers and staff shared their successful ideas and problems with one another.

Original Designs, Inc., Long Island, NY

National Sales Manager, 1985–1990

- Started as a sales representative for TOLA. Developed 30 new accounts in this virgin territory. After four months, promoted to the corporate office.
- Personally called on 50 key accounts including mass merchandisers (Service Merchandise, Montgomery Wards), wholesalers, department store chains (Macy's, Saks Fifth Avenue) and retailers (Zales, Gordons, Kay's, Finlay) resulting in more than $4 million in sales per year.
- Created numerous promotional programs including the "Diamond Total Weights," which increased annual volume by 33%.
- Hired and trained a new sales force of Regional Sales Managers in both sales and operational techniques.
- Designed new MIS systems to increase sales information on specific items and trends.

Zale Corporation, Dallas, TX

Jewelry Manager, 1984–1985

- Managed 40 people in the fine jewelry department of this flagship catalog showroom.
- Assisted Regional Vice President in troubleshooting at other showroom locations.

EDUCATION:

Certificate, Harvard Business School, Boston, MA
"Management Strategies for the Small Firm"
M.A. Northeastern University, Boston, MA
B.A. University of Iowa, Iowa City, IA

PERSONAL:

Interests include traveling, reading, needlepoint and aerobics.

Broadcast Letters

Up to this point, I've been candid about my preference for tailored cover letters. However, not everyone agrees with my viewpoint. A number of job seekers (and their career counselors) believe they should tell as many people as possible that they're available for new opportunities. They think the quantity of the letters they generate is more important than the quality (tailored content) of each one. Consequently, they write one carefully constructed letter (or letter and resume) and send it unsolicited to employers, search firms and various other contacts. They know they're playing a numbers game, but they assume that sending out 500 letters will generate a 1 to 5 percent response rate. This means they might receive 5 to 25 phone calls or letters asking for more information.

People do land jobs this way, even though the chances of any one letter leading directly to a new position are slim. If you decide to try this approach, you can either send a generic cover letter and resume or combine the two in a broadcast letter. A broadcast letter's main purpose is grabbing a reader's interest and encouraging him to respond. Since it replaces a resume, it must describe experience in greater detail than in a typical cover letter. And to intrigue readers and beat the usual response rate, it often includes a clever opening remark or philosophical statement. This approach may strike some recruiters as avant-garde, cavalier or flaky, but it may pique the interest of others enough to schedule an interview.

Advantages of Broadcast Letters versus Cover Letters and Resumes

Most job seekers assume that sending cover letters and resumes to potential employers and search firms is a poured-in-concrete tradition. However, the road less traveled offers certain advantages over the typical letter/resume combination. Broadcast letters:

☆   Are shorter than a letter/resume combination. If you're planning a major direct-mail campaign, a broadcast letter will get your message across more quickly than the alternative, saving you time, paper and, possibly, postage.

☆   Provide more information than a typical letter.

☆   Allow you more flexibility to discuss your experience than the usual chronological resume, which requires listing all of your experience by job title, starting with your last job first. A functional resume also provides this type of flexibility, but many HR and search executives assume that job seekers who use them are trying to hide something. Candidates who send broadcast letters that omit dates of employment won't suffer the same stigma because readers aren't anticipating a specific format.

☆ Are unique. Relatively few people use broadcast letters, so you'll automatically stand out by sending one in lieu of a letter/resume combination.

Disadvantages of Broadcast Letters

As with many of life's paradoxes, what helps in one circumstance may be a hindrance in another. While broadcast letters are shorter than cover letter/resume combinations and provide added flexibility, many corporate recruiters and executive search firm professionals aren't interested in seeing anything but chronological resumes. When they receive your broadcast letter, they won't appreciate your individuality. In fact, they may be resentful about not getting the information they need, in the format they expect. Because they're deluged by correspondence from job seekers, they have no compunction about round-filing you.

As with any risk you take to differentiate yourself from your competition, sending a broadcast letter may be perceived as unconventional—even unprofessional. To clarify the issue, ask yourself: If I really like this type of letter, but the person who receives it doesn't, do I truly want to be part of his team? Sending a broadcast letter may automatically eliminate you for some openings, and heighten your marketability for others, depending on the personalities of the employers. Only you can decide if this self-selection process is a plus or a minus.

Broadcast Letter Target Groups

There are several schools of thought about where to target broadcast letters. Some people want to tell everyone they know—friends, fellow alumni, country club and tennis buddies, friendly acquaintances, neighbors, professional organization colleagues, members of their church or fraternal organization—that they're seeking a new position. Others call these people by phone, saving their broadcast letters for individuals they don't know, such as company representatives and headhunters.

By talking with a variety of people who regularly receive correspondence from job seekers, I've concluded that it's best to use broadcast letters to entice line managers and recruiters at contingency firms to call. Executives at retained search firms are firmly in the chronological resume corner. Broadcast letters don't give them enough information to satisfy their specific needs. HR professionals also aren't comfortable with approaches that deviate from the traditional cover letter/resume combination.

Selecting the Individuals to Receive Your Broadcast Letter

As with any good cover letter, a broadcast letter should be personally addressed. If you aren't hunting for a specific person as you would when sending a tailored letter, it's easy to find plenty of people to receive your correspondence. For instance, if you're planning a direct-mail campaign designed to reach several hundred executive search professionals, you should:

☆ Locate a copy of *The Directory of Executive Recruiters* (1998, Kennedy Publications, Fitzwilliam, NH).

☆ Decide how many letters to send.

☆ Determine how you'll choose your recipients, either by industry, profession or geographic area.

☆ Select the specific firms and individuals who'll receive your letters.

Use this process to develop mailing lists from directories of professional organizations, executives, companies or any other group that might be helpful in your job-search campaign. The Appendix includes some resources that can help you get started.

Creating a Database

Once you've decided whom to contact, put their names, addresses and phone numbers into a database that can serve two main purposes:

1. To mail-merge each of the entries with the text of the letter.
2. For making follow-up contacts, if you have the time and inclination.

How you enter names into a database depends on how sophisticated you want to be and whether you'll refer to them again. If you plan to use the names only once, an alphabetical listing is all you'll need. If you want to track responses by certain categories, or follow up by mail or phone, you can classify them by profession, industry, geography, size of company, level of contact, date sent or other characteristics. Obviously, the more categories you have, the more complicated your database will be.

Most word-processing software has a database management component for mail-merging and other purposes. Read your owner's manual to learn how to input and sort the names by categories.

Candidates who don't have the computer equipment or software to create a database can contact a vendor who'll do so for a fee. Many already have appropriate lists in their computers. Talk to these firms about their procedures and costs, then pick one that suits your needs, time frame and budget.

The Mail-Merging Process

The days of printing or copying hundreds of the same letter, then typing in individual names and addresses, are long gone. This process is not only tremendously time consuming, but the final results look very unprofessional. If you're doing a major direct-mail campaign, always use a computer and a laser or state-of-the-art ink jet printer to create hundreds of original documents and envelopes. This individualized approach won't guarantee that you'll emerge a prime candidate, but neglecting to send crisp, clean, professional letters will eliminate you in a minute.

Be sure to use high rag content stationery and envelopes and first-class stamps on all your letters. Bulk mail may save money, but a first-class stamp makes your letter seem important. If you cut corners by using third-class postage, readers will probably assume the same letter is going to hundreds or thousands of other people and, consequently, isn't worth their time.

Even when you're playing a job-search numbers game, it's important to give targeted recipients a feeling of exclusivity. How do you feel when a bulk-mail letter arrives stamped "Confidential" on the front, while a message inside claims you're one of a chosen few to receive it? Do you believe this statement? Not likely. In fact, you're probably offended by the implied assumption that you're gullible enough to swallow this line.

Broadcast Letter Components

In addition to the usual heading, inside address, closing and signature, broadcast letters have three essential components:

☆ An initial quip or paragraph used to "hook" the reader's attention.

☆ A section describing highlights or aspects of your experience that match the reader's needs, otherwise known as "the meat."

☆ "The call to action," a closing paragraph or statement encouraging the recipient to call you for more information.

The Hook

Since your broadcast letter is being sent unsolicited to companies and search firms, it's important to capture readers' interest quickly. Otherwise you risk losing them altogether. Since you're mailing the same letter to a large number of people, you can't use the tailoring techniques suggested for cover and market letters. Find another, more innovative way to keep them reading. Using a catchy phrase, sentence or short paragraph like the examples that follow is one approach:

> Are you tired of programmers who spend a year or two with your company, then leave? If you are interested in finding a committed software professional who thinks loyalty is a virtue, read on.

> Customer service is more than a business tool. It's a mission. If your customer service efforts are falling short of your expectations, you need a manager whose primary goal in life is building relationships that surprise and delight your clients. You need someone like me.

ROBERT HALF'S RESUMANIA

One candidate sent an employer a seven-page letter that had this eye-catching first paragraph: "Where do babies come from? The Stork brings them. Everybody knows that. They are not found under toadstools early in the morning, like some people say. Nobody gets up that early."

This job seeker was hoping to show that he didn't think like other people. I sure wouldn't debate him about that.

Even the venerable Peter Drucker says American business is in a state of chaos. If you are looking for a leader who can keep his head when those around him are losing theirs, I'm your man.

These openings are blatantly self-serving and, from most people's perspectives, downright boastful. That's what makes them fresh and thought provoking. While readers may think these opening statements show tremendous chutzpah, they may be sufficiently intrigued to continue reading, which is exactly the outcome you want.

If you can't bring yourself to take the preceding approach, try writing a more businesslike first paragraph that refers to industry trends or a generic problem that many companies are trying to solve. Here are some typical examples:

A recent *Wall Street Journal* article says that businesses must sensitize their employees to the diverse attitudes and expectations of their colleagues and customers or risk losing prospective associates and sales to more savvy competitors. If you have a client company that is concerned about its ability to build successful teams or compete in the global marketplace, perhaps I can be of service.

Human Resources used to be a department full of people whose main function was building trust with all company employees. But in the past 5 to 10 years, its role has changed. Now HR professionals must have great people skills *and* be experts in employment law, health-care programs, complicated compensation and pension plans, and a variety of other complex issues no responsible management team can afford to ignore. If you've decided it's time to increase your corporation's expertise in these critical HR areas, perhaps we should talk.

The Meat

The bulk of your broadcast letter will summarize job-related experiences that might interest your entire group of readers. Because you aren't tailoring this letter to a specific job or company, make this section generic enough to attract a number of organizations.

This part of your letter replaces your resume. It should describe your experience in narrative format, rather than the bullet points of a typical resume, and may include references to your career philosophy or mission. On pages 230–233 are examples of a broadcast letter and a good resume using the same experience. Note how they spotlight many of the same achievements, yet look quite different.

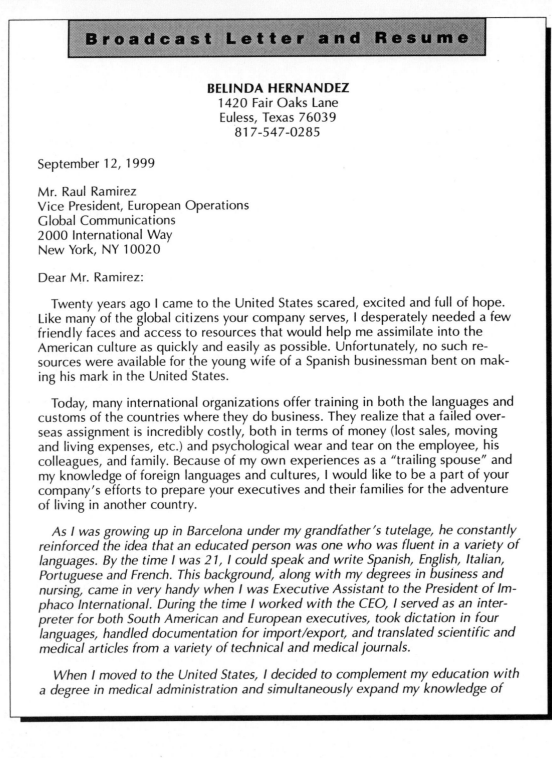

Broadcast Letter and Resume

BELINDA HERNANDEZ
1420 Fair Oaks Lane
Euless, Texas 76039
817-547-0285

September 12, 1999

Mr. Raul Ramirez
Vice President, European Operations
Global Communications
2000 International Way
New York, NY 10020

Dear Mr. Ramirez:

Twenty years ago I came to the United States scared, excited and full of hope. Like many of the global citizens your company serves, I desperately needed a few friendly faces and access to resources that would help me assimilate into the American culture as quickly and easily as possible. Unfortunately, no such resources were available for the young wife of a Spanish businessman bent on making his mark in the United States.

Today, many international organizations offer training in both the languages and customs of the countries where they do business. They realize that a failed overseas assignment is incredibly costly, both in terms of money (lost sales, moving and living expenses, etc.) and psychological wear and tear on the employee, his colleagues, and family. Because of my own experiences as a "trailing spouse" and my knowledge of foreign languages and cultures, I would like to be a part of your company's efforts to prepare your executives and their families for the adventure of living in another country.

As I was growing up in Barcelona under my grandfather's tutelage, he constantly reinforced the idea that an educated person was one who was fluent in a variety of languages. By the time I was 21, I could speak and write Spanish, English, Italian, Portuguese and French. This background, along with my degrees in business and nursing, came in very handy when I was Executive Assistant to the President of Imphaco International. During the time I worked with the CEO, I served as an interpreter for both South American and European executives, took dictation in four languages, handled documentation for import/export, and translated scientific and medical articles from a variety of technical and medical journals.

When I moved to the United States, I decided to complement my education with a degree in medical administration and simultaneously expand my knowledge of

Belinda Hernandez   Page 2

the English language. While attending college, I worked 18 hours per week at the school language lab teaching students both Spanish and French. At the department chair's request, I recorded tapes, still in use today, that illustrate the difference between Mexican and South American Spanish accents.

Shortly after completing my degree, I became Executive Assistant to the Director of Marketing at Diamond Triangle Petroleum. There I served as a simultaneous translator for meetings and teleconferences for Spanish, English and French-speaking professionals; handled correspondence in Spanish, French, Italian and Portuguese; taught Spanish to company engineers who were going to be stationed in South America; and translated sales and advertising literature and engineering operations manuals from English to Spanish.

When the energy industry experienced massive downsizing in the mid-1980s, I moved into a liaison position with a regional transit agency, which used my medical and business knowledge in transporting handicapped individuals throughout the metropolitan area. During my seven years with SMART, I continued to do a lot of translation and interpretation, particularly for the Hispanic community. One of my most interesting assignments was serving as the interpreter for the Governor of Monterey, Mexico, when he and his entourage visited SMART to learn more about our program for handicapped citizens.

Now that my family is raised and I am free to relocate or travel, I would like to devote my career to helping people around the globe adjust and thrive wherever they are doing business. Having lived in Spain, England, France and the United States, I count myself as a citizen of the world who is comfortable in adapting to any culture. And through my volunteer work as a trained mediator, I've refined my communications skills to work effectively with individual personalities, whatever their culture.

If your organization is looking for a seasoned professional to help select and coach your employees and their families for overseas assignments or work with your sales staff in the nuances of negotiating with people of other cultures, please give me a call. I would like to assist your firm in making the global marketplace a more user-friendly environment for all its constituents.

Sincerely yours,

Belinda Hernandez

BELINDA HERNANDEZ
1420 Fair Oaks Lane
Euless, Texas 76039
817-547-0285

OBJECTIVE

Teaching Spanish and/or ESL courses for the Dallas County Community College District.

APPLICABLE EXPERIENCE

In England developed own course curriculum and taught pro-bono English classes to the Spanish/Italian staff while at Fulbourn Hospital studying Psychiatric Nursing.   (2 years)

While a full-time student at Tarrant County Junior College Northeast Campus Hurst, worked 18 hours weekly at the language lab helping students with Spanish and French. Recorded lessons on tapes illustrating differences between Mexican and South American Spanish accents. To my knowledge, tapes are still in use.   (2 years)

At Imphaco International in Barcelona, Spain, as Executive Assistant to the President: (11 years)

Served as interpreter for business executives from South America and Europe.

Translated scientific articles from the American Medical Association, *Psychology Today,* and many other technically and medically-oriented publications.

Took dictation in four languages.

Handled documentation for import/export of pharmaceutical products.

At Diamond Triangle and Beta as an Executive Assistant: (2 years)

Handled correspondence in Spanish, French, Italian and Portuguese with businesses in foreign countries.

Translated sales and advertising literature and engineering operations manuals from English to Spanish.

Taught Spanish to engineers and other staff twice per week.

Provided simultaneous translations in meetings and teleconferences among Spanish, English and French-speaking professionals.

Belinda Hernandez   Page 2

As the Administrative Liaison for Special Services at SMART: (7 years)

   Presented the HandiRides program in Spanish to the Hispanic community and its agencies.

   Took minutes of public meetings and translated them into Spanish.

   Served as department liaison with community leaders, politicians, governmental and social service agencies.

   Served as the interpreter for the Governor of Monterey, Mexico, and his aide, when they visited SMART to learn about its transportation program for the disabled community.

   Translated SMART information for the community from English to Spanish.

As a freelance Contractor for Accento, The Language Company: (2 years)

   Translated technical, medical and legal material into five languages.

   Interpreted undercover tapes used as evidence for the court system.

   Translated a videotape about HIV and other communicable diseases for OSHA, timing the Spanish dialogue so it could be dubbed into the already-completed English version.

   Taught Spanish to groups of professional people.

Also tutored private students in Spanish using my own curriculum.   (2 years)

EDUCATION

Business Degree (equivalent to a B.S.) University of Barcelona, Spain

B.S. in Administration, Southwestern Medical University, Dallas, Texas

Psychiatric Nursing (LVN), London, England

Certified Mediator, Civil and Family, Dispute Resolution Service, Tarrant County, Texas

PERSONAL

Born and raised in Barcelona, Spain. Temporarily lived in England and France. U.S. naturalized citizen.

The Call to Action

Because broadcast letters are sent to hundreds of people, you can't follow up on every one of them. Consequently, you'll have to depend on interested recipients to initiate personal contact. Your final paragraph or call to action needs to be a strong statement reiterating why you both should get to know each other better. In Belinda Hernandez's letter, her final sentence is her mission statement. It describes her career commitment from this time forward and her reasons for dedicating herself to it.

Some other call-to-action statements might look something like these:

Now you have my experience in a nutshell. I think you will agree we have a great deal in common in terms of wanting to make our cities safe and responsive to the needs of their citizens and visitors. My track record in law enforcement and my demonstrated commitment to reducing crime make me an ideal candidate for your police force, especially if you are looking for professionals known for their integrity and genuine concern for the neighborhoods they serve. If you think I might help in your efforts to make a difference in your city, please give me a call.

Ever since I was a young boy growing up in the inner city, I've wanted to teach children and serve as a role model in helping them become proud, productive adults. Now that I have graduated with my degree in math education, I

ROBERT HALF'S RESUMANIA

There's never any reason to say in a resume or cover letter how wonderful the resume and its writer are. A resume should stand on its own. The material contained in it should be relevant and give a clear, unencumbered picture of the candidate. Here are two statements from the cover letters of people who evidently don't agree:

"I am certain you will agree that once you read this resume, and have an opportunity to speak with me in person, you will find me a cut above anyone else competing for the same job with you."

Or, "I don't usually toot my own horn, but in this case, I will toot away."

Fine, but the job we have open is for an accountant, not a musician.

am finally ready to fulfill my mission. Please give me the opportunity to be a part of your team, where I know I can provide teenagers with the tools to overcome the destructive forces of the "hood" and move into mainstream society.

Broadcast Letters from Real People

Here's what Don Overton of Media, Pennsylvania, says about why he wrote the following broadcast letter:

I am an engineer in my 50s and have rethought the whole problem of how to get attention from the decision makers in a company. Since I have a suspicion that their secretaries have been told to either automatically send resumes to the HR person for disposition or trash them immediately, I wanted to get my information past these gatekeepers by eliminating the resume altogether.

Also, I decided that managers and executives want to know what I can do for their company and want to examine experience in an easy-to-read manner without all the normal resume rhetoric. So, I came up with the attached resume letter for broadcast mailings that has been much more successful. I include a self-addressed postcard when I send a letter to a particularly important company as an inducement for the reader to reply. I have had at least eight interviews and over 40 personal responses from this format.

DONALD W. OVERTON
496 North Shelbourne Road
Media, PA 19064
610-946-2446

9 June, 1999

Mr. Big Shot, President
XYZ Corporation
7th and Golden Streets
Remote, PA 18000

Dear Mr. Shot:

I have taken the liberty of contacting you directly since you are best aware of the current and future business plans of XYZ Corporation. This letter is to introduce myself to you so you can determine how I may be beneficial to your company. In today's difficult economic and business climate, it is even harder to compete with domestic and foreign companies than in the past. While you must reduce costs by eliminating waste from business and manufacturing functions, it is even more important to use new technology and improve worker effectiveness to become a leader in your marketplace. Being successful in the near future requires a diversified staff adept at quickly solving product, process and manufacturing challenges while quickly and accurately addressing business and personnel problems.

I believe I can assist your company in pursuing new technical and managerial opportunities because of my diverse engineering, manufacturing and supervision background. I have worked with several sizes and types of industries, in various stages of development, and with metals, ceramics, composites and polymers. I have actual experience with the many processes listed below, some of which may be of direct interest to your company:

Equipment procurement, from hand tools to major capital equipment investments—Research, cost justification, evaluations, testing, negotiating, installation, start-up, qualification, operating procedures and P.M.

Product and materials procurement—Specifications, vendor research, audits and evaluation, product standards dev. and testing, cost and quality comparisons and negotiations.

Product development—Personal and published customer and product market research, product specifications, process or vendor cost analysis and delivery estimate.

Donald W. Overton   Page 2

Fixture development—Welding, brazing, machining and EDM.

Materials development, technical evaluation and selection—Low carbon steel
     sheet, tool steels, high silicon aluminum alloys, ceramic shapes, ceramic
     and Al metal matrix composites, precious metals, brazing and soldering
     alloys, Misc. low temp. Sn alloys and misc. polymers, elastomers, and
     adhesives.

Product and process cost analysis—Process dev., process improvement and
     revaluation, job analysis and definition, total cost development, equip-
     ment and personnel forecasting, and make-or-buy decisions.

Project management—Process dev. and qualification, facilities and plant lay-
     out, equipment installation and start-up using Std. PERT or Microsoft
     Project software.

Products manufacturing, consumer and industrial—Electronic heat sinks and
     packages; misc. rolled strip and punched and formed shapes; double-
     sided, fine line printed circuit boards; semiautomatic MIG and TIG
     welded shapes; polymer/metal powder composite shapes; ceramic tape
     casting; high quality die cast parts, and precious metal and pewter cast
     small parts.

Process control—Use of manual and computer MRP2 process, inventory,
     scheduling, and systems control. SPC evaluation.

Manufacturing systems—Process and quality control, scheduling, MRP2, JIT
     and TQM.

Quality engineering—Manual or auto dimensional measurements, thermal
     and moisture accelerated environmental testing, and mechanical, sur-
     face finish, vacuum lead, and in-process inspection techniques along
     with SPC analysis.

Machining metals and ceramics—Supervised production machining and
     model shops using standard equipment plus diamond toolgrinding, CNC
     machining centers, lapping and wire EDM equipment.

P.C. literacy—Lotus 1-2-3, Microsoft Word, Microsoft Project, Drafix CAD,
     and Harvard Graphics.

Personnel supervision and budgeting—Engineers, technicians of production
     and quality reports, computer services, manufacturing personnel, and
     admin. services. Personnel selection, training, and discipline.

Donald W. Overton   Page 3

While the above list touches on some of the categories where I am either an authority or have functional skills, there is much more I can accomplish by combining some of these materials and processes with good organizational and communication expertise, business experiences, and person-to-person encounters. I have a B.S. in Met. Nuclear Eng. from a respected engineering school and undergraduate and graduate level business administration class work which complements over 20 years of manufacturing, production, project and program management, manufacturing operations, production systems analysis, and plant management. However, I will consider a senior engineering position in these fields, if there are real growth opportunities.

In summary, I can make technical and organizational improvements, get new products into the marketplace, reduce costs, improve quality and productivity, and attack new challenges to be more competitive. You may already know a technical or major project that requires additional attention to accelerate results. Only you can judge what your company needs right now and in the coming years. If you feel you want a closer look at my background or are interested in using my skills now or in the near future, please call me at the above number for more detailed discussions. Or, simply return the attached postcard, and I will contact you or someone you recommend to discuss my abilities in relation to your company's needs.

However, if you have no immediate need for additional managerial or technical staff, perhaps you can direct me to a professional associate outside your company that may be in need of additional help. Thank you for your time and any assistance. I'm looking forward to hearing from you very soon.

Sincerely yours,

Donald W. Overton

ERNEST VILLANOVA
456 Ruggland Terrace
Springfield, OH 43055
216-841-9236

June 1, 1999

Ms. Taunee Besson
Career Dimensions
6330 LBJ Freeway
Dallas, TX 75240

Dear Ms. Besson:

After a 17-year career with a major sales and distribution company and a short stint heading my own marketing firm, I have seen many examples of great leadership and some that have not been up to the challenge. What separates the truly successful from the "wannabes" is the way people feel about their contributions to the goals of the corporation. While Total Quality Management (TQM) has been around for many years, successful implementation has been illusive to many more than would choose to admit it. This failed effort has resulted in a great deal of unrealized potential, and poor communication has left those expected to carry out the process with questions about the real objective. I'm sure you agree that creating a comfortable environment makes the work more interesting and fun while reducing stress. And, when the entire unit gains a stake in the outcome, the probability of improved efficiency increases. By now you have deduced that one of the things I enjoy most is developing capable people.

I have participated in changes that have transformed an industry. While many of these changes supported minor segments, many affected the ability of independent retailers to maintain and expand market share. As a result of a clear vision, an understanding of each person's role in the process, and a team desire to actively collaborate, we took business strategies from words to action on world-class scale. My experience in sales, marketing and distribution, at both the wholesale and retail levels, have enhanced my ability to anticipate outcomes and lead effectively. I am enthusiastic about using this unique blend of experience in an organization driven by the quest for added value and legendary service.

If you are looking for a Vice President/General Manager who can motivate a team to implement plans with multiple priorities that not only meet, but exceed growth and financial goals, I am the person who can deliver those expectations and more.

May we talk?

Ernest Villanova

LARRY M. URBAN
3819 Hidden Harbour Drive
Melbourne, FL 32935
407-882-0747

March 28, 1999

Mr. Robert Darwin
Northern PhoneCom
14815 Northpark Blvd.
Charlotte, NC 28216

Dear Mr. Darwin:

The art of teaching and the need for motivational instructors will ALWAYS be essential to the population at large. As a professional with over 12 years of experience in educational administration, marketing, personnel, and finance, and 20 years of teaching and language translation of English to Spanish and Spanish to English, I am currently seeking new challenges in INTERNATIONAL BUSINESS AND TRAINING MANAGEMENT.

Select career highlights include:

- Serving as a successful manager supervising schools with multiple departments, staffs of up to 25 employees, and hundreds of students.

- Teaching and creating courses, revising and adapting training programs, implementing methods of study, and supervising teachers' work habits and teaching methods.

- Creating and implementing policies and procedures used very successfully in corporations.

- Gaining a comprehensive knowledge of computers sales, export/import, customer support and satisfaction.

Currently, I serve as the President/CEO/General Manager for Centro de Capacitacion Bilingue, Inc. which is a training/vocational/educational center I started in Venezuela. I am responsible for all aspects of a business operation and the specifics of running a higher-level learning institution. From the company's inception, I have:

- Established a corporation that commands the highest respect and approval from the community, state authorities, and the population at large.

Larry M. Urban   Page 2

- Increased profits by over 1000 percent in seven years by introducing new procedures and areas of training now being imitated by my competition.

- Established new systems for control of student fees and attendance.

- Increased income while keeping taxes low.

- Created a translation department for an important tourist magazine.

- Attained the status of the only licensed translator by both federal government and state authorities in the eastern part of the country.

I believe I am a person who can serve you in a variety of capacities. I would be pleased to meet with you personally to discuss possible options. Please give me a call (or leave a message) at the number shown above.

Sincerely,

Larry M. Urban

George K. Kloppenberg

6123 Green Manor Drive
Louisville, KY 40219

502-387-6857 (H)
502-481-0777 x242 (W)

January 10, 1999

Mr. Fernando Fernandez
President
Intrex Corporation
1000 First Street
Harrison, NJ 07029

Dear Mr. Fernandez:

In God We Trust, all others must bring data!

Division Managers at Dahlstrom were expected to manage "by the numbers." My whole-hearted acceptance of this expectation, reinforced by my open, participatory leadership style, contributed substantially to my successful stay there.

As **DIVISION MANAGER with P&L responsibility for $10 million in annual sales,** I achieved significant operational and financial improvements by fostering an atmosphere of open communications, trust and mutual respect. Working directly with our managers and supervisors, I applied over **20 years of manufacturing management experience** to lead a focused factory with cellular production, ISO 9002 driven quality systems, and continuous improvement teams. Our management group reduced cycle times 50 percent and direct labor 36 percent, improved inventory turns 50 percent and increased on-time delivery from 10 to 90 percent, while maintaining quality levels at 98 percent.

Previously, as **General Manager of a 170-employee plant,** I led a team of managers who developed and maintained continuous flow manufacturing, work cells and SPC, while reducing cycle times, inventory and floor space, and continually refining our MRP system (AskManMan) to conform to a JIT environment.

Since I am currently in an outplacement mode, my intention is to gain your assistance in two ways:

- **Determine potential positions at your company.**
- **Enlist your help to discuss employment possibilities in your area and to find new networking resources.**

I plan to call within ten days to ensure you received this and to determine your willingness to participate in my job-search effort. **I appreciate your consideration.**

Sincerely,

George K. Kloppenberg

"By the way, our office space is at a premium right now, so we've made temporary accommodations for you."

11

Thank-You Notes and Other Job-Search Correspondence

The majority of job seekers think cover letters are the most important component of effective job-search correspondence (excluding resumes). However, don't underestimate the role other letters play in developing relationships with potential employers and in helping you start a new position on the right foot. The most prominent of them is the thank-you note.

Thank-you notes are appropriate follow-ups for networking appointments and interviews. When someone is kind enough to give you a significant amount of time, it's only polite to acknowledge your appreciation.

A thank-you letter, composed to be more than a bread-and-butter note, also can serve a strategic purpose. After a networking appointment, sending a thank-you letter can be an excellent way of telling your interviewee what you plan to do next. Instead of leaving a relationship dangling without momentum or closure, your thank-you note can move you toward an interview, help you tactfully decline the option of exploring career possibilities or leave the door open for you to communicate at a later date. And writing a thank-you note after an employment interview explaining why you're interested in and ideally suited for the position can mean the difference between receiving an offer or not.

Let's take a look at some instances when a thank-you note can make an important impact on your job search.

Three Types of Networking Thank-You Notes

If you're an active networker, it's likely that you'll talk with a variety of people during your job search. With some, you'll form a mutual admiration society and want to cement relationships. Others will only vaguely interest you. The rest will have little or nothing in common with you or what you want in your career. If you plan to use your thank-you letters as strategic job-search tools, you can't adopt a cookie-cutter approach. Each thank-you note must be tailored to its recipient.

When customizing your letters, your first step might be to divide them into three categories:

1. The "thanks-but-no-thanks" note.
2. The "don't-be-surprised-if-I-call-you-again" note.
3. And the "our-relationship-is-destiny" note.

Each type of letter has a different purpose and combination of components. But regardless of which you choose during your job search, such letters are the easiest, most logical form of follow-up you can use.

The "Thanks-but-No-Thanks" Note

This letter should be sent to a networking contact who has been kind enough to meet with you but has little to offer in terms of job opportunities, ideas or further contacts. When writing this thank-you note, you're showing appreciation without encouraging further communication. In general, one paragraph thanking the individual for her valuable time and information will suffice.

ROBERT HALF'S RESUMANIA

Let me share with you a portion of a letter written by a job seeker to an employer who'd given the job to someone else:

"After I hung up the phone with you, I realized you had lied to me about why I wasn't chosen for the job. You said you wanted someone with experience at another company. That doesn't make any sense. You said your accounting system was difficult to understand. If I had worked at another company, I would want to do things the way that another company did them, which would make it hard for me to understand your system. Not only that, if I had worked for another company and was leaving to go to work for you, that would say that I wasn't a dependable, steady employee, and probably wouldn't stay with you very long. In other words, not having worked for another company would be an advantage, not a negative reason for turning me down. Also, I thought you wanted a hard worker. Someone with experience isn't likely to work as hard for you as someone without experience. And finally, I assumed you wanted somebody who would be happy working in an accounting department. Somebody who gave up a job obviously wasn't happy, and wouldn't be happy with you either.

"If you wish to reconsider, I can be reached at . . . ."

Aside from obviously faulty logic, the tone and purpose of the letter is totally inappropriate.

Thanks-but-No-Thanks Note

800 Blue Mist Road
Kimberly, Alaska 99631
907-343-7798
January 22, 1999

Mr. Daniel Trihoe
President
Trihoe Environmental Strategies
2222 Northern Lights Way
Juneau, Alaska 99631

Dear Mr. Trihoe:

   Thank you for getting together with me to discuss the continuing efforts to prepare for the spills in Prince Edward Sound. I really appreciate the information you gave me concerning the various groups involved in this mammoth task and their current strategies. Good luck in your quest to maintain pristine beauty and economic viability of the national treasure.

Sincerely yours,

Robert Sampson

Be sure to include your address, phone number and e-mail address on every thank-you note you send, even if it's a tactful one-paragraph dismissal. You never know when someone who seemingly holds no opportunity has a relative or friend who's trying to fill the job of your dreams. If you ensure that everyone who gets a thank-you note can reach you, you won't inadvertently lose a key referral.

The "Don't-Be-Surprised-If-I-Call-You-Again" Note

This second type of networking thank-you is geared for contacts whom you enjoyed meeting, who are involved in projects that interest you, but who have nothing to offer at this point. These letters include three main components:

1. A paragraph on what you find particularly admirable or intriguing about the contact or his company, industry or job.

2. A few sentences highlighting how your background, skills and interests parallel what the person does or seeks in a successful colleague.

3. A paragraph stating how you expect to continue your research but might like to contact the person again to ask more refined questions or pursue an opportunity.

This thank-you helps keep the door open without guaranteeing future contact. It also gives this individual implicit permission to call you if an interesting opportunity becomes available.

Don't-Be-Surprised-If-I-Call-You-Again Note

2300 Bellmeade Place
Columbia, SC 29303
803-789-4455
March 23, 1999

Ms. Laura Lee Caruthers
VP of Marketing
Granite Office Systems
4 Robert E. Lee Blvd.
Columbia, SC 29303

Dear Laura Lee,

Thank you so much for getting together with me to talk about how the role of office systems distributors is evolving in this area. I particularly appreciated your genuine concern for keeping your customers in touch with state-of-the-art developments, while recognizing their need to upgrade equipment only as their internal requirements and budget justify it. Your philosophy represents a true commitment to customer service and is relatively rare in an industry where bottom-line results often take priority over long-term business relationships.

In our discussion about my career direction, I was really pleased to hear you say that good sales professionals can sell almost anything if they have the intrinsic people, planning and perseverance skills and a hunger to constantly learn more about their products. If this enlightened attitude is gaining favor among manufacturers, I can easily segue into other similar product areas.

As I mentioned during our appointment, I am planning to continue my research on a variety of high-tech products and services before targeting my specific career goal. As I refine my ideal job description, I may give you a call to expand upon some issues we've already discussed or to explore a possible new opportunity. Don't be surprised if you hear from me again in the not-too-distant future.

Sincerely yours,

Cindy McDonald

The "Our-Relationship-Is-Destiny" Note

This is the kind of thank-you note all job seekers long to write because it means they've struck career gold on a recent networking appointment. Eureka! You've found a great company where you might land a challenging position reporting to the mentor of your dreams. Obviously, this extraordinary situation deserves an extraordinary thank-you note—one that's reserved for the most exciting opportunities.

Like the don't-be-surprised note, the relationship-is-destiny letter begins with a complimentary paragraph describing something you genuinely admire about the reader or organization. Because the two of you have formed a mutual admiration society, this paragraph should be an especially enthusiastic statement about why you'd like to join your reader's team.

The second paragraph should make an outstanding case for why the company and your interviewee might be interested in having you on board. If you've done a good job of information interviewing, you'll know exactly what skills, personality traits and values are desired by your potential employer. Paragraph two should spotlight which of your accomplishments match those of an ideal candidate.

The final paragraph should state specifically what you plan to do next. For instance, you may:

☆ Confirm the date and time for an impending employment interview.

☆ Use your note as a cover letter for a requested resume, and say you'll call next week to confirm its arrival and discuss the next step.

☆ Thank your contact for suggesting names of colleagues you should meet, then update him on your efforts to see them.

☆ Tell your interviewee you appreciate his offer to discuss potential opportunities for you with his team, and that you'll touch base in a couple of weeks to learn the results of his conversations.

☆ Mention that you've given your recent meeting much thought and have a proposal to discuss with him. You'll call in a week or so to make an appointment for a meeting.

These are a few scenarios that can evolve from a positive networking appointment. Whatever the outcome, send a thank-you note that shows you're motivated and promotes a lasting relationship.

Our-Relationship-Is-Destiny Note

Sally Hines
200 Frankfort Drive
Evanston, Illinois 60202
708-113-2424

April 30, 1999

Ms. Susan Calvecchio
Partner
Calloway, Couthron and Calvecchio
2300 East First Street
Springfield, IL 62702

Dear Susan,

   I really appreciated your getting together with me to discuss how recruiting interns helps your firm maintain the calibre of its work and promote healthy growth. From what you have told me, it's clear your organization is interested in the whole person, not just his ability to log billable hours. While we both know that billing hours is how lawyers survive and profit, some firms are so committed to 60- to 70-hour weeks that their partners and associates have no time for anything else. It's refreshing to discover an organization which realizes that too much hard work can kill the goose that lays the golden eggs, or at least, retard its production.
   I was also pleased to learn that your approach to finding the best interns resembles the one my admissions team uses to select students most likely to benefit from our programs at Northwestern. Many talented young people apply for admittance to the university, but we don't have the resources to accept all of them. Consequently, our selection process must favor those individuals who will take greatest advantage of their educational experience and serve as excellent representatives for us as they move through their careers.
   Calloway, Couthron and Calvecchio must also consider which intern candidates are most likely to be successful within the law firm and eventually become prominent in their field of expertise and their community. As we discovered, your criteria for determining the most appropriate candidates and Northwestern's are very similar.
   As you seriously consider establishing a formalized human resources department, I am enclosing my resume for your "pending" file. Now that we've deemed ourselves official friends, let's get together about once a month to catch up on each other's activities and compare notes on our latest recruiting efforts. I'll call you in a couple of weeks to find out when both of us can meet for lunch. Talk to you soon.

                                         Sincerely,

                                         Sally Hines

Enclosure

Our-Relationship-Is-Destiny Note

Amber Blaha
7140 University Place
Evanston, Illinois 60201
(708) 328-7073
(214) 931-8888

March 22, 1999

Mr. Jim Martin
Regional Market Director, HRC
Ernst & Young LLP
2121 San Jacinto Street
Suite 500
Dallas, Texas 75201

Dear Mr. Martin:

I appreciated the opportunity to speak with you on Tuesday about Ernst & Young and the Human Resource Consulting group.

I have really enjoyed meeting with members of the HRC group. Obviously its highly intelligent and professional staff is the main reason why consulting has become such a large part of the services Ernst & Young provides. The work sounds very challenging, and I believe the high expectations that accompany such a challenge lead to excellent results. I also really enjoyed speaking with you. From our talk, I gained a strong sense of Ernst & Young's dedication to bringing only the best people on board. I enjoyed the challenge of such a candid discussion and welcomed the chance to show you what I am truly "all about."

I feel strongly that I have the initiative, intelligence and common sense that characterizes Ernst & Young consultants. And I think my education and internship experience have given me a strong foundation from which to build a significant career. Most importantly, I am satisfied only when I produce exceptional work. I believe this quality would make me a valuable asset to your company.

I will be in Dallas until March 26 when I return to Chicago. If you have more questions, I would be glad to answer them. I look forward to hearing from you soon.

Sincerely,

Amber Blaha

Networking Thank-You Notes from Real People

Milt Plowright
Right Associates
50210 Claybrook Avenue
Baton Rouge, LA 70806
504-247-8283

March 2, 1999

Ms. Taunee Besson
President
CAREER DIMENSIONS
6330 LBJ Freeway, Suite 136
Dallas, TX 75240

Dear Taunee:

Thank you for the opportunity to meet with you on February 27 to explore your thoughts relating to career counseling.

As a result of our discussion, I made a decision to concentrate my efforts at this time in outplacement. Furthermore, I have implemented a plan to enhance my outplacement skills and will market them appropriately.

Taunee, I appreciate our frank and open discussion, and suggest we keep in touch.

Sincerely,

Milt Plowright

Networking Thank-You Notes from Real People

Amber Blaha
7140 University Place
Evanston, Illinois 60201
(708) 328-7073
(214) 931-8888

March 22, 1999

Ms. Laura Rickover
Ernst & Young LLP
2121 San Jacinto Street
Suite 500
Dallas, Texas 75201

Dear Ms. Rickover:

I appreciated the opportunity to speak with you Tuesday about Ernst & Young and the compensation practice.

I was really impressed by the level of responsibility and autonomy consultants have with their clients. It seems like you have had significant opportunities to develop your skills and even bring in your own clients to the business. In addition, the presentations, research, and compensation tools you use for your projects sound very interesting. I think it is great that Ernst & Young gives people the opportunity to develop a career that addresses both their interests and aptitudes.

I found it very helpful to speak with you about the actual tasks a senior staff consultant and staff consultant perform. Also, I appreciated getting your point of view about lifestyle issues such as travel and work hours. Ernst & Young seems to strike a good balance between life inside and outside the office.

I really enjoyed our discussion and hope to talk with you again sometime soon.

Sincerely,

Amber Blaha

Other Uses for Networking Thank-You Notes

As you network, you'll talk to many contacts by phone or modem, rather than face-to-face. These people deserve a thank-you note just as much as those you've met in person, especially if they give you a hot lead or offer information that's hard to get. If you doubt the etiquette of thanking someone who's given you job-search advice, choose the abundance alternative. Brighten their day and risk breeding a little contagious good feeling with an unexpected but genuine show of appreciation.

To Type or Write by Hand

People often agonize over whether to type or handwrite a thank-you note, and whether to send it on business stationery or personal notepaper. For the record: It simply doesn't matter. The most important thing to remember about thank-you notes is to send one as soon as possible. If you think a typed note on printed letterhead is more businesslike, boot up your computer and go to it. If you enjoy jotting personal notes to friends and acquaintances on Crane's monogrammed note cards, curl up in your favorite easy chair and start writing. Professionals in our stroke-deprived culture get so few compliments from each other that they might even welcome a note scribbled on the back of your latest to-do list.

Thank-You Notes for Employment Interviews

There are several ways to categorize interview thank-you notes. However, we'll concentrate on three types:

1. The "I-want-the-job" note.
2. The "I-don't-want-the-job" note.
3. The "overcoming-employer-or-client-concerns" note.

The "I-Want-the-Job" Note

This employment interview thank-you note is similar to the enthusiastic letter you send after a networking appointment that has real potential. In your first paragraph, compliment the interviewer or her company. In your second, mention how your background, skills and personality traits parallel what the potential employer (or client) is seeking. And, in the third paragraph, state your intention to remain in touch until she makes her decision.

Among the typical interview thank-you notes that follow, several were prepared by Larry Frantz and Richard Hirsch, whose letters throughout this book are excellent examples of how to finesse an employment or consulting relationship.

"I-Want-the-Job" Thank-You Notes by Hirsch and Frantz

3270 Dana Drive
Dallas, Texas 75220
214-352-2400
Beeper: 324-2400

July 20, 1999

Ms. MARTHA C. COCHRAN
Executive Vice President
GENERA HOMES of TEXAS
Dallas/Ft. Worth Division
1431 Greenbelt Drive
Suite 700
Irving, Texas 75038

Dear Martha:

I appreciate your seeing me on Monday to discuss if Genera and I would be a good match. I was impressed with your warmth, friendly manner and your interest in ac-quainting job candidates with several Genera managers. The more we can learn about each other, the better decision we will collectively make on the viability of a long-term business relationship.

During our interview, I told you a good deal about my background and approach to sales. In reading *Update Builders Report,* I noticed that the company also believes strongly in offering a quality product, attending to details and going the extra mile for its clients. Because these things are so important to me, it's critical that I join an organization whose philosophy agrees with mine.

I look forward to hearing from you in the next week or so. If you haven't contacted me by Tuesday, I will call you to touch base on where we stand at this point and where we need to go from here.

Sincerely yours,

Richard A. Hirsch

3270 Dana Drive
Dallas, Texas 75220
214-352-2400
July 14, 1999

Mr. Mike McGruder
General Sales Manager
GENERA HOMES OF TEXAS
Dallas/Ft. Worth Division
1200 Greenbelt Drive, #700
Irving, TX 75038

Dear Mike:

Thank you for getting together with me to discuss a sales position with Genera. I was very impressed with the company's philosophy on customer service and its commitment to finding and keeping outstanding professionals.

Frankly, I was amazed at the speed and efficiency of your home-building process and the fact that any punch list items are fixed within three days. Based on my extensive experience working with builders, your attention to customer needs is extraordinary.

For the past 14 years, starting when I was 16, I have had a successful career in selling products and services to customers who demand the best value for their money. I think I am most effective with people who ask tough questions and want to know why they should buy from me.

As far as I'm concerned, good sales techniques are highly transferable. They work whether you are selling remodeling projects, high-ticket retail items, or new homes. If you find out your clients' needs, show them how your product (home) matches their requirements, offer an excellent value and always follow through on your promises, you will make the sale and generate referral business at the same time.

Because of many years of experience in interior design and home sales, I have an extensive network of realtors who enjoy selling new homes. If I work for Genera, I will bring both my expertise in sales and my contacts in the real-estate business to your firm.

As I said in my interview, I want to work for Genera. I think your company and I have a lot to offer each other and would make an excellent match. Perhaps if you can't hire me now, there are some things I could do prior to your next opening to prove I would be an asset for your company.

I will call you Tuesday 7/20/99 to set up a time to explore some options. I look forward to talking with you soon.

Sincerely yours,

Richard A. Hirsch

LAWRENCE G. FRANTZ
6535 Northpoint Drive
Dallas, Texas 75248

September 7, 1999

Mr. L. H. Robinson
President and Chief Executive Officer
Triple Drilling Company
5956 Cognac Lane, Suite 1500
Dallas, TX 75225-9004

Dear Dick:

I appreciated the opportunity to spend some time with you and learn more about Triple. The IPO prospectus was very complete and thorough, but there is no substitute for talking with the boss to learn what the company is really like. And it may be motherhood and apple pie to some, but to me, words like quality company, safe working environment and a CEO with integrity are critical.

If I understand what you are looking for, you want a financial professional to help you determine the appropriate capital structure for Triple. You would like to have the confidence that you have access to the capital to grow the company the way you want without being dependent on your European owner. You are perhaps less concerned about whether your investor relations and human resource functions are upgraded, but you seemed willing to listen to suggestions in those areas.

You expressed concern that it had taken some time before you were able to schedule our interview. This is a very important step you are about to take, and I think you should be as deliberate as you need to be. Judging from my impression of Allen, you already have some quality people, and you want to be certain your CFO is consistent with that tradition.

I am very enthusiastic about working with Triple. It looks like a fine company and I am sure I could help make it even better. I would be willing to consider either a full-time CFO position, or as an option, you may wish to try a part-time consultant for say, six months. A consulting relationship would give us both an opportunity to get comfortable with each other with an option to make it permanent.

Thanks again for your time.

Sincerely,

Larry Frantz

Lawrence G. Frantz
6535 Northpoint Drive
Dallas, Texas 75248

March 18, 1999

Ms. Katharine Kinney
Planning and Administration
Growtex Corp.
4111 Lemon Way
Dallas, TX 75237

Dear Katharine:

I really enjoyed our lunch meeting yesterday. You are interesting, articulate and, obviously, very intent on learning all you can about investor relations.

Growtex also sounds like a fine, professionally-run organization. This is exactly the kind of company and management I would like to have as a client, if you believe you have some tasks where I might help you.

As a start, it would be useful for me to get some idea of what you have been saying to analysts for the past year. Please send me a copy of as much of the following material as you have available:

1. A draft of your annual report text (in whatever shape it's in now)
2. Any interim reports issued since you went public
3. All press releases post IPO
4. A copy of the slides used on the road show (and any subsequent presentations if the slides were different from the road show)
5. All analyst reports or comments about Growtex.

I would be happy to give you some feedback on whatever you send me. I believe a good way to get to know a possible client is to see what he has written and a good way for you to get to know me is by the quality of feedback I give.

In the meanwhile, please call me with any questions you might have. You ask good questions and I love a challenge!

Sincerely,

Larry Frantz

"I Don't-Want-the-Job" Note

It's often appropriate to decline a position, even before it's offered. If you're sure you don't want an offer in the short or long term, or have decided to accept another position, tell your interviewer as soon as possible. He'll appreciate your candor and concern for his time, which otherwise would have been wasted in the futile pursuit of a disinterested candidate. Because you never know when your paths may cross again, it's a good idea to treat him with the kindness and respect you'd want if you were being rejected.

Perhaps you've heard of "the sandwich formula," often used by managers, colleagues, friends and relatives who have bad news or need to offer constructive criticism. The premise behind this approach is: A piece of bad news sandwiched between two bits of good news is a lot easier to take than the bad news alone.

What kind of good news can you use to maintain a friendly relationship with a potential employer? Consider the following possibilities:

☆ The people working for/with him are fortunate to have a manager who's both an expert in his field and a dedicated mentor.

☆ His company's commitment to high-quality products, customer service, employees, innovation or community involvement is truly exceptional.

☆ His staff's camaraderie is a model for productive team work.

☆ His dedication to the bottom line never sacrifices his company's mission.

If these don't fit, mention other admirable attributes. Just think about what you most respect about your interviewer and her organization, then use it as the bread in your "I-don't-want-this-job" sandwich.

Valerie Freeman, owner of Imprimis, thinks the letter on page 263 is a great example of how to reject and compliment a potential employer at the same time.

I·Don't·Want·the·Job Note

Jean Silverman
800 East Colony Drive
Carrollton, TX 75006
214-306-8823

March 20, 1999

Imprimis
Attn: Valerie Freeman
         President
5550 LBJ Freeway, Suite 15, LB52
Dallas, Texas 75240

Dear Ms. Freeman:

Thank you for making time yesterday to meet with me concerning the ACE Director position. I can appreciate the busy schedule that you must have and feel fortunate to have had your quality time to discuss this position with you.

I am very impressed with what I know of Imprimis and feel it is a first-class operation. However, another opportunity has come to fruition and I have accepted it.

The staff that I met over the past few weeks has been extremely proud and happy to be working with WORDTEMPS. That is an excellent sign of dedicated management.

Thank you again for allowing me to meet with you.

Sincerely,

Jean Silverman

cc: Anita Marina

The "Overcoming-Potential-Employer-or-Client-Concerns" Note

Occasionally you may have an uneasy feeling that a potential employer or client is uncertain about your qualifications for the job, or that you've neglected to explain why you are his *ideal* candidate. Rather than throwing your hands in the air and settling for a mediocre posture, use your thank-you note to address the issues that still need closure.

For instance, suppose your interviewer says he's looking for someone with more experience in XYZ. Strengthen your position by spotlighting in your letter how you coordinated several key XYZ-type projects, which gave you more experience than you originally mentioned.

Suppose your problem is the opposite—you're perceived as being overqualified. In this case, explain that you're willing to accept a lesser position because you believe it offers intriguing challenges or because you're tired of burning your candle at both ends and want a less stressful job that requires fewer hours.

Other issues to address may include your background and adaptability for tackling a different industry, product, company size or culture; the discrepancy between your current compensation and what the potential position offers; your willingness to relocate (especially overseas); the possible philosophical clashes between your manager's style and your own. In short, a thank-you note is a useful vehicle for resolving any problems because it allows you to put your argument on paper and make strategic use of the sandwich approach. The following "overcoming-potential-employer-or-client-concerns" thank-you notes are from real people. Do you think they succeeded in overcoming their interviewers' objections?

CLAYTON COLLINS
2815 Perry Court
Manassas, VA 24501
804-596-5376

August 30, 1999

Mr. Clint Roster
Iontech, Inc.
1434 Green Drive, Suite 5005
Lassiter, VA 22101

Dear Clint:

I enjoyed our visit this afternoon and want to thank you for your time and interest. At this time, I believe it would be beneficial for both of us to address your reservations concerning my joining your team at Iontech.

As I understand, there are two main issues you are pondering about my ability to help Iontech enter its new market niche. First, have my selling skills eroded during the years I served as the president of Candor Group? Second, will I be satisfied with a position as a "SALESMAN?" or more to the point, will I put forth the effort required to succeed in this endeavor?

On the first point, let me assure you, the main responsibility of a leader of a small technology company is selling. As Iontech introduces its new family of integrated application development products, it will be confronted with many of the same challenges that I have already faced, such as how to convince prospective customers that this new technology will help them address real business problems with cost-justifiable solutions, or how to recruit strategic partners who can provide profitable distribution channels for Iontech in the partners' unique niches.

While I acknowledge your concern about my desire for a position as a "SALESMAN" for Iontech, I do not share the view that the position is just a salesman. As we discussed in your office, I am evaluating possible positions using the following four criteria (order not significant):

- Its potential for compensation.
- Its geographic location.
- Its product(s) and/or service(s).
- Its responsibilities/positions.

The opportunity at Iontech leads in at least two and perhaps three of these categories.

Clint, I am excited about your company's technology, its market, which I believe is the next major growth segment for the software industry, and the chance to be associated again with a clear leader in this arena. I trust that this letter will successfully address your concerns. I look forward to the appropriate next steps with you and your immediate supervisor.

Sincerely,

Clay Collins

Lawrence G. Frantz
6535 Northpoint Drive
Dallas, Texas 75248

February 3, 1999

Mr. J. Ward Smith
President and Chief Executive Officer
Biomed Control, Inc.
9200 Webb Chapel Road, Suite 500
Dallas, TX 75220

Dear Ward:

Thank you for the opportunity to make a proposal to you for my assistance with your investor relations. I know from my experience, and from discussions with other investor relations people this program will work to broaden your coverage by analysts.

You and A.J. expressed some concern over whether there are enough potential analysts to make Phase II of my program viable. A check with a directory shows there are 133 buy-and-sell-side firms that follow health care. Because of multiple health-care analysts in the same firm and the exclusion of smaller firms from this particular directory (but available in others), I would estimate there are 300 health-care analysts. While I recognize not all of those analysts would be interested in Biomed Control, the advantage of Phase II of my proposal is it would cost you nothing for those analysts who are not interested in talking to me about your company. I feel my proposal is reasonable in estimating 90 analysts or 30 percent of the total population would be interested in hearing about your company.

I look forward to talking with you about your trip to New York.

Sincerely,

Larry Frantz

The Acceptance Letter

Without a doubt the most enjoyable job-search letter is the one at the end of the process: the acceptance letter. Yet most people are so relieved to finally land a new position, they neglect to compose the landmark document that acknowledges their search is over and a new phase of their career is beginning.

Like thank-you notes, acceptance letters can be formulaic and full of bland platitudes, or they can specifically describe your understanding of the responsibilities and rewards of your new position. While the thought of an employment contract makes many managers fear a potential lawsuit, your written acceptance can serve the same purpose as this legal document without creating the accompanying paranoia. Indeed, before our society became so litigious, the main purpose of an employment contract was simply to outline the mutual expectations of the involved parties so that everyone clearly understood the basis for the relationship. Your acceptance letter can still do this without the nasty baggage associated with a contract.

Advantages of a Letter of Acceptance

☆ It feels sooo good to write.

☆ It clarifies your and your employer's understanding of exactly what you've agreed to. Perhaps you've noticed how no two people seem to recall events or conversations the same way. Or their recollections of an event may be correct, but their interpretation of it differs. Filtered perceptions and misinterpretations often occur in interviews when both parties are trying to impress one another and encourage a budding relationship. Although neither person means to misrepresent himself, misunderstandings may occur nonetheless.

If you write an acceptance letter stating your understanding of your job responsibilities, compensation, reporting relationship, and anticipated (but not assured) future, you give both yourself and your manager a "constitution" for starting your new venture. If your employer reads it and finds your perceptions differ from his, you and he can set the record straight before the original miscommunication snowballs, possibly destroying your relationship.

A letter of acceptance is a benchmark for describing where you began your career at the company. As your career progresses, you can use it before or during performance appraisals, raises or promotions to illustrate how your responsibilities have increased. Or if your career seems stymied, it can serve as a gentle reminder of the first time you and your manager discussed your future.

While this letter isn't an official contract, it will probably go into a permanent employment file that human resources keeps under lock and key. If a disagreement over your responsibilities arises, you have a historical document to back you up. (Unfortunately, if your relationship with your manager deteriorates enough to need the letter, it's probably too late to salvage your job.)

A Word of Warning

Because so many companies have been sued for breaking implicit contracts, your manager may get nervous when he sees your letter. If you detect such a concern, reassure him about your motives and offer to destroy it. But keep in mind that his paranoia about being sued may stem from actual events, not just horror stories in the business media.

A good manager is a good communicator who'll appreciate your efforts to assure a good start. He doesn't need to worry about litigious misunderstandings because he's able to resolve misperceptions before they become problems. Good supervisors rarely land in court.

Writing Your Letter of Acceptance

In your acceptance letter, include the various issues that impact your decision to take the position. These include your job title, start date, location, salary or commission and potential bonuses, responsibilities, relocation package if applicable, reporting relationship, and opportunities for growth (if you perform up to expectations). As your manager reads it, he can compare his recollections with yours and either confirm your thinking or act immediately to resolve any differences.

Your letter should be a genuine, enthusiastic and friendly summary. Since it serves as the semiofficial document for starting a mutually beneficial relationship, it should sound collegial, not adjudicative.

The following example is a typical letter of acceptance.

Acceptance Letter

Bradley Greenman

780 Terrace Drive   **Seattle, WA 98104**   **206-456-2905**

November 20, 1999

Ms. Susan Tannenbaum
Managing Partner
Rincon Taylor
2100 Friendship Place
Seattle, WA 98104

Dear Susan,

I am really pleased to accept your offer of employment for the position of Senior Accountant at a starting salary of $4,000 per month commencing January 2, 1999. While I look forward to taking a little time off during the holidays, I will appear bright and early at 2100 Friendship Place first thing next year.

Based on our interview discussions, I look forward to working directly with you and Cramer Fitzgerald on the firm's largest domestic accounts. Because I have extensive experience in audits and tax returns for Fortune 500 companies, I should be able to hit the ground running and relieve you and Cramer of the tax work for these firms by the end of the first quarter. Then both of you will have more time to concentrate on the company's international client base, which we all agree has tremendous potential for future growth.

As I mentioned in our prior conversations, I plan to make Rincon Taylor my business home for the long term and look forward to growing in my responsibilities as the company increases its clients. I would eventually like to be involved in some international accounts, both because I am working on an MBA in International Business, and because I believe the future of the firm will be predicated on our serving global organizations.

Thank you for choosing me to be a part of your team. I am most enthusiastic about the opportunity to work with you while making a contribution to Seattle's best accounting firm.

Sincerely yours,

Bradley Greenman

The Landing Letter

There's one more letter to compose after you write your acceptance letter: a note to your key networking contacts. We'll call it the *landing* letter in honor of Right Associates, a Philadelphia-based national outplacement firm that gives its outplacement candidates a landing party when they accept a new job. The party celebrates the job seeker's success and informs fellow searchers of his achievement.

As you network when you're looking for a job, you'll become acquainted with numerous people who are genuinely interested in your search and its outcome. When you finally *land* a new position, you'll want to send them a note about your good news. They'll enjoy hearing of your success and feel gratified that you decided to tell them about your new job personally.

While you're at it, be sure to give them your new title, company, business address and phone number. If it doesn't take too long to be printed, send them a new business card for their Rolodex. Now that these fellow professionals have developed an interest in your career, stay in touch with them. Call each of them about once a quarter and get together for lunch, golf or some other relationship-building activity. In today's job market you never know when you or they may have to seek another opportunity. *A good network is a terrible thing to waste.*

The following great landing letter was written by a fellow Mortarboard alumnus who called me when he decided to relocate back to Texas. When he landed his new job, he sent me this letter.

RODNEY SCHLOSSBURG
401 EAST 34TH STREET
NORTH TOWER—23K
NEW YORK, NEW YORK 10016

October 19, 1999

Taunee Besson
Career Dimensions
6330 LBJ Freeway, #136
Dallas, Texas 75240

Dear Taunee:

Thank you for talking with me this past summer in connection with my interest in relocating to Texas. Your advice and encouragement helped keep me on track.

I am pleased to let you know that I have accepted an offer with McGowen Communications, the big cellular communications company (that operates as Cellular 2000). I will be the marketing director—responsible for business-to-business and consumer marketing in Austin, Central/East Texas and Louisiana. The position is based in Austin.

Thanks again for all your help! I hope we get to chat in person at some point in the next few months—especially now that I'll be back in Texas by the end of the month.

Sincerely,

Rodney Schlossburg

Other Follow-Up Letters

Sometimes landing the new position or contract may take several months or more. While you can't be badgering potential employers or clients with weekly calls, you can send occasional notes to reinforce your ongoing interest in the opportunity. If possible, write to them for some reason other than your need for a job or contract. Some typical "hooks" people use for follow-up letters include:

☆   I saw an article about your company in *The Wall Street Journal*, local paper or national business magazine.

☆   I ran into a mutual friend the other day who said you were buried in a big project (on a month-long assignment in Tokyo, just won $25,000 in the lottery, had a baby girl).

☆   Congratulations on winning the Baldridge Award, Entrepreneurial Business of the Year, Corporate Citizen Award or Cattle Baron Ball funding.

☆   I was looking through my mutual fund's annual report and saw your company listed. I noticed that its stock is doing well on Wall Street, your IPO was very successful or there was a recent 2 for 1 stock split.

☆   I know you're interested in science fiction (old Corvettes, Nancy Drew, etc.) and I thought this article or book might intrigue you.

If possible, include the referenced article with your letter, or mail only the article with a sticky note saying, "I saw this and thought you might like a copy." Be sure to sign your name.

Our champion of follow-up, Larry Frantz, wrote the next three letters.

Lawrence G. Frantz
6535 Northpoint Drive
Dallas, Texas 75248

February 15, 1999

Mr. J. Ward Howell
President and Chief Executive Officer
Biomed Control, Inc.
9200 Webb Chapel Road, Suite 500
Dallas, TX 75220

Dear Ward:

I noted your stock moved up very quickly on Wednesday and Thursday last week. Though I am sure you appreciate the improvement, you probably would have preferred the reason to be related more to the fundamentals of your business and less on market exigencies.

You and A.J. expressed some concern that Phase I of my proposal was a lot of money just to educate me about your business. I wanted to be sure you realize what else I would be doing for you during those initial two months. Though I strongly believe it is important for any spokesman for your company to know it well, you would have the following additional benefits from my initial involvement:

1. A list of over 100 analysts who are ideal targets for interest in your company.
2. A survey of holders and analysts familiar with Biomed to see what the market's perception is.
3. A package of charts on Biomed guaranteed to pique the interest of analysts.

I look forward to talking with you further on how I can help get you the analyst exposure you need.

Sincerely,

Larry Frantz

Lawrence G. Frantz
6535 Northpoint Drive
Dallas, Texas 75248

February 21, 1999

Mr. Ray Wilson
Triple Drilling Company
5956 Cognac Lane, Suite 1500
Dallas, Texas 75225-9004

Dear Ray:

I enjoyed meeting you at last week's NIRI luncheon and getting caught up with what's happening at Triple. As we discussed, I was very impressed with Dick and Allen when I interviewed for the CFO job in September 1998. Subsequent to that meeting, I decided to spend full time on my investor relations consulting business. IR was part of my job at Hope Energy and I really enjoyed it. If I can help you in any way, either as a consultant or as just someone to bounce around a problem with, please give me a call (387-7450).

Meanwhile, I hope to see you at future NIRI meetings. They are a good group of people and I know you will get a lot out of the meetings.

Sincerely,

Larry Frantz

Enclosure: Biographical Summary

Lawrence G. Frantz
6535 Northpoint Drive
Dallas, Texas 75248

February 11, 1999

Ms. Katharine Kinney
Planning and Administration
Growtex Corporation
4111 Lemon Way
Dallas, TX 75237

Dear Katharine:

Congratulations on the very good earnings you just reported. It certainly makes the investor relations job easier when you have this kind of success. But the company really needs us IR types when the results are not so good, and that time eventually comes for all companies.

One of the frustrations we all encounter is the variety of ways in which various newspapers report earnings. Due to differences in the treatment of extraordinary items, accounting adjustments and pro forma restatements, analysts can get very confused if they rely on published reports. In your case, for example, three different newspapers reported three different prior year net income figures for Growtex. *The Wall Street Journal,* the *New York Times,* and the *Dallas Morning News* reported fourth quarter net income as $2,715,000, $215,000 and $3.3 million and full year net income as $7,692,000, $5,192,000 and $10.9 million, respectively. That is quite a difference! Unfortunately, there is not much that can be done to prevent such discrepancies. All we can do is be sure existing shareholders and analysts who follow the company get the story from us, not from the newspapers.

I would be happy to discuss with you some other thoughts I have on this problem. Give me a call at 972-387-7450.

Sincerely,

Larry Frantz

Enclosure: News Reports

Appendix

Guide to Researching the Job Market

To help you focus on specific areas of research, codes are provided. Most of these resources are available at your local public library.

C = Company   O = Occupation
I = Industry   E = Executive Search Information

Code	Guides
C	**Almanac of American Employers: A Guide to America's 500 Most Successful Large Corporations** Alphabetical profiles of major corporations, including information about benefits, job turnover and financial stability.
C	**Billion Dollar Directory: America's Corporate Families** Lists over 7,800 U.S. parent companies and their 44,000 foreign and domestic subsidiaries. Organized alphabetically by name of parent company.
C, I, O	**Business Periodicals Index** Gives references to published stories and articles in a variety of periodicals about people and corporations, industries and companies.

C, O   **Career Guide: Dun's Employment Opportunity Directory** Specifically targeted to those just beginning their career. Describes job prospects at hundreds of companies.

C, I   **Consultants and Consulting Organizations Directory** Lists consultants by name of organization, location and fields of specialty.

C   **Corporate Annual Reports** Publicly held corporations produce these handsome booklets to highlight their financial status, promote their products and services, and publicize their involvement in community and charitable activities. Because annual reports are authored by the firm itself, they are slanted to be as positive as possible. However, the information they provide is well worth reading as long as you keep this positive "spin" in mind.

C, I, O   **Directories in Print** Contains descriptions of all published directories: what they list, who uses them and who publishes them.

C   **Directory of Corporate Affiliations,** "Who owns whom?" Discusses specific mergers and acquisitions and names companies on the NYSE and Fortune 500.

C, I, O   **Directory of Directories** Includes more than 200 directory data bases as well as subject and title indexes on business and industrial directories, professional and scientific rosters.

E   **Directory of Executive Recruiters** Lists over 2,800 executive search firms and offices. Helps you identify recruiters based on the function or industry they serve, geographic location, firm name, key contact name or type of search assignments accepted.

C   **Directory of Services** A guide to social service agencies in the city or community area.

C   **Dun & Bradstreet Million Dollar Directory** A listing of approximately 160,000 U.S. businesses. Listings appear alphabetically, geographically and by product classification.

C   **Dun & Bradstreet Reference Book of Corporate Managements** Contains data on officers and directors of U.S. companies with the highest revenues; notes dates of birth, education and business positions held.

I, O   **Encyclopedia of Associations** Names national and international organizations of all types, purposes and interests; includes headquarter addresses, telephone numbers, chief officials. Indicates placement committees and added details on possible position leads.

I, O   **Encyclopedia of Associations: National Organizations in the U.S.** Lists 23,000 local and national associations, professional clubs and civic organizations by categories; includes key personnel and indexed graphically.

C, I   **Encyclopedia of Business Information** Lists each industry's encyclopedias, handbooks, indexes, almanacs, yearbooks, trade associations, periodicals, directories, computer databases, research centers and statistical sources.

O   **Enhanced Occupational Outlook Handbook** Contains descriptions of 250 occupations, along with the nature of the work, qualifications, salary and employment outlook; and sources of more information.

E   **Executive Recruiters of North America** A resource directory of executive search firms. Particularly useful in organizing your direct-mail campaign.

C   **Fortune Double 500 Directory** Lists the 500 largest corporations, as well as the 500 largest U.S. nonindustrial corporations and the top 100 service companies in diversified financial services and banking—all arranged in annual sales.

C, I, O   **Gale Directory of Publications** Lists national, local and trade magazines alphabetically and by state.

O   **Guide for Occupational Exploration** Answers questions concerning skills, duties, interests, qualifications, working conditions and DOT numbers for thousands of jobs.

C, I, O   **Guide to Special Issues and Indexes of Periodicals** Alphabetical listing of consumer, trade and technical periodicals.

C   **Hoover's Handbook of American Business** More than 500 in-depth company profiles.

C,I,O   **Job Hotlines USA** Lists over 1,000 job hotlines in a variety of companies across the United States.

E   **Kennedy's Pocket Guide to Working with Executive Recruiters** A pocket addition to the *Directory of Executive Recruiters*. Gives you guidelines and other important information about *how* to work with executive search firms.

C, I, O   **Magazines:** *Forbes, Business Week, Fortune, Inc., Money, Financial World,* and so on.

C, I   **Manufacturer's Guide** Lists local/state companies by type of industry and product.

C   **Moody's Complete Corporate Index** When you are really interested in a lengthy description on a particular company, this publication is for you. If you want to know a company's history, Moody's provides the details—from financial information to when the company was founded.

C, I   **National Directory of Addresses and Telephone Numbers** Contains addresses and telephone numbers of business establishments, organizations, hotels, schools, hospitals, throughout the country. Also contains a valuable listing of trade publications.

I, O   **National Trade and Professional Associations of the United States** Lists more than 7,600 associations, addresses, officers and a brief history. Also ranks associations by financial size.

C, I, O   **Newspapers:** *The Wall Street Journal,* local business journals, metropolitan dailies (especially the business section), *Barron's, USA Today.*

O   **O-Net Dictionary of Occupational Titles (DOT)** This reference gives detailed information for almost 1,200 occupations, covering nearly 100% of the U.S. workforce. It cross-references the Dictionary of Occupational Titles, the Occupational Outlook Handbook, and other major references, and includes information on earnings, education, tasks, skills, related jobs and much more.

C,I,O   **Online Services** Although information and available services are constantly changing, several online services offer valuable job-search information. For example, America Online offers articles and other information about companies you might want to research. Online services often have job listings and templates of resumes, as well as other types of job-search information. On the Internet, look for Monster.com. See also the sites listed in Chapter 8.

C, I, O   **Publications of governmental agencies** Such as the Bureau of Apprenticeship and Trade, Small Business Administration, Department of Commerce, Department of Labor.

C, I   **Sources of Business Information** (University of California Press) Excellent sources for all fields of business. Basic research methods are described. Contains a detailed index

C, I, O   **Standard & Poor's Register of Corporations** A three-volume guide. Volume I: Corporate Listings—addresses, telephone numbers, names, titles, public companies. Volume II: Directors and Executives—lists individuals serving as officers, directors, trustees and partners and their principal business affiliations. Volume III: Indexes—color-coded sections relating to Standard Industrial Classification Index and Codes, Geographical Index, Corporate Family Indexes, new companies and individuals appearing in current edition.

C, I   Your **stockbroker or investment counselor** can provide detailed information on specific companies and industries.

C   **Thomas Register of American Manufacturers; Thomas Register Catalog File** By looking up a particular product or service, you can find every company that provides it in this 23-volume publication. Published annually, this reference also includes data on branch offices, capital ratings, company offices and addresses and phone numbers.

I, O   **Trade and professional journals** To find the ones that pertain to your needs, ask the librarian or consult the Business Periodicals Index headings under "occupations," "office workers" and "professions" (individually named). There are hundreds of these focusing on individual industries and careers.

I   **U.S. Industrial Outlook** (Department of Commerce) Published yearly, this reference contains information on 350 industries including trends, pressing issues, and long-term forecasts.

C, I   **Value Line Investment Survey** A monthly updated guide on business trends. Lists public companies, officers and new items. Offers opinions on the stock market and advisability of owning 1,700 stocks.

C, I   **Ward's Business Directory of U.S. Private and Public Companies** As you might imagine, the directory lists both firms that are traded on stock exchanges and those that aren't. Each very brief reference includes the company's name, address, phone number, its officers, SIC code and its products or services.

C   **Yearbook of International Organizations** Lists 27,000 international organizations active in at least 3 countries. Indexed by name, address, and description.

C   **Yellow Pages**

Index

A

Acceptance letters, 267–269
Accomplishments, writing about, 33–35
Address, 23
Ads:
   call-in responses, 106–107
   interpreting, 94–96, 102–105
   key words, 94
   online, 188–196
   writing a letter, 96–100
Andrews, Karen, 146–147
Anger, curbing, 39
Attention getters, 128

B

Baum, Gary, 181
Blind ads, 26

Block style, 25

Block style, 25
Brevity, 37
Broadcast letters, 224–242
   advantages, 224–225
   database, creating a, 226–227
   disadvantages, 225
   target groups, 225–226
Buzz words, 35–36

C

Candidate interviews, 127
CareerMosaic, 189–190
Careers.wsj.com, 190
CareerWEB, 181–182, 191
Choosing whom to contact, 67–69
Closing, 33
Computer equipment, 186
Copies, 33

D

Demands, making, 39–40
Direct-mail:
  campaigns, 67–91
  writing letters, 73–91
Directory of Executive Recruiters, The,
    134, 226
Do's and don'ts, 33–41
  accomplishments, 33–35
  buzz words, 35–36
  humor, use of, 36
  negative information, 38–39

E

Electronic bulletin board postings,
    214–216
E-mail, 186, 188, 189, 195, 198
Employers:
  choosing, 67–69
  researching, 69–72
Enclosures, 33
Errors, 38
Evaluation form, 158–160
Examples:
  block, 25
  breaking the rules, 114–115
  indented, 24
  newcomer, 112–113
  you-want-I-have, 116–117
Expectations, 62–64

F

Fax number, 23
First paragraph, 27–28
  ad, 28
  direct mail, 27–28
  networking, 27
  referral, 27
Follow-up letters, 245–275
Formats, 22–23, 40–41
  block, 25
  indented, 24
Frantz, Larry, 81–83, 272
Freeman, Valerie, 133–135, 140, 262

G

Global Information Systems, 159–161
Greeting, 26–27, 97
Guidelines for cover letters, 146–147

H

Handwritten notes, 217
Heading, 23
HeadHunter.NET, 190
Help-wanted ads, 93–122
Hirsch, John, 159–160
Hot lines, job, 107–108
Humor, use of, 36

I

Imprimis group, 133
Indented style, 24
Information:
  interview evaluation form, 158–160
Inside address, 23, 97
Internal corporate letters, 203–217
Internal job search, reasons for,
    204–205
  finding jobs, 205–207
Internet, 179–201
  access, how to, 186

access providers, 186–187
bibliography, 201
definition, 187
glossary of terms, 196–201
job listings, 189–191
netiquette, 187–188
users for employment purposes,
    182–185
Inventory skills, 48–60

J

Jargon, use of, 35–36
Job hot lines, 107–108
Job Hotlines USA, 107
Job listings, 189–191, 211–216
Job search aids, 191–194

K

*Kennedy's Pocket Guide to Working with
    Executive Recruiters,* 135
Korn/Ferry International, 126

L

Landing letter, 270–271
*Lexicon of Intentionally Ambiguous
    Recommendations, The,* 63
Locating jobs, internal, 205–207
Lord, David, 134

M

Market letters, 219–223
Monster Board, The, 190
Morrison, Robert, 126, 132

N

Name dropping, 35
NationJob Network, 191
Negative information, handling, 38–39
Netiquette, 187–188
Networking contacts, 153–177
    how to use, 154–155
    information from, 155–158
Networking contacts, online, 185

O

Online Career Center (OCC), 180, 186,
    189, 195, 196
Organizational assessment, 127

P

Philosophy of writing, 21–22
Phone number, 23
Position specification, 127
Posting systems, 211–216
Preprinted headings, 23
Process-oriented approach, 3

Q

Qualifications, determining, 43–65
Quetico, 126
Quiz, 7–9
    answers, 9–19

R

Reasons for writing, 2–3
Recommendations, 62, 64–65

Recruitment, 127
References, 61–65
    check of, 127
Resumania, 30–31, 36, 37, 38, 39, 45,
        61, 70, 81, 96, 98, 145, 157, 228,
        234, 247

S

Seaquist, Don, 181
Search firms, 125–139
    contingency, 133–139
    employer pays, 126–127
    letter examples, 130–132, 137–139
    retained, 126–132
Search strategy, 127
Second paragraph, 28–29
    ad, 31–32
    direct mail, 29–31
    lead follow-up, 29
    networking, 29
Skills, identifying:
    accomplishments history, 44–46
    inventory, 48–60
    references, 61–62
Synder, Kristin, 181

T

Tailoring your letter, 21–33
Taylor, Jeff, 195
Temporary agencies, 140–144
Thank-you notes, 245–266
Third paragraph, 32–23
Thornton, Robert, 63
Tools, 41

U

Usenet groups, 201

W

Waddle, Peter, 181
Warren, Bill, 186, 189, 196
Westberry, David, 126, 133
World Wide Web, 180, 182, 186, 187,
        189, 191, 194

4 WEEKS *FREE* OF

THE WALL STREET JOURNAL.

For your career and your future

Our first section gives you a quick, accurate read of your business day.

Keep your finger on the pulse of the day's major business, economic and financial news -- from the U.S. and around the world. Breaking stories. Current issues. Straight, unbiased reporting. Vital news that helps you stay focused, up to date and on top of your job.

In Marketplace consumer and business interests are the issues.

Technology, Marketing, Law, Enterprise, And More. The Market place section expands your knowledge in many key areas that can help you make the right moves for your company and for you personally. From consumer trends and thinking to innovative corporate strategies, you'll get insight and ideas you can use to build your career and shape your future.

Money & Investing: A wealth of financial information you can bank on

The Journal is the preeminent source for coverage of the day's financial markets, with personal and professional strategies for getting ahead. Helpful charts, easy-to-read stock quotes, plus our renowned investment columns provide timely information to help you make the most of every opportunity.

31